Primal Philosophy

Primal Philosophy

Rousseau with Laplanche

Lucas Fain

ROWMAN & LITTLEFIELD
Lanham • Boulder • New York • London

Published by Rowman & Littlefield
An imprint of The Rowman & Littlefield Publishing Group, Inc.
4501 Forbes Boulevard, Suite 200, Lanham, Maryland 20706
https://rowman.com

6 Tinworth Street, London SE11 5AL, United Kingdom

Copyright © 2021 by Lucas Fain

All rights reserved. No part of this book may be reproduced in any form or by any electronic or mechanical means, including information storage and retrieval systems, without written permission from the publisher, except by a reviewer who may quote passages in a review.

British Library Cataloguing in Publication Information Available

Library of Congress Control Number: 2020944134

ISBN 9781538146187 (cloth) | ISBN 9781538148396 (pbk) ISBN 9781538146194 (epub)

In the bosom of superstition where reason has no force, philosophy must necessarily take on a mysterious air in order to gain credence.

—Jean-Jacques Rousseau, *Fragment 38*

Contents

Acknowledgments ix

1 The Wager of Rousseau 1
2 Philosophy in Crisis 15
3 Rousseau's Intervention 55
4 Primal Philosophy 113
5 Philosophy and Responsibility 161

Abbreviations and Works Cited 181
Index 195
About the Author 205

Acknowledgments

This book is, above all, a work of philosophy. Its publication marks an act of resistance against the contemporary forces of neoliberalism, which have increasingly restricted the scope of what is produced in departments of philosophy today. Rousseau is typically considered an outlier. Laplanche is known mainly to specialists as the disciple-turned-rival of Jacques Lacan, and more widely perhaps as the coauthor with J.-B. Pontalis of the encyclopedic *Vocabulaire de la psychanalyse*. Against all odds, the combination of Rousseau with Laplanche amounts to something of a double-dog dare against the ruling conventions of academic philosophy. It is therefore with tremendous gratitude that I wish to acknowledge the individuals and institutions that made it possible for me to complete the work contained in this volume.

Foremost, I thank my mentors, Jeffrey Mehlman and the late Stanley Rosen, two teachers with very different perspectives, without whom I would not have ventured the core ideas for this book when I was a graduate student in the University Professors Program at Boston University. The present text bears little resemblance to my doctoral dissertation, but Stanley Rosen taught me how to read the history of philosophy as an ongoing conversation among philosophers, while Jeffrey Mehlman continues to inspire a style of reading that can be compared only to Freud's fundamental rule of psychoanalysis.

The intellectual horizon of my research expanded significantly during a postdoctoral appointment in the Committee on Degrees in Social Studies at Harvard University, where I benefitted from conversations with many outstanding colleagues, among whom I mention Scott Staring and Rodrigo Chacón, two friendships forged as if in a furnace. I am also grateful to Richard Tuck for his spirited tenure as chair of the program.

When Stanley Rosen passed away, C. Allen Speight picked up the torch. I am deeply thankful for his enduring support of my scholarship. Humphrey

Morris, whom I first met as an Affiliate Scholar at the Boston Psychoanalytic Society & Institute, was instrumental to advancing my education in psychoanalysis, not least through his leadership of the Harvard University reading group on Psychoanalytic Practices. Daniel Guevara made possible three quarterly research appointments, which allowed me to complete the manuscript at the University of California, Santa Cruz.

The publication of this book owes special gratitude to the relentless encouragement of Gregory Fried. He brought the manuscript to the attention of my editor, the visionary Frankie Mace, who understood immediately what I had set out to accomplish. Among teachers past and present, my studies have been indelibly marked by Daniel O. Dahlstrom, Francisco J. Gonzalez, Jonathan Lear, Reginald Lilly, Moishe Postone, and the work of Richard Velkley. I am also grateful to Michael Zank for arranging a research appointment in the Elie Wiesel Center for Jewish Studies at Boston University, where I finalized the typescript.

Part of chapter 2 uses material reproduced with permission from "Heidegger's Cartesian Nihilism," *The Review of Metaphysics* 64, no. 3 (March 2011): 555–79. The cover image of Hugues Chassonneris' *carte à jouer*, "Jean-Jacques Rousseau, tenant le *contrat Social*," is generously provided by the Musée de la Révolution française—Domaine de Vizille.

Finally, this book could not have been written without the inexhaustible love of my parents, Jerry and Jane; my sister, Ellice; family and friends too many to name, in solidarity with Andy Rohr, Joe Roche, Michael Chapman, Brian Marrin, and Mark Mitrovich. I wish Amy Stein were here to see it. My grandfather, Sidney Beserosky, would have been delighted. However, it is to the memories of Edith Beserosky and Millie Fain Schneir that I dedicate this volume. As the two matriarchs of my immediate family, they taught us how to live. I trust this sentiment will not be lost on readers of Rousseau.

Lucas Fain
Boston, March 2020

Chapter 1

The Wager of Rousseau

I. FOR THE CONTEMPORARY FATE OF PHILOSOPHY

Fifteen years after his death, in the heat of the French Revolution, a set of playing cards appeared with an image of Rousseau printed among the deck. Such *cartes de la Révolution* were not uncommon, as figures of liberty, equality, and fraternity were made to replace the traditional kings, queens, and jacks of the ancien régime. More uncommon are the details of this image, stamped by Hugues Chassonneris in 1793. An aged Rousseau is labeled the Sage of Clubs, recalling his fondness for botany, as he peels out of his Armenian robe with the *Social Contract* extended in hand. If the *Révolution* was to be a gamble, this card would speak to a central wager of Rousseau's thought: the ambition to replace the rule of despots with the wisdom of the Sage. In Rousseau's vision, the Sage appears in the guise of a Lawgiver who inaugurates in a people not only the principles of the social contract, but also the motivation to contract with others, the will to will generally, the will to will the general will. As Rousseau remarked with regard to securing this motivation: a people brave enough to "recover and defend its freedom would amply deserve that some *homme sage* teach it to preserve it."[1] With this playing card, then, Rousseau is recognized as that *homme sage*, that *sage instituteur*, he called the Lawgiver.[2]

The Sage and the Lawgiver appear unified in Rousseau's thought by the teaching of freedom. Yet this depiction of Rousseau the Lawgiver-Sage opens up a question concerning the difference between the Sage and the Philosopher, hence, the Philosopher and the Lawgiver. Even the term "Philosopher" is suspect, as Rousseau chastised the "tranquil slumber" of the *philosophes* for whom the inward life of reason suppressed the source of all the social virtues, pity or compassion, the "first sentiment of humanity."[3]

For Rousseau, philosophy presents itself as a problem, as much spiritual as ethical or political. But if the Rousseau depicted by Chassonneris should turn out to be, neither Sage nor *philosophe*, but a genuine *philosopher*, then the conventional difference between wisdom and the love of wisdom might also be applied with equal force to the ideal of the Lawgiver. At the very least, it becomes necessary to consider the mythic status of the Lawgiver-Sage and whether wisdom itself belongs to a kind of *mythos*, not unlike the multiplicity of images Rousseau produced of himself under the commandment inscribed on the Temple at Delphi.

Such images tend to stare back at their author, as Rousseau admitted late in life—in the voice of the Solitary Walker, speaking on the topic of lying, no less—that the injunction *know thyself* was not as easy to follow as he had once believed in his *Confessions*.[4] With respect to the tension between wisdom and the love of wisdom, Chassonneris' Rousseau thus presents a question of fundamental importance, not only for understanding the aim and scope of Rousseau's philosophical-political project, but also for relating the significance of this project to the history of philosophical conceptions of philosophy after Socrates. One important aspect of this question concerns whether the effort to ascend philosophically, toward *logos*, does not terminate inevitably in the production of a *mythos*. For if reason translates itself inevitably into myth, what consequences follow from the genesis of philosophy to the responsibility of the philosopher?

It may seem that the possibility of philosophy itself threatens to invert the trajectory from *mythos* to *logos*, which defines the characteristic experience of philosophy in ancient Greece through its permutations in the modern West. Along related lines, readers of Horkheimer and Adorno will recall their thesis in *Dialectic of Enlightenment* (1944/1947) whereby "myth is already enlightenment; and enlightenment reverts to mythology."[5] Insofar as "enlightenment" means "liberating men from fear and establishing their sovereignty," the dialectic of enlightenment indicates the conversion of this aim into its opposite, captured most notably in their observation that "the fallen nature of modern man cannot be separated from social progress."[6] For the visionaries of the Frankfurt School, the emancipatory myth of enlightenment gave way to the totalitarian domination of scientific rationalism and the social tyranny of the culture industry. It is therefore striking that Rousseau's name appears only once in this text, in a passing reference to the Marquis de Sade's scorn for Rousseau's defense of political equality, while precedent for Horkheimer and Adorno's famous thesis concerning the self-destruction of enlightenment has its origin in the argument of Rousseau's prize-winning *Discourse* of 1750: that advancements in the arts and sciences do not yield, but rather reverse, moral or political progress.[7] Stated in terms closer to Horkheimer and Adorno: if myth is enlightenment and liberation is myth, to be enlightened is to produce the conditions of one's own domination. Faith in enlightenment is likewise a symptom of mass delusion. Technical advancements in the arts and sciences lead directly to self-forgetting and misery.

The intensification of self-forgetting and misery serves to affirm the historical inversion of Socratic philosophy, which takes its bearings from the promise of happiness achieved through self-knowledge. If we wish to know the fate of philosophy in relation to its modern history, it is therefore necessary to know if this inversion is the inevitable consequence of a certain practice of philosophy, as the answer to this question has everything to do with how we understand the meaning of philosophy itself. In the spirit of Chassonneris' *carte de la Révolution*, the wager of this book is accordingly to show how the work of Rousseau intervenes at a critical and indeed pivotal moment in the historical fate of philosophy—not only in his time, but also our own.

I therefore lead with the following suggestion. If the contemporary fate of philosophy is tied to the historical inversion of Socratic philosophy, and if Rousseau is crucial to explaining the subordination of philosophic happiness to self-forgetting and misery, then the effort to comprehend the contemporary fate of philosophy must presuppose some understanding of Rousseau's relation to Socrates. That Rousseau was indebted to Socrates is well known, which is not to say a platitude.[8] From the opening lines of the *First Discourse*, Rousseau proposed to write in the voice of "an honest man who knows nothing and esteems himself none the less for it."[9] At the same time, he authored this text in the name of "un Citoyen de Genève." When the Academy of Dijon asked in the October 1749 *Mercure de France*, "Has the restoration of the Sciences and Arts contributed to the purification of Morals?," Rousseau therefore answered in the voice of a citizen who knows nothing and esteemed himself nonetheless. This statement can be read in two ways: from the standpoint of the citizen who recognizes the virtue of humility in matters of philosophy or politics, or from the standpoint of the philosopher who recognizes the danger of citizens who refuse to admit their ignorance. It could be said, in this regard, that the practice of ignorance expresses the responsibility of the philosopher, insofar as philosophy in the Socratic sense refuses both the reduction of wisdom to specialized knowledge in the arts and sciences and the replacement of ignorance by what Rousseau called a "dangerous Pyrrhonism."[10]

Of course, by communicating this teaching through the voice of "un Citoyen," Rousseau emphasized the political end of Socratic ignorance—especially, its demand to question "enlightened" opinions about the de facto goodness of enlightenment. Moreover, by writing in the voice of a Citizen, Rousseau aimed to traverse the irreducible distance between the "approbation of a few Wise men" and the "approbation of the Public."[11] For Rousseau, it was a high imperative to speak persuasively to the public, for one cannot convey an effective moral teaching if it penetrates only philosophic minds. This is why in the penultimate paragraph of the *First Discourse* Rousseau identified himself with those he called the *hommes vulgaires*, the "ordinary people, to whom Heaven has not vouchsafed such great talents and whom it does not destine for so much glory."[12] Of course, Rousseau was not a simple *homme vulgaire*, and the oratory of the Citizen demands to be read against Rousseau's admission in the preface, where he aligned himself with those few wise men who write for times and places beyond their own. Thus, writing in the voice of a Citizen, Rousseau appears as a teacher of the multitude who "should leave to others the care of instructing Peoples in their duties."[13] To borrow a line from Nietzsche, whatever is profound loves a mask.[14] As Chassonneris evidently knew, the rhetoric of Rousseau the Citizen and *homme vulgaire* expresses the public teaching of Rousseau the Sage.

It is now the latter that I am most concerned with. When trying to define the wisdom at which philosophy aims, it is useful to draw the line at Socrates. Before the Oracle at Delphi inspired Socrates to examine himself in conversation with others, *sophia* in the ancient world was broadly associated with a kind of expertise or "know-how," namely, knowing how to do good in something. There was *sophia* about shipbuilding, music, medicine, cosmology, athletic skill, political rule, and so on.[15] While the *Histories* of Herodotus record the earliest reference to *philosophia* around the fifth century BC, it was the Socratic innovation to make knowledge of the good itself the highest aim of wisdom.[16] Since *eudaimonia* signifies the elevation of spirit which expresses the highest good for human beings, the possibility of human happiness depends upon knowledge of the good. Philosophy in the Socratic sense is thus a certain kind of striving, organized around a lack, the highest aim of which concerns the discovery of happiness through wisdom, which in turn depends upon knowledge of the good. Restated according to the standard Socratic thesis: virtue is knowledge; happiness is knowledge of the good.

Turning back to Rousseau, it could be said that in the domain of practical affairs the figure of the Sage exemplifies knowledge of the good, characterized by sound judgment rendered prudent by experience. In this sense, the *homme sage* or "Wise Man" embodies the completion of philosophy in the achievement of practical wisdom. Leaving to one side the question of theoretical knowledge about the order and intelligibility of the whole, this description corresponds exactly to that of the Lawgiver in the *Social Contract*. There, Rousseau described an individual of "superior intelligence; who saw all of man's passions and experienced none of them; who had no relation to our nature yet knew it thoroughly; whose happiness was independent of us and who was nevertheless willing to care for ours; finally, one who, preparing his distant glory in the progress of time, could work in one century and enjoy the reward in another."[17] Indeed, this account is not unlike Rousseau's statement of his own authorial intention in the preface to the *First Discourse*—his first mature publication. Thus, commenting on his submission to the Dijon Academy's 1750 essay competition, Rousseau remarked:

> Here is one of the greatest and most beautiful questions ever raised. This *Discourse* is not concerned with those metaphysical subtleties that have spread to all departments of Literature, and of which the Programs of Academies are not always free; it is concerned, rather, with one of those truths that affect the happiness of humankind.
>
> I do not care whether I please Wits or the Fashionable. There will always be men destined to be subjugated by the opinions of their century, their Country, their Society: Some men today act the part of the Freethinker and the Philosopher who, for the same reason, would have been fanatics at the time of the League. One ought not to write for such Readers when one wants to live beyond one's century.[18]

Rousseau would, of course, go on to win the prize and further glory. But what both the author of the *First Discourse* and the Lawgiver of the *Social Contract* share in common is a responsibility for the possibility of human happiness, on the one hand, and, on the other, the intention to have one's teachings last beyond one's century. Taken together, this responsibility for happiness joined with transcendent wisdom recalls the fundamental aim of philosophy in the initial Socratic sense. This is despite Rousseau's general refusal to call himself a "philosopher," with a modest exception appearing in the *Dialogues*, where the character Rousseau says of Jean-Jacques: "I doubt that any philosopher ever meditated more profoundly, more usefully perhaps, and wrote more in so little time."[19] This line is obviously spoken in character—and when the character Rousseau quotes Jean-Jacques directly, he recalls Jean-Jacques' pronouncement: "I am neither a philosopher nor austere."[20] Taken together, these observations suggest that when Rousseau wrote in the voice of a Citizen, he wished to bolster not only his egalitarian political doctrine, but also his contrast with *la clique philosophique* or *la cabale philosophique*, in the same spirit that the character Rousseau identified Denis Diderot with sarcasm as *le philosophe Diderot*.[21] Thus, in contrast to the *philosophes* with whom Rousseau associated the degeneration of philosophy, he preferred to call himself a "man of paradox," a "friend of virtue," or a "friend of the truth."[22] To be sure, it is a profound paradox that Rousseau wished to renew the spirit of Socrates by declining the appellation of *philosopher*.

II. THE DESTRUCTION OF PHILOSOPHY

Today, when talk persists about the "overcoming of metaphysics" or the "end of philosophy," a question remains to be confronted about the status and fate of Socrates. In one version of a response, we may be asked to consider whether Socratic philosophy is still relevant to the contemporary epoch, or whether it is better treated archeologically, as a curio of the past. According to these suggestions, either the Socratic lessons have already been learned or the lessons themselves are no longer worth learning. In either case, the implicit problem is itself rooted in the past, in the so-called quarrel between the ancients and the moderns. This expression refers originally to a literary debate—dramatized by Jonathan Swift in *The Battle of the Books* (1704)—about the superiority of ancient or modern poetry. Several movements collected under the banner of Enlightenment later expanded this debate to address a more fundamental question about the virtues of ancient civilization, against the modern enterprise to secure freedom and material comfort through the conceptual mastery of nature and society.

To condense a breadth of history: after the introduction of scientific rationalism into the intellectual discourse of the seventeenth century, the controlling categories of the eighteenth century became that of liberty and prosperity. The desire to secure equal rights to private property and the pursuit of happiness gave rise to revolutions in both America and France. With the spreading abolition of formal inequalities, the stage was set for the entrenchment of democratic capitalism in the nineteenth century, along with the antagonistic unfolding of revolutionary Marxism and its tendentious elevation of equality over liberty, beginning with the Paris Commune of 1871.

As history pushed into the twentieth century, the ambitions of the modern Enlightenment gave way to Nietzsche's claims about the death of God and the crisis of European nihilism. Max Weber's studies of bureaucracy and the disenchantment of the modern West along with Durkheim's thoughts on social anomie, the decline of religion, and the crisis of moral mediocrity were soon followed by the work of Heidegger, who spurned the age of modern technology by announcing the *Destruktion* of metaphysics, the end of philosophy, and the need for a new beginning of thinking. In general effect, these pronouncements were not unlike those of Wittgenstein's parallel efforts to destroy the traditional methods of philosophical rationalism,[23] coupled with his attendant affirmation that philosophy should not seek to explain, but merely describe.[24] Leaving aside the appeals of Wittgenstein to mysticism and Heidegger to *Gelassenheit*, both of which demand openness to mystery, it is astonishing that despite their vast thematic and methodological differences, the Anglo-American and European traditions of philosophy were—in alignment with the thesis of Horkheimer and Adorno—participants in an inversion of the Enlightenment, which had two of the world's leading thinkers conclude: in the case of Wittgenstein, all talk about "happiness" is "nonsense,"[25] and, in the case of Heidegger, the pursuit of "happiness" is "the greatest nihilism."[26]

In the present context, the meaning of "happiness" is less at issue than its abandonment as the end of philosophic inquiry. The word in German used by both Wittgenstein and Heidegger is *Glücklichkeit*. Wittgenstein called it "nonsense" because all attempts at definition terminate in tautology. If I say: "I desire happiness because I wish for what is 'good' or 'harmonious' or 'right,'" these reasons return to "happiness." It seems that language runs up against a limit. The investigation cannot push further.[27]

By contrast, when Heidegger called "happiness" the "greatest nihilism," it was to challenge the view of Nietzsche that nihilism means the lack of having "goals" (in German: *Ziele*), in the sense belonging to "the long misunderstood *telos* of the Greeks."[28] The highest human *telos* in the Greek sense is, of course, *eudaimonia* or "happiness." Yet Heidegger argued that having goals closes off our possibilities and so conceals the truth of being. More radical than Nietzsche for whom the human will would rather will nothingness than nothing at all, Heidegger takes nihilism to mean abandoning the truth of being for the goals of "happiness," which manifest themselves in the modern epoch as the desire for machination and distraction—that is, the "greatest nihilism," greater even than the destruction of religious institutions and the murder of people.[29]

From the Socratic standpoint, Heidegger invokes a double displacement of the original attachment of philosophy to happiness. In the age of machination, the highest *telos* in the Greek sense is lowered to complacent satisfaction. "Happiness" expresses the goal of making material pleasures available to all, but this goal conceals a deeper wish not to have goals at all. Still worse than the abandonment of goals is our concealment of our ownmost possibilities, which means, for Heidegger, the dread of confronting a radical decision: to persist under the conditions of domination by the metaphysical crisis of the West or to confront the opening of a new historical beginning. The height of "happiness" in the Greek sense is therefore lowered, then replaced by the freedom of decision.[30]

To restate all of this succinctly, in the place of "happiness" both Wittgenstein and Heidegger sought the destruction of philosophy, with the result that happiness was replaced by freedom—but freedom from wisdom or the love of wisdom. In effect, the reduction of "happiness" to either "nonsense" or "nihilism" amounts to the admission that philosophy in the Socratic sense is, or has become, impossible.

III. ROUSSEAU, THE PIVOT

Rousseau is an unlikely figure to associate with an inquiry into the possibility of philosophy. Most often he is thought of as a political philosopher and literary genius. But Rousseau is of special interest to this late modern version of "the quarrel" because he represents an effort to not only invigorate the spirit of Socratic philosophy against the corrosive effects of the Enlightenment, but also, and even more so, because he occupies a pivot point within the history of Western philosophy. On one hand, he offers an incisive critique of the scientific foundations of the Enlightenment, while on the other, he sows the intellectual seeds of the Kantian and post-Kantian philosophies of freedom, which have dominated the modern and contemporary philosophical landscapes. While he looks back to ancient principles of Socratic, Spartan, and Roman virtue, he simultaneously looks forward, not to a reactionary return to the past, but toward the long nineteenth century efforts to fasten the aims of Enlightenment to a doctrine of self-legislative reason, inspired largely by his doctrine of the general will. In opposition to Hobbes' antecedent notion of freedom as the absence of external impediments, the influence of Rousseau can be summarized by the thesis of the *Social Contract* that freedom means "obedience to the law one has prescribed to oneself."[31]

By the end of the twentieth century, the continuation of Rousseau's Post-Kantian legacy might be represented best by Jürgen Habermas, whose theory of communicative action salutes the inherent normativity of language—its function to communicate—as the final form of the Kantian categorical imperative: to treat the humanity in others and oneself never merely as a means, but always as an end in itself. According to this formula, the treatment of others or ourselves as a mere means puts the will in contradiction with itself, as it undermines the capacities of spontaneity and autonomy which determine our humanity. Likewise, the communicative function of language is put into contradiction with itself when its function to communicate is distorted or abused. Yet the imperative to communicate cannot itself determine the content of what is said. For example, the imperative to make ourselves understood by one another cannot itself distinguish the discourse of fascism from that of modern liberalism—unless it presupposes the impossibility of discourse with our enemies.

Moreover, despite his effort to convert Kantian moral philosophy into a normative theory of practical discourse, Habermas has never provided a transcendental deduction of the normativity of language. I suspect this is because grounding the normative end of communication would require a deduction of the a priori identity of language and reason, that is, the historically entrenched assumption of Aristotle that the human being is by definition the *zōon logon echon* for whom the terms "speech" and "reason" are almost interchangeable.

On this point, Habermas agrees in principle with Wittgenstein about the need for silence.[32]

Ultimately, what Habermas replicates of Kant resolves in a form of methodological decisionism, which owes its legacy to Descartes' initial plan to found a science of morality on the model of mathematical certainty.[33] But whereas Descartes pursued a method of doubt inspired by the experimental sciences, Habermas substitutes a theory of linguistic intersubjectivity for Kant's original decision to ground morality on the principle of noncontradiction, as expressed in the alternate formula of the categorical imperative: to accept as moral only those maxims that can be willed a universal law. As Kant's phrasing indicates, the principle that one cannot both will and not will at the same time and in same the respect undergirds every formulation of the moral law. Likewise, in the Habermasian theory of communicative rationality, oppositional voices speaking simultaneously enter a formal contradiction and cancel each other out. At bottom, Kantian moral theory and its Habermasian counterpart both presuppose the validity of formal logic and its suitability for moral reasoning. Yet the principle of noncontradiction cannot tell us why we should prefer noncontradiction to its opposite—or whether we should ignore a plurality of logics. The Kantian science of morality is, accordingly, no more reasonable than the arbitrary choice of formal logic.

These remarks serve to indicate a fundamental problem consisting in the resolute decision, characteristic of Enlightenment, to subordinate the aims of Socratic philosophy to modern doctrines of individual and political freedom secured by the rhetoric of scientific certainty. In this connection, it is a paradox of Rousseau that he wished to preserve the Socratic spirit of philosophy against the excesses of Enlightenment, while at the same time he offered Kant and his successors a definition of freedom as autonomy, which could serve as the starting point for a critique of Cartesian rationality—the understanding of reason as *ratio*, a mere instrument of calculation. In its place, Rousseau's insight into the self-legislative freedom of the individual paved the way for Kant to redefine reason in terms of its capacity to freely give itself moral or political ends. However, in choosing to submit ourselves only to reasons that we have authored, the free employment of rationality finds its highest end, not in "happiness," but in the preservation of its own self-legislative freedom. Of course, the aim of Kantian moral philosophy is not to make us happy, but to make us good. But this same attempt to make us good results in sundering the good—or an account of the human relation to the good—from the foundations of moral reasoning. As Kant himself stated toward the end of the *Groundwork* (1785): "There is for us human beings no possibility at all for an explanation of how and why the universality of a maxim as a law, and hence morality, interests us."[34] At the extreme limit of Kantian practical philosophy there is thus an arbitrary resolution—or better, a leap of faith.

IV. FOR THE FUTURE OF PHILOSOPHY

Philosophy is impossible if it cannot explain the basis of its reasoning or justify its end. Yet this describes the precise situation of philosophy in the long epoch of Enlightenment, which has seen the original aim of Socratic philosophy plunged into the abyss of "nonsense" or "nihilism," defined respectively by Wittgenstein and Heidegger.

Among the most striking features of the contemporary movements that have organized around the call for a "postphilosophical" (often termed "postmetaphysical") culture is the widespread denial of any universally valid starting point for thinking about the possibility of philosophy itself. If philosophy is possible at all, its possibility is actualized by a pure act of the will, which appears much closer to a leap of faith than an erotically induced pursuit of wisdom. This is largely due to the revolution against metaphysics, which denies that the discipline of free thought can appeal to principles, grounds, or foundations in order to legitimate its assertions—and this is because the very notion of legitimacy is said to rest upon the flawed assumption of an enduring rational order, which has since given way to the shifting sands of historicism and twentieth-century hermeneutics. This condition is again described by Nietzsche as a form of nihilism, defined in the *Nachlass* of 1887 as the consequence when "the question 'Why?' finds no answer."[35] If the question "Why?" finds no answer, then all attempts at explanation are futile, and speech is no better than silence. For anyone with ethical or political concerns, this assertion will be especially troubling, as it denies that ethical or political questioning can yield binding principles or an answer to that most Socratic question: "How shall I live?" In his 1962 *Nietzsche et la philosophie*, Gilles Deleuze called our independence from such questions: "Irresponsibility—Nietzsche's most noble and beautiful secret."[36]

The study of Rousseau contained in this book takes its bearings from the claims of nihilism to render philosophy impossible. If philosophy is impossible, then it makes no sense to speak about the responsibility of the philosopher. One could talk about the responsibility of the intellectual or the poet or the technician or the pundit, in the way one talks about routine tasks or social functions. One could also speak in the manner of Rousseau about allegorical figures like the Citizen, the Lawgiver, the Solitary Walker, and the Sage—the last of which he ranked among the "Preceptors of Humankind."[37] But since the possession of wisdom is not the same as the love of wisdom, the responsibility of the wise cannot be the same as the lover of wisdom.

For the contemporary champions of postphilosophical culture, these statements will sound like a language game. Everything turns on the meaning of "philosophy." Since the word obtains no final meaning, our understanding of the term must be interpreted in a way that corresponds to the time and place in which we live. This is another way of saying that in a postphilosophical epoch the responsibility of the philosopher gives way to correspondence with history, resolving ultimately in the historically contingent—and finally arbitrary—decision for obedience or resistance to convention.[38] To be sure, an inquiry into the possibility of philosophy leads inevitably to reflection on the meaning of philosophy itself. But again, there is no "in itself" for the proponents of postphilosophical culture—and this is because, as Richard Rorty put it, there are no "final vocabularies."[39] The meaning of philosophy can be changed simply by its being redescribed.

The view presented here is different. I shall not propose to reinvent the meaning of philosophy. Instead, I will investigate the possibility of philosophy itself through an examination of Rousseau's Socratism, taken as an intervention in the recent discourse of philosophy, which has been so ready to proclaim an end to the "epoch of philosophy." The bulk of this study is contained in the third and fourth chapters, which advance an interpretation of Rousseau's thought on the meaning of a genuine *first philosophy* in light of Jean Laplanche's seminal effort to put the psychoanalytic understanding of the human being on new foundations through a critical retrieval of Freud's original theory of seduction. It is the wager of this book that reading Rousseau together with Laplanche will open up a way to rethink the foundational question of philosophy, not in terms of the decisionistic rationality of Enlightenment, but through a process of seduction which explains the erotogenesis of philosophic wonder. It is a corollary of this wager that the general theory of seduction developed by Laplanche can help us to complete Rousseau's account of the possibility of philosophy, with a view to the challenge it presents for the method of Cartesian first philosophy. At issue is the decisionistic character of Cartesian thought and the culmination Descartes' legacy in the nihilistic consequences of Heidegger's decision to found the future of thinking on a radical return to the question of being. Stated in short: the seduction of happiness, not the forgetting of being, is at stake for the future of philosophy. In the final chapter, I then build on this account in order to address the contemporary importance of Rousseau for thinking about the responsibility of the philosopher in the aftermath of Heidegger's disastrous revolution in, or against, philosophy. As a propaedeutic to that end, the next chapter surveys the crisis conditions of philosophy in the twentieth century, with a focus on the responses of Theodor Adorno and, more recently, Alain Badiou to the question concerning the possibility of philosophy after Heidegger. This chapter sets into clear relief the claims concerning the "end of philosophy" to which Rousseau's heretofore largely unknown and unappreciated critique of Descartes prepares a response.

Rousseau made his name by being the first to expose a fundamental contradiction in the Enlightenment between the progress of scientific rationalism, on the one hand, and the pursuit of happiness and freedom, on the other. As these opening remarks have shown, the pursuit of freedom by the methods of scientific mastery sunders happiness from the aim of philosophy—with the ultimate result that the pursuit of freedom demands freedom from philosophy. By invoking the question of the possibility of philosophy in a study of Rousseau, I propose to show how Rousseau can illuminate not just the late modern abandonment of happiness as the end of philosophic inquiry, but, more positively, how philosophy can legitimate itself through a return to the question of happiness, understood by Rousseau as the founding question of philosophy.

NOTES

1. Rousseau, OC 3:391/SC 78.
2. "Sage instituteur," OC 3: 384/SC 72; "lawgiver" (législateur), OC 3:381ff/SC 68ff.
3. Rousseau, OC 3:156/SD 153. See note 21.
4. Rousseau, OC 1:1024/R 28.
5. Horkheimer & Adorno, DA 13/xvi.
6. Horkheimer & Adorno, DA 15/3; 11/xiv.
7. Horkheimer & Adorno, DA 120/98: "Only a misanthropist like Rousseau could assert such a paradox, because being so very weak himself, he wished to pull down to his level those to whose height he could not ascend."
8. See, esp., Orwin (1998). By contrast, Williams (2007) recognizes the importance of Plato for Rousseau, but remains wedded to a notion of "Platonism," which attempts to defend Rousseau's "commitment to transcendent ideas as the ultimate authority for moral and political arguments" (xxvii). In the readings of Plato and Rousseau presented here, I subscribe neither to this notion of "Platonism," nor to the conflation of Plato and Socrates, which appears as a constant throughout Williams' text.
9. Rousseau, OC 3:5/FD 5.
10. Rousseau, OC 3:9/FD 8. Cf. OC 3:12–14/FD 11–13.
11. Rousseau, OC 3:3/FD 4.
12. Rousseau, OC 3:30/FD 27.
13. Rousseau, OC 3:30/FD 27.
14. Nietzsche, BGE §40.
15. For *sophia* as "know-how," see Hadot (1995) 2002, 17–18. For the broad use of *sophia* in the classical period, see Lloyd (1987), 83ff.
16. Elsewhere, through a reading of Plato's *Symposium* with Herodotus's *Histories*, I have shown the influence of Solon on the Socratic-Platonic unity of happiness and philosophy. See Fain (2015).
17. Rousseau, OC 3:381–82/SC 68–69.
18. Rousseau, OC 3:3/FD 4.

19. Rousseau, OC 1:791/D 101.
20. Rousseau, OC 1:838/D 137.
21. "La clique philosophique," OC 1:506/C 424; "la cabale philosophique," OC 1:569/C 476; "le philosophe Diderot," OC 1:789/D 99. Cf. Rousseau's 18 August 1756 letter to Voltaire, written in "the tone of a friend of the truth speaking to a Philosopher" (OC 4:1059/LtV 232); and in response to a letter from Christophe de Beaumont, dated November 18, 1762: "[. . .] *without being a true philosopher;* (Oh, I agree! I have never aspired to that title, to which I acknowledge I have no right; and I am surely not renouncing it through modesty.) *a mind endowed with a multitude of knowledge* (I have learned to be ignorant of multitudes of things I believed I knew)" (OC 4:1004/LtB 81).
22. "Man of paradox," for example, OC 4:928/LtB 22, OC 4:1004/LtB 81; OC 4:323/E 93; OC 3:230–31/LtP 223. "Friend of virtue," for example, OC 4:931/LtB 24; OC 4:1059/LtV 232. "Friend of the truth," for example, OC 4:348/E 110; OC 4:962/LtB 48, OC 4:965/LtB 51; OC 4:968/LtB 53; OC 4:1059/LtV 232; OC 3:107/ Bordes 110. Cf. OC 3:82/FD 72.
23. Heidegger and Wittgenstein both use the language of "destruction" to describe a process of dismantling the historically ingrained conceptual presuppositions of "metaphysics" and "traditional philosophy" (e.g., beings are "what is," words say "what is"). For comparison, see Wittgenstein's remark, reminiscent of Francis Bacon's seventeenth-century aim to purge the "idols" of the mind: "All that philosophy can do is to destroy idols. And that means not creating a new one—say in the 'absence of an idol'" (BT §88, p. 305). See also Wittgenstein, PI I.50, 55–58, 118; CV 19. Cf. Heidegger, GdP 31/23: "*Destruktion*" is "a critical dismantling (*Abbau*) of the traditional concepts, which at first must necessarily be employed, down to the sources from which they were drawn." See also Heidegger, BdZ 103: "The phenomenological *Destruktion* of ontology and logic amounts to a critique of the present time."
24. See, for example, Wittgenstein, PI I.109, 124, 126.
25. Wittgenstein, NB 77–78 (29.7.16, 30.7.16), 117. See also Wittgenstein LoE.
26. Heidegger, BzP 139/109. Cf. Heidegger, U-XII-XV 159/123, 224–25/176–77, 270/214.
27. This example is drawn from Wittgenstein, NB 78 (30.7.16). See also Wittgenstein, TLP 6.421, 6.53, 7.
28. Heidegger, BzP 139/109. Cf. Heidegger, GaP 38–39/28: "Τέλος means 'end' in the sense of 'completedness,' not 'aim' or even 'purpose.'" Heidegger abandons εὐδαιμονία as the "highest" human end because he abandons the interpretation of ἀγαθόν, "the good," as a "value" (GaP 43/31; 69/48). Instead, Heidegger interprets εὐδαιμονία as "the being-completed of being-here, the *very being-possibility of being-here itself*" (GaP 95/65; 96–97/66–67 [Heidegger's emphasis]). For Nietzsche, see KSA 4:76/Z 60; NF 355–56/WP §20.
29. Heidegger, BzP 139/110. Stated in full, this disturbing remark from the period 1936 to 1938 reads:

> The essential determinant of "nihilism" is not whether churches and monasteries are destroyed and people are murdered or whether this ceases and "Christianity" is allowed to

go its way. Instead, what is determinant is whether one knows or even wants to know that precisely this tolerance shown to Christianity, and Christianity itself, as well as the loose talk of "providence" and the "Lord God," no matter how sincere the individuals may be who speak thus, are mere ways of escape and mere predicaments in *that* domain one does not wish to acknowledge or give validity to as *the* decisive domain regarding historical being (*Seyn*) or historical non-being (*Nichtseyn*).

30. Consider, for example, Heidegger, U-XII-XV 159/123: "What is '*good*' is not the 'pleasant,' nor what brings 'happiness,' nor the beneficial, nor the useful, nor the obligatory, nor a mere value; instead, it is the steadfastness of Dasein in freedom on the basis of an affiliation with historical being." Cf. Heidegger, GaP 43/31, 61/43. See also Heidegger, B 45–47/37–39; esp., 46/38: "Decision is not decision between 'being' or 'non-being' of man but between the truth of being of any possible being and the machination of 'beings in the whole' that are abandoned by being."

31. Rousseau, OC 3:365/SC 54.

32. As a theorist of the formal pragmatics of communication, Habermas draws an explicit limit to the possibility of grounding the "discourse theory of ethics" in "an a priori transcendental deduction along the lines of Kant's critique of reason" ([1983] 1990, 116; 39, 118–19, 129–30). The normativity of language is consequently enforced, not by transcendental arguments or empirical evidence, but the hortatory rhetoric of universal and necessary conditions for establishing the ideal speech situation. This amounts to an admission that the validity of the theory of communicative action is contingent upon the choice not to have existential enemies—a veritable absurdity.

33. Descartes, *Discours de la méthode*, A-T 6:7–8. The problem of Descartes' "decisionism" is elaborated in chapter 2.

34. Kant, GMS 460.

35. Nietzsche, NF 350/WP §2.

36. Deleuze (1962), 25/21.

37. Rousseau, OC 3:29/FD 26.

38. This is a particular consequence of the "weak thought" of Gianni Vattimo. See, for example, Vattimo (2009) 2011: "The event (of Being) to which thought has the task of corresponding in the age of democracy is the mode in which Being is configured on an ongoing basis in the collective experience" (21). Cf. Vattimo (2003) 2004: "A philosophy that does away with first principles, or rather that actually comes into being as theoretical recognition of the unfoundedness of thought, is the most appropriate response—the most verisimilar, the best attuned—to the epoch of late-modern pluralism. To correspond to the times is also a responsible form of commitment" (39); "if we do wish truly to correspond to the dissolution of principles, then it would appear that we really have no choice except to set about constructing an ethics of finitude. [. . .] An ethics of finitude tries to *keep faith* with the discovery that one's own provenance is 'located,' in a way always and insuperably finite, without forgetting the pluralistic implications of this discovery" (43–44). It bears emphasis how, for Vattimo, an ethics of finitude is practiced as an arbitrary leap, an act of faith.

39. Rorty (1989), 73–95.

Chapter 2

Philosophy in Crisis

I. THE END OF PHILOSOPHY

The end of philosophy has been announced many times. Among the cultists of postmodernism, it was the recent fashion to declare that philosophy is dead.[1] Proclamations about the completion of philosophy, the destruction of philosophy, and even the exhaustion of philosophy, all express the wish of philosophic thinkers to abolish the demand of philosophic inquiry. This wish may be as much personal on the part of the individual philosopher (or "thinker"), as it is historical, in that philosophy defines a Greco-Western project of improving human life. To announce the "end of philosophy" is thus to take a stand on the success or failure of that project. At stake is nothing less than the future of philosophy itself.

In order to appreciate the contemporary importance of Rousseau for rethinking the future of philosophy, it will be necessary to say something more about the ways in which philosophy may end. The fundamental alternatives are two in number. The first involves completion, the second involves destruction. Under the banner of completion, the clearest proclamation comes from Hegel, for whom philosophy ends with the dialectical unity of thinking and being: the achievement of absolute knowledge about the intelligible order of the whole. Under the banner of destruction, I have already mentioned the names of Wittgenstein and Heidegger. In the case of Wittgenstein, philosophy finds its limit in the logical form of speech, whereas for Heidegger the end of philosophy is achieved opposite to Hegel, by dismantling the unity of thinking and being, hence, the conceptual determination of being as presence, which conceals the primordial truth of being. This is why Heidegger regarded the Hegelian Absolute as "the final suppression of the basic question."[2] For Heidegger, as much as Hegel, the end of philosophy bears heavily on the future of humanity—and for both much hangs on the destiny of metaphysics in the tradition initiated by Aristotle.

Let us postpone the question of being qua being for a moment. Though vastly different in their claims, the alternative arguments for completion or destruction all share a common consequence in that they each command a transformation in our attitudes about happiness as an object of philosophical desire. If we accept the Hegelian version of the history of philosophy, the end of philosophy culminates in the transcendence of superficial "happiness" or *Glückseligkeit* into universal *Befriedigung* or "satisfaction."[3] On one hand, this conceptual arrangement presupposes the lowering of ancient *eudaimonia* to the satisfaction of desires and inclinations, as Kant had earlier accomplished by subordinating happiness to freedom as the end of reason.[4] On the other hand, the conversion of subjective "happiness" into universal "satisfaction" presupposes the return of teleological completedness, which Kant had emptied from the end of practical reason. Thus, whereas Kant frees the individual to be free within the bounds of moral law, the Hegelian completion of philosophy can be understood in terms of a dialectical sublation consisting in Kant's negation of ancient eudemonism and the negation of this negation by the satisfactions of absolute knowledge and universal freedom won through a world-historical struggle for mutual recognition in the ethical state. With the end of philosophy, and so the end of history, the personal happiness of the classical philosopher is transformed into a perfected version of bourgeois society.

If we accept the view of Wittgenstein, by contrast, ethical speech is "nonsense." We may regard happiness as something mystical and demanding of respect. But the insufficiencies of language lead to silence.[5] There is nothing more to say.

Conversely, in the case of Heidegger, the Socratic pursuit of happiness and wisdom is replaced by a hortatory rhetoric of authenticity and anxiety. Through resolute attunement to our mortal finitude, there is an opportunity to escape the bourgeois state of Hegel, which functions like a trap. Well before Heidegger deployed an ontological critique of machine technology, Kierkegaard had diagnosed the social problem of modernity when he showed how modern commercial society transforms the Hegelian demand for recognition so that "envy becomes the negatively unifying principle in a passionless and very reflective age."[6] Kierkegaard was not speaking of reflection as contemplation, but as the desire to see ourselves esteemed in the eyes of others who desire the same esteem. Kierkegaard's solution, familiar to both Wittgenstein and Heidegger, was to inspire a leap inward into silence. It was hoped this "religious inwardness" would shatter the mirror of reflection.[7] In Wittgenstein, this same appeal to silence reappears as a reverential disposition toward the nonsense of ethical and religious speech, whereas in Heidegger the influence of Kierkegaard is inflected in the silent call of conscience, which tears us from the inauthentic chatter of the crowd. By revealing our mortal finitude as our ownmost possibility, the call of conscience turns us, not upward toward the unchanging Ideas of Plato, but forward toward the future and the authentic anxiety of being-here.[8]

Now, attendant to the drama of completion and destruction, there is yet a third way in which philosophy may end—namely, with its gradual replacement by the specialized sciences. In this spirit, the late mathematician and cosmologist Stephen Hawking argued that the failure of philosophy to keep pace with developments in the natural sciences meant that "philosophy is dead."[9] If the lifeless body of philosophy has not been ushered from the university curriculum, as is happening with alarming frequency today, it is likely to be liquefied into programs of humanities and social justice, or repurposed as the handmaid to theoretical physics, linguistics, neurocognitive science, and the like.

This is the positivist legacy in modern philosophy, which may be traced to the seventeenth century turn of Francis Bacon, who wished to see philosophy become a systematic natural science. Its overarching purpose: "the glory of the Creator and the relief of man's estate."[10] Indeed, Bacon hoped that advancements in the sciences would wake us from the dream of philosophy originating in ancient Greece. "As for the philosophers, they make imaginary laws for imaginary commonwealths, and their discourses are as the stars, which give little light because they are so high."[11] To chart a path into the future, we do not require the stargazing of Plato's Socrates, but rather knowledge of the stars and their patterns in the sky. So, it seems that with the scientific Enlightenment, philosophy was already dead.

II. RESPONSIBILITY IN CRISIS

In confrontation with Heidegger, the Marburg neo-Kantians, and the Vienna School inspired by Wittgenstein, the young Theodor Adorno began his career at the University of Frankfurt by wondering aloud about the fate of "great philosophy" in his 1931 inaugural address, "*Die Aktualität der Philosophie.*" Meaning both "actuality" and "relevance," the *Aktualität* that Adorno spoke of concerned the historical standing of philosophy within the crisis conditions of the twentieth century. Thus, he argued, "Every philosophy which today does not depend on the security of current intellectual and social conditions, but instead upon truth, sees itself facing the problem of the liquidation of philosophy."[12] In this seminal lecture, Adorno defined the "relevance" and "actuality" of philosophy in terms of its capacity to give a systematic account of the intelligible whole. The problem is "whether, after the failure of the last great efforts, there exists an adequacy between the philosophic questions and the possibility of their being answered."[13] Since, for Adorno, the idea of truth is synonymous with totality, and since totality is not observable without remainder, what passes for truth is partial at best or illusory at worst. In either case, the power of thought is insufficient to grasp the "totality of the real," and truth degenerates into correspondence with the current moment—the so-called security of current intellectual and social conditions.[14] As Adorno put the point twenty years later through a reversal of Hegel in *Minima Moralia* (1951): *"Das Ganze ist das Unwahre"* (The whole is untrue).[15] The tradition of *philosophia perennis* is but a dream, and the liquidation of philosophy can be avoided, but only by converting it into a form of *Deutung* or "interpretation," in contradistinction to science, defined as *Forschung* or "research."[16] The difference consists in the paradox that "philosophy persistently and with the claim of truth, must proceed interpretively without ever possessing a sure key to interpretation," whereas research "assumes the reduction of the question to given and known elements where nothing would seem necessary except the answer."[17] Thus, whereas the separate sciences accept the results of their investigations on the basis of existing evidence, the work of interpretation proceeds by a process of *Vernichtung* or "annihilation," which aims at the elimination of the traditional philosophical questions, beginning with the question of the whole.[18]

Fifteen years after the publication of *Minima Moralia*, Adorno's concern for the fate of traditional philosophy persisted with the publication of *Negative Dialectics* (1966), a text which opens with a section called "The Possibility of Philosophy" (*Zur Möglichkeit von Philosophie*). Obviously reminiscent of his inaugural address of 1931, this expression appears only once throughout the entire volume, as a response to the fall of Hegel after Heidegger. More specifically, this heading marked Adorno's wish to occupy a position analogous to that of Kant, whose *First Critique* was addressed to the "possibility of metaphysics after the critique of rationalism."[19] After Heidegger, it is not simply a question of the possibility of metaphysics. It is more radically a question of the possibility of philosophy. What this means for Adorno is in effect a repetition of the thesis that he introduced in 1931 and pressed into increasing refinement, with the final version worked out in the "theory of negative dialectics."[20]

Adorno began as follows: "Philosophy, which once seemed obsolete, lives on (*erhält sich am Leben*) because the moment to realize it was missed. [. . .] Having broken its pledge to be at one with reality or the point of its immediate production, philosophy is obliged to criticize itself ruthlessly."[21] The task of negative dialectics is to discover how—after the end of philosophy, after the supposed end of history—philosophy is still possible. Yet the meaning of "philosophy" is ambiguous because Adorno's answer to the question is conditioned by his thoroughly historicist conception of philosophical activity. Because philosophy cannot but appear within the context of a determinate social reality, its pretense to offer transhistorical solutions to the great philosophical questions is itself a high deception.[22] From the decline of great philosophy into interpretation, Adorno's appeal to interpretation gains specificity and rigor as the practice of negative dialectics. In turn, the practice of negative dialectics, defined as "the epitome of negative knowledge," involves turning the work of interpretation against itself in order generate an attitude not unlike the one Foucault later called—in reference to the spirit of Enlightenment—an ethos of permanent critique.[23] Beyond the end of "great philosophy," the tradition "lives on" as a mode of ruthless self-criticism made urgent by the impotence of reason and its most striking failures in the face of world-historical violence.

Adorno's basic attitude toward the failures of philosophy did not change after World War II. However, the events at Auschwitz made it impossible to speak about the "security of current intellectual and social conditions."[24] Instead, "Auschwitz demonstrated irrefutably that culture has failed."[25] The Hegelian thesis that promised the reconciliation of metaphysics and history has produced neither freedom nor satisfaction, but rather violence and domination. Adorno continues: "That this could happen in the midst of all the traditions of philosophy, art, and the enlightening sciences says more than merely that these traditions and their spirit lacked the power to take hold of men and change them. There is untruth in those fields themselves, in the self-sufficiency that is emphatically claimed for them."[26] In the face of such untruth and false autonomy, it becomes necessary to reflect on the responsibility of thinking after the collapse of great philosophy.

The way forward for Adorno is succinctly captured in the final section of *Minima Moralia*, provocatively titled "*Zum Ende*," literally, "Toward the End." Having abolished the Hegelian Absolute by the insufficiencies of reason, Adorno writes in closing: "The only philosophy which can be responsibly practiced in face of despair is the attempt to contemplate all things as they would present themselves from the standpoint of redemption."[27] For Adorno, this means fashioning "perspectives," in the style of Nietzschean *Perspektiven*, in order to "displace and estrange the world" by revealing it as indigent and distorted as it will appear one day in the messianic light." Adorno adds: "This alone is the task of thought (*Denken*)."[28]

In language that recalls Heidegger's subordination of philosophy to thinking, thinking for Adorno is opposed to philosophy as responsibility is opposed to irresponsibility. However, Adorno complicates things by turning this interpretation against itself in a way that is characteristic of the method of negative dialectics. On one hand, he calls the practice of responsible thinking "the simplest of all things, because the situation calls imperatively for such knowledge." On the other hand, he says, "it is also the utterly impossible thing, because it presupposes a standpoint removed, even though by a hair's breadth, from the scope of existence."[29] Because the events of history have both exposed and confirmed the impotence of philosophy, the imperative to redeem thinking requires that we look at things from a messianic standpoint. What is "simple" is to recognize that the fundamental disjunction between metaphysics and history requires us to disband with the illusion that reason is competent to comprehend the whole. It is, accordingly, the impotence of reason in the face of its own incompetence that engenders the demand for responsible thinking. Thus, the messianic enters as the standpoint of redemption and thinking is redeemed through its responsible confrontation with absolute unreason, that is, what Adorno called in the register of Hegelian dialectics: the nonidentity of concept and object.[30]

In short, responsibility means viewing the world from the standpoint of redemption. Yet, Adorno also called the redemption of thinking "utterly impossible."[31] It is impossible because the endeavor to think from a messianic standpoint—the very effort to remove oneself from the immediacy of the world or one's "felt contact with its objects"—requires the production of a critical perspective that is inevitably debased by "the same distortion and indigence which it seeks to escape."[32] This is the unavoidable problem of interpretation. The partiality of perspectival thinking inevitably distorts the object of critique, and this distortion risks degenerating into ideology through its alienation from concrete reality.

However, this is not an insurmountable problem for Adorno. While the partial character of interpretation exposes an aporia between the need for redemption and the inevitable risk of distortion, this same aporia makes Adorno align himself with Kant against Hegel in his effort to inaugurate a new epoch of responsible thinking. Because the reconciliation of thinking and being—hence, the reappropriation of totality—is impossible, the Kantian "thing in itself" returns as the nonidentical remainder which engenders responsibility. Concisely stated, the impossibility of redemption is itself redeemed by practical moderation. It is not "the question of the reality or unreality of redemption" that matters, but "the demand thus placed on thought."[33] Thus, *Minima Moralia* concludes: for thinking to become responsible, it must "comprehend even its own impossibility for the sake of the possible."[34]

This statement is essential to Adorno's critique of Heidegger and should be examined through its relation to the Heideggerian motto that "possibility is higher than actuality."[35] At stake for Adorno is the correct response to the Heideggerian "cult of being," which, by retreating into the truth of being, aims to escape the paradox of Enlightenment: the "universal fear that our progress in controlling nature may increasingly help to weave the very calamity it is supposed to protect us from."[36] On this point, Adorno argues that the

Heideggerian retreat into being determines a "subjective mode of conduct," which causes us to identify with a "sense of impotence."[37] What Adorno calls "impotence" is, for Heidegger, the authentic mode of being-in-the-world, defined as the resolute anticipation of Dasein's ownmost possibility, namely, its death. "Anticipatory resoluteness" (*vorlaufende Entschlossenheit*) thus describes our authentic relation to the future as openness to the possibility of having possibilities, whereas the inauthentic mode is grounded primarily in the actualities of the world into which Dasein is thrown and projects its possibilities.[38] Possibility is therefore higher than actuality, for Heidegger, because the genuine meaning of the world takes its bearings from the future.

The purely phenomenological character of this analysis prohibits Heidegger from making distinctions of rank between authentic and inauthentic modes of being-here. However, inauthentic being is clearly problematic because it forecloses our authentic reception of the future and our choice of possibilities. Still, another problem appears as soon as we ask how the connection between possibility and authenticity prepares us to choose one possibility or another. If our genuine possibilities are revealed to us by the silent call of conscience, and if the call of conscience turns us toward the resolute anticipation of our ownmost possibilities, then it seems we are paralyzed by anticipation. Authentic anticipation renders us impotent to choose. This is why, in Adorno's terms, the Heideggerian "cult of being" teaches "impotence."

On the topic of *choice*, Heidegger writes in *Being and Time* that "freedom (*Freiheit*) [. . .] *is* only in the choice of one possibility, that is, in tolerating (*im Tragen*) one's not having chosen the others and one's not being able to choose them."[39] Otherwise stated, freedom manifests itself in the space of decision: the opening up of possibilities for choice.[40] In the sense that Dasein is the being for whom its very being is an "issue," Dasein issues its own possibilities, hence, its own criteria for action or inaction.[41] Freedom is accordingly freedom from any independent standard by which to judge a choice right or best. As a matter of lived practice, the only thing that matters is the capacity to tolerate the choice, which may be as much a test of intestinal fortitude as it is courage or strength.[42]

It is a devastating irony that the space of decision in which Dasein becomes "responsible" (*schuldig*) terminates in the height of irresponsibility.[43] For Heidegger, responsibility means choosing to have a conscience. In becoming responsible, Dasein learns that it is, or has the capacity to become, answerable (*verantwortlich*) to itself as that entity which calls itself to itself.[44] On this point, Simon Critchley has observed how Heidegger's account of responsibility amounts to an "existential echo" of Kantian autonomy.[45] Whereas the Kantian formulation of autonomy consists in *Willkür* (the power of free choice) choosing itself as *Wille* (the logical structure of the will), Heideggerian responsibility consists in *Entscheidung* (decision, the authentic potentiality of choice) choosing itself as *Entschlossenheit* (the existential structure of anticipatory resoluteness).[46] In this precise manner, Kantian autonomy and Heideggerian responsibility exhibit analogous autarchic structures. Moreover, the Heideggerian analysis underlies and explains the problem of Kantian decisionism discussed in chapter 1. In this connection, Heideggerian responsibility expresses the *possibility* of Kantian morality. But whereas Kantian morality forbids the willing of maxims in violation of the categorical imperative, Heideggerian responsibility provides us with no criteria at all for guiding our actions. Because possibility is the negation of actuality, all factors leading to authentic being terminate in paralysis or resolute indecision. It follows that freedom without decision is pointless, whereas decisions without prudence are completely reckless.[47]

By contrast, Adorno claims that for thinking to become responsible it must comprehend its own impossibility or fundamental limitation, namely, its ultimate failure to grasp the truth defined as the intelligible whole. However, this leads to a paradox. By adopting a messianic standpoint, thinking becomes responsible for the whole precisely through its incapacity to comprehend it. The whole therefore becomes foundational for responsible thinking, insofar as it functions as the perspective according to which the world appears in the messianic light: indigent, distorted, fragile, and damaged.[48] When Adorno further states, "beside the demand thus placed on thought, the question of the reality or unreality of redemption itself hardly matters," it is not the quasi-theological standpoint that is essential to making thinking responsible. Instead, responsibility is produced by what Adorno called the task of thought: "To gain such perspectives without arbitrariness or violence, entirely from felt contact with its objects."[49] The messianic light does not come from above—outside of time or history. Rather, through concrete engagement with the world it shines through the nonidentity of thinking and being in the production of perspectival experience. As the interrogation of thinking and the comprehension of its "inevitable insufficiency," the messianic standpoint supplies the promise of ethical responsibility.[50]

III. BROKEN PROMISES

For Adorno, contra Heidegger, the reckless character of authentic resoluteness is moderated by the messianic negation of concrete historical reality. Against Heidegger's motto that possibility is higher than actuality, impossibility is higher than possibility because the messianic standpoint illuminates, not the good at which all things aim, but the negative space to imagine a less damaged life. Nonetheless, the heteronomous demand of a nonidentical other subverts the autarchic structures of freedom in Kant and Heidegger. Paradoxically, the free assent to the messianic perspective generates a condition of heteronomy because the demand of the other is produced out of the immanent activity of thinking "entirely from felt contact with its objects."[51] As Adorno put the point in *Negative Dialectics:* "We are not to philosophize *about* concrete things; we are to philosophize *out of* these things."[52]

Adorno's example *par excellence* is again Auschwitz, which supplies the materiality for a "new categorical imperative"—namely, "to arrange thoughts and actions so that Auschwitz will not repeat itself."[53] In a passage that bears reading against the abstract systems of Kant and Heidegger, Adorno writes: "Our metaphysical faculty is paralyzed because actual events have shattered the basis on which speculative metaphysical thought could be reconciled with experience."[54] This statement applies equally to Heidegger's existential analytic of conscience as it does to Kant's metaphysics of morals.[55] In either case, the impotence of abstract thinking calls for our immersion in the affective experience of concrete reality—in effect, a return to pretheoretical ordinary experience, "which does not begin by taking a standpoint."[56]

By thinking out of the particularity of a historically determinate situation, the freely adopted messianic perspective creates an impossible demand for redemption, and hence the possibility of a genuine future that is not predetermined by the conditions of the present. On this account, ethical experience is not produced by an act of self-legislative freedom. Rather, it is created out of the free assent to a heteronomous demand. To evoke Adorno's use of rhetorical chiasmus: freedom engenders heteronomy; but heteronomy engenders freedom. By comporting ourselves toward an impossible demand, we make it possible to think beyond the strictures of the existing material conditions. This is what it means to think the impossible for the sake of the possible.

Despite this portal of hope, Adorno is nevertheless equally deflationary about the possibility of human happiness as he is about the possibility of philosophy. While philosophy lives on as the responsible thinking of negative dialectics, happiness has a much more uncertain fate. At best, Adorno calls upon the *promesse de bonheur* of aesthetic experience, invoked originally by Stendhal. However, the rule of negative dialectics requires Adorno to treat Stendhal's formula negatively, as a "broken promise."[57] The reasoning is the same as that concerning the paradox of the whole. Whereas the ineffable part of the whole guarantees the possibility of thinking beyond the partiality of a given situation, it is likewise the temporary satisfaction of needs and inclinations that prefigures the impossible ideal of lasting happiness beyond temporary enjoyments.[58] It follows, for Adorno, that because any mortal experience of happiness (*Glück*) is "false" (incomplete or contaminated by ideology), the promise of happiness "must be broken in order to keep it."[59] Indeed, the promise of happiness is kept alive by our inability to achieve it.

As for the specific function of aesthetic experience, it opens up the *promesse de bonheur* through sensual appeals to utopia in music, literature, the visual arts, and so on. In Adorno's words, "art thanks existence by accentuating what in existence prefigures utopia."[60] In this way, it is the function of artworks to "detach themselves from the empirical world and bring forth another world [. . .], as if this other world were an autonomous entity."[61] Leaving aside the normative question about whether this ought to be the function of art, to say nothing of the critical question concerning distinctions between successful and unsuccessful creations, aesthetic experience has the potential, the *dunamis*, to hold open the promise of happiness by its dialectical negation of the empirical world. Yet this promise degenerates as art becomes increasingly critical of its utopian distance from praxical reality. One could point, for example, to the visceral and deeply disturbing work of Paul McCarthy, whose signature style of performance art and multimedia installation combines the idiom of the culture industry with scenes of suburban alienation, self-mutilation, and family trauma blended into an undrinkable swill of *Kulturkritik*. His world is not simply dystopian, it is uninhabitable. In this exact sense, "The force of negativity in the artwork gives the measure of the chasm separating praxis from happiness."[62] For McCarthy, the dark underbelly of bourgeois modernity breaks the promise of happiness while intensifying terror and depravity.

Of course, *Minima Moralia* was said to issue from a "melancholy science" which "relates to a region that from time immemorial was regarded as the genuine (*eigentliche*) field of philosophy."[63] This region, we are told, is *die Lehre vom richtigen Leben*, "the teaching of the right life."[64] Adorno does not speak of *das gute Leben*, "the good life" of classical philosophy. Instead, the replacement of the "good" with the "right" reflects the subordination of classical philosophy to scientific method beginning around the turn of the seventeenth century. To take as an example, knowledge of the good signifies the highest point of erotic ascent for Plato, whereas Hobbes and Kant deduce notions of right from axiomatic principles and methods: the fear of violent death in Hobbes, the freedom of self-determination in Kant. It follows that as an inversion of the "gay science" so conceived by Nietzsche, the "melancholy science" of Adorno puts the category of the "good" under a double erasure. That is to say, the promise of happiness is broken twice. First, the philosophical good is replaced by methodological right. But with the untethering of life from the good at which philosophy aims, the teaching of the right life has "lapsed into intellectual neglect, sententious whimsy, and finally oblivion."[65] Adorno laments: "What the philosophers once knew as life has become the sphere of private existence and now of mere consumption."[66]

If the good belongs to "what the philosophers once knew as life," Hobbes serves as an example of a modern for whom the highest good of the classical philosophers is lowered to bodily preservation; hence, the ideology of self-preservation: the founding principle of modern natural right. On the assumption that survival alone is not enough, Locke soon modified Hobbes to include the right to comfortable self-preservation—especially, the right to property from which follows a division between the sphere of publicly regulated activities and the sphere of private enjoyments. With Locke, and so Thomas Jefferson, author of the U.S. Declaration of Independence, the conversion of philosophy into method secures the right to pursue happiness, but not the right to be happy. Rather, the conversion of philosophy into method shunts the good life of the philosophers into separate forms of public and private *Richtigkeit*, that is, moral-juridical "rightness."

With Adorno, the capitalist exploitation of modern commercial society now subverts even the right to pursue happiness. Rather, the sphere of private enjoyment is converted into one of mere consumption: "an appendage of the process of material production, without autonomy or substance of its own."[67] Under such conditions: "Life does not live."[68] "Life has become appearance."[69] And: "There is no right life in falsity" (*Es gibt kein richtiges Leben im falschen*).[70]

This emphasis on "life" is philosophically significant for at least two reasons. First, the subordination of the good to the right corresponds with the destruction of happiness and the death of philosophy—two important symptoms of the decadence of human life in bourgeois modernity. Second, by following the Marxian turn toward an immanent critique of human life under the structural conditions of capitalist society, Adorno attaches the fate of philosophy to both a determinate time in history and the historically determinate method of Marxian critical theory. History, not philosophy, is accordingly the teacher of moral-juridical right. Again, Hobbes is instructive. Quoting from his discussion of Thucydides, if the "principal and proper work of history is to instruct and enable men, to bear themselves prudently in the present and providently toward the future," and if "men profit more by looking on adverse events, than on prosperity," then their "miseries do better instruct, than their good success."[71] The subordination of happiness to misery is thus legitimated by the pedagogical use of history. The aim is to teach human beings as they are, not as they ought to be. Hence, prudence is obtained by knowledge of the past, and history functions as a kind of melancholy science, which teaches futural responsibility.

Yet the use of history as a method of pedagogy implies not simply the education of prudence by history, but the replacement of prudence by method.[72] Prudence does not come from individual experience or grassroots understanding. Rather, it is inherited through a codified account of the past. On one hand, we are provided a method and an archive. On the other, there is no method for the prudent application of the method. The urgent question is how, without prudence, we are supposed to decide against one method for another. It seems that we require an archive for the application of archives.

To be clear, the immediate point is not that we require the revival of philosophy to positively answer the question of the "good" or the "right." Instead, I want to indicate how Adorno's radical historicism reproduces the methodological problem of decisionism that was witnessed in Kant and Heidegger. For that matter, this problem is already visible in Hobbes' decision to make self-preservation the founding principle of modern natural right. While Hobbes makes rhetorical appeals to the fear of violent death, and thus our want for peace, the basis for these appeals (indeed, the meaning of terms like "nature," right," and "reason") rests on nothing but the sovereign power to decide. As Hobbes formulates this thesis in *The Elements of Law* (1650): "Seeing right reason is not existent, the reason of some man, or men, must supply the place thereof; and that man, or men, is he or they, that have the sovereign power."[73]

To the extent that Adorno attempts an answer to the sovereign power of decision, he follows Hobbes by appealing to our sense of misery.[74] But this requires an appeal to something beyond method, to that which can account for the needful turn to history. Ordinarily, we would call this an appeal to something like prudence or compassion, that which Adorno called the standpoint of redemption. But since neither prudence nor compassion nor a standpoint of redemption can be at once the postulate and product of a scientific method, the appeal to melancholy science splits into aporia. Adorno's rhetoric of responsibility conceals the inner recklessness of a purely willful decision. As in the earlier but parallel case of Hobbes, the elevated importance of history dissolves the pursuit of happiness into the mitigation of misery—and so follows the end of philosophy: in Adorno, the science of redemption; in Hobbes, the science of domination.

Without an account of the possibility of philosophy itself, the doctrines in which it issues may be remanded to what Richard Rorty called a "transitional genre."[75] By this he meant a kind of weigh station between the antiquated faith in God and the emergence of a postphilosophical literary culture to follow after the epochal rejection of transhistorical "truth." As in the exemplary case of Adorno, the transformation of philosophy into melancholy science and its refinement as negative dialectics is justified by the failure of philosophy to fulfill the promise of Enlightenment. History does not lead to happiness or wisdom, but to the eternal return of impotence and misery. The dream that individual and political freedom could be obtained by the technical mastery of nature and society is accordingly reversed into the nightmare scenarios of capitalist domination and totalitarian violence. In sum, the rhetoric of Enlightenment has betrayed itself as rhetoric without justification. With history as its judge, it seems the entire Greco-Western project must be made to stand trial for its crimes against humanity. The verdict: guilty. The penalty: death. Its only redemption: an afterlife as negative dialectics where "philosophy is obliged to criticize itself ruthlessly."[76] As the manifest expression of a melancholy science, this call for the self-humiliation of philosophy appears as the symptom of a sadomasochistic fantasy organized around a return of the repressed demand for happiness. Can we not say the same for compulsions to repeat the end of philosophy?

IV. RAISING THE DEAD

Among contemporary philosophers, the voice of Alain Badiou has been among the most prominent to oppose the claim that philosophy is dead, that its history has come to an end, or that we now inhabit a postphilosophical epoch. But whereas philosophy lives on, for Adorno, as the responsible thinking of negative dialectics, Badiou argues in his *Second Manifesto for Philosophy* (2009) that "by definition, philosophy, when it truly appears, is either *reckless* or it is nothing."[77] As a final preface to the study of Rousseau, let us examine this statement alongside Badiou's suggestion that "the future of philosophy always takes the form of a resurrection." As Badiou further states: "The great declarations about the death of philosophy in general, or of metaphysics in particular, are most likely the rhetorical means to introduce a new path, a new aim, within philosophy itself."[78]

To this point, I have been developing the thesis that the presumptive end of philosophy culminates in either the achievement or abandonment of some permutation of "happiness." In Hegel, the achievement of happiness as satisfaction accords with the complete articulation of the science of wisdom, whereas in both Heidegger and Adorno the death of philosophy coincides with the abandonment of happiness and a new beginning of thinking. Two responses subsequently follow from the death of philosophy: a rhetorical call for responsible thinking, which, in the examples of Heidegger and Adorno, betrays an inner recklessness, or, in the case of Badiou, an externalization of recklessness which expresses the resurrection of philosophy. In the former, the reckless core of responsibility manifests itself as a resolute decision to return to the pretheoretical ground of thinking. In fact, Adorno and Heidegger agree on this axial point: that a return to the origin of thinking is necessary to reverse the progress of modern nihilism. However, this is also where they depart. For Heidegger, nihilism is defined by the concealment of the original Greek revelation of being as *alētheia*, whereas for Adorno nihilism describes the failure of idealism to prevent the self-destruction of Enlightenment. It follows that for Heidegger the confrontation with nihilism leads directly to the thinking of being, whereas for Adorno it leads to the embedding of thinking in material history.

This difference also measures the exact point of disagreement from which Adorno leveled his 1931 attack on Heidegger.[79] As he announced in his inaugural address at the University of Frankfurt, "that question which today is called radical and which is really least radical of all [is] the question of being itself" (*der Frage nach Sein schlechthin*).[80] Because the question of being must be abstracted from the events of material history, Adorno argued that Heidegger perpetrates a "deception of the beginning."[81] In Adorno's language, the return to being is a "false" beginning because an abstraction from the material conditions of human experience is secondary to the material reality from which it abstracts. Moreover, in the authentic mode of anticipatory resoluteness, Heideggerian being is pregnant with possibility. Yet the revelation of ontological possibility is accomplished only by the negation of ontic actuality. Thus, detached from the material conditions of lived experience, life becomes "false"; and there can be "no right life in falsity" because the thinking of being can be neither right nor wrong. Emptied of value, it can be nothing but the existential excrescence of time. The question of being is therefore "least radical" because it emerges from a process of abstraction, which is itself "derived from the methodologization of philosophy."[82]

Badiou's effort to restore the possibility of philosophy takes place largely through a confrontation with the conflict between Adorno and Heidegger. After all, Heidegger was not guilty of simply failing to resist the atrocities of German Nazism; as we know today, he was expressly eager to think the politics of National Socialism through the ontological awakening of a new beginning of thinking. But whereas Adorno saw the disaster of World War II as evidence of the incapacity of great philosophy to confront world-historical violence, Badiou rejects the suggestion that philosophy should therefore be condemned to an afterlife of masochistic self-criticism. It is rather a mistake to concede the future of philosophy to Auschwitz. Instead, we require a reexamination of the conditions upon which the possibility of philosophy may rest. So Badiou writes in his first *Manifesto for Philosophy* (1989):

> I do not claim that philosophy is possible at every moment. I propose a general examination of the conditions under which it is possible, in accordance with its destination. That history's violence can interrupt it is an idea which cannot be given credence without closer examination. It would be to concede a strange victory to Hitler and his henchmen to declare outright that they had managed to introduce the unthinkable into thought and so terminated its architectured exercise.[83]

There are two thoughts contained in this passage. On one hand, Badiou rejects the thesis of Adorno that after Auschwitz philosophy in the "architectured" or systematic sense is impossible. On the other hand, Badiou denies that philosophy is possible at every historical moment. Instead, it requires the appearance of certain conditions called "truth procedures," of which he names four: science, politics, art, and love. The possibility of philosophy depends upon its specific relation to these four conditions at a given time in history. For this same reason, the world-historical violence that both Adorno and Heidegger trace to the machinations of rationalist metaphysics cannot itself point to the end of philosophy. Instead, there is an important separation between philosophy and history, where the possibility of philosophy is determined by the historical configuration of its conditions. In turn, these conditions determine the immediate destination of philosophy. As Badiou remarks, recalling Hegel, the task of philosophy is "to think its time by putting the state of procedures conditioning it into a common place."[84]

On this view, philosophy depends upon but is irreducible to the generic conditions of "truth" in science, politics, art, and love. In the *vocabulaire* of Badiou, "truth" does not signify the revealing power of *alētheia*, as it does for Heidegger, but rather a relation of *fidelity* to an *event*—about which I shall say more in a moment. It will follow for Badiou that philosophy is neither "a production of truth," nor does it produce "truths."[85] Instead, philosophy consists in a conceptual site which thinks the mutual implication of truths at a given time in history. The result of "suturing" philosophy to one or more of its conditions is consequently a perversion of philosophy.

I note in passing that Badiou liberates this notion of the *suture* from Jacques Lacan, for whom it designates the supplementing of a lack within a signifying chain. Badiou appropriates this notion to indicate the closure of a void between philosophy and its conditions. The problem of the suture thus concerns the fateful consequence of binding philosophy to a truth in science, politics, art, or love. In the context of Adorno, for example, the suturing of philosophy to the political atrocity of Auschwitz destines philosophy to impotence before its messianic conversion into negative dialectics. In a different sense, for Heidegger, the interpretation of philosophy as metaphysics results in suturing the Greco-Western tradition to a science of being qua being rendered as the metaphysics of presence. Heidegger's ambition to desuture the future of thinking from the history of metaphysics has the further consequence of suturing the alethic thought of being to the truth condition of art—specifically, poetry in the Greek sense of *poiēsis*, understood "in the highest sense" as the primordial mode of "bringing-forth."[86] In the controversial case of Heidegger, moreover, the resurrection of philosophy as poietic "thinking" makes it possible to suture the new beginning of thinking to the poetic destiny of the German *Volk* and hence the fascist politics of National Socialism. This *disaster* is exactly why it is imperative for Badiou to *desuture* philosophy from its conditions—a fact made all the more urgent through Badiou's alignment of his project with Heidegger's original insight that "philosophy as such can only be re-qualified on the basis of the ontological question."[87] On this crucial point, Badiou differs sharply from Heidegger on the meaning of ontology and its relation to philosophy.

As we know, for Heidegger, Greco-Western philosophy has fallen under the dominant sway of traditional ontology, which equates the science of being qua being with the study of "being an object" (*Gegenstandsein*).[88] So formulated, traditional ontology asks the metaphysical question, "What are beings?," which covers over the more primordial question, "What is being?" Because traditional ontology treats being in the mode of an object, its effort to discover the fundamental meaning of being (beingness, *Seiendheit*) is interpreted in reference to some notion of a highest being (*das Seiendeste*). The paradigmatic case appears in the doctrine of "Platonism," which designates Heidegger's name for the way metaphysical questioning subordinates the revealing power of *alētheia* to a notion of *eidos* or *idea*. In a manner that brings together the ontological and theological aspects of Aristotelian metaphysics—the longstanding question whether *prōtē philosophia* concerns being qua being or the being of the prime mover—the so-called Platonistic determination of "beingness" as "objectness" likewise consigns the thinking of being to a thinking of oneness and ultimately the one. In turn, the figure of the one establishes the paradigm of what is thinkable over and against the originary process of the unconcealment of being. This point is condensed in a note appended to Heidegger's second volume of Nietzsche lectures from 1939/1946: "The one as unifying unity becomes *maßgebend* [authoritative, normative, decisive] for the subsequent determination of being."[89]

Badiou's effort to desuture philosophy from ontology takes aim at this precise point concerning the metaphysical domination of the one. Thus, picking up on the compound sense of *maßgebend* as "authoritative," "normative," or "decisive," Badiou argues in "The Question of Being Today" (1998) that "it is because of the normative function of the one in deciding being that being is reduced to the common, to empty generality, and is forced to endure the metaphysical predominance of the entity (*l'étant*)."[90] The central question concerns whether it is possible to break the decisive bond between being and the one, "without thereby ensnaring oneself in Heidegger's destinal apparatus," which sutured the destruction of metaphysics to "the unfounded promise of a saving reversal," heralded as much by the call for a new beginning of thinking as it was in Heidegger's late admission that "only a god can save us."[91]

It is a serious problem, for Badiou, that Heidegger's confrontation with the epoch of modern nihilism destines the future of thinking to a pathetic expression of nostalgia, the glorification of "return," and a pious wish to be saved. At the level of "ethics" or practical comportment, this problem is also reflected in Heidegger's treatment of the human being as a victim. In the last analysis, Heidegger renders us largely powerless, as the saving power must come from somewhere beyond the human, with a measure of influence that could belong only to a god. In fact, on this point there is no major difference between Adorno and Heidegger. The human being is fundamentally impotent and in need of redemption.

Moreover, by casting the human being as "the being who is capable of recognizing itself as a victim,"[92] Heidegger's thought appears as a certain culmination of Hobbes. But whereas, for Hobbes, the fear of violent death underlies the natural right to self-preservation, Heidegger *radicalizes* the principle of mortal finitude such that the governing principle of natural right appears transformed as the source of authentic being-toward-death. In a parallel sense, both Hobbes and Heidegger require a *decision* at the point of mortal finitude: in Hobbes, the transfer of liberty to a sovereign; in Heidegger, a leap into the primordial experience of being. Apropos to either case, the reduction of the human to a "being-for-death" (*être-pour-la-mort*)[93] has led Badiou to argue that ethical discourse becomes nihilistic when it equates the ethical subject with the harm that can be done to it. This of course resonates with Nietzsche's complaint about the enervating effects of slave morality. But whereas Adorno rejects Heidegger's "pathos of authenticity"[94] in exchange for the messianic hope of redemption, Heidegger defies Nietzsche by requiring devotion to a "god." As he wrote in the *Beiträge* of 1936/1938: "How few know that god waits for the grounding of the truth of historical being (*Seyns*), and thus for the leap of the human being into Da-sein."[95]

V. ONTOLOGY AND ETHICS

In order to free philosophy from the history of ontology as metaphysics, so determined by the normative character of the one, Badiou ventures to rethink the relation between ontology and philosophy beginning with an ontology of the multiple. Specifically, in the monumental work of *Being and Event* (1988), Badiou submits that his "entire discourse originates in an ontological decision (*la décision ontologique*); that of the nonbeing of the one."[96] There are in fact two decisions at stake. First, the decision in agreement with Heidegger that the future of philosophy must be assessed on the basis of the ontological question. Second, the decision in favor of answering the ontological question with the axiomatic priority of the nonbeing of the one—as authorized by the basic assumptions of Zermelo-Fraenkel set theory. Together these two decisions implement Badiou's most concise statement of his philosophical intention: "To *resume* the thread of modern reason, to take *one more step* in the lineage of the 'Cartesian Meditation.'"[97] Or as he also claims: "To rediscover a foundational style, a decided style, a style in the school of a Descartes."⁹⁸ As we shall see, this "decided style" will describe the *reckless* character of Badiou's resurrection of philosophy.

Let us note, however, that Badiou's Descartes is not the one who sought to found philosophy anew on the local certainty of the *cogito: ubi cogito, ibi sum*, "where I think, there I exist."⁹⁹ Any attempt to found philosophy upon the singularity of the *cogito* would amount to yet another instance of the metaphysical domination of being by the one. Instead, Badiou's Descartes is the one who, in the *Discourse on Method*, endeavored to reform the moral writings of the ancient pagans by replacing their loose foundations of sand and mud with the more solid foundation of mathematics.¹⁰⁰

It is important to emphasize the sense in which Badiou follows in the tradition of Descartes by intending to found the future of philosophy—including moral philosophy or what Badiou calls "ethics"—upon a renewed mathematical rationalism derived from set-theoretical conceptions of the multiple and the infinite. For that matter, Badiou's ethical doctrine, the "ethic of truths," will attempt to succeed where Descartes had failed—namely, by entrenching a doctrine of ethics in the formula: "mathematics *is* ontology."¹⁰¹ In order to situate the significance of Badiou's effort to resurrect the possibility of philosophy from the destroyed history of metaphysics, let us look closely at his decision to form allegiance with Descartes—with a focus on the relation between ontology and ethics, on the one hand, and ontology and philosophy, on the other.

Starting with the relation between ontology and ethics, Badiou's "ethic of truths" describes the process through which one becomes the subject of a truth by pledging fidelity to an event. On this view, ethics begins with a decision; and there can be no ethics "in general" because a subject is produced through the act of becoming faithful to the insurgency of an event; an eruption the *new* which is always relative to a *particular* situation.

In Badiou's technical sense, an event is anterior to the subject. Subjects do not cause events; events are not revealed by subjects; the actions of subjects are not responsible to preexisting norms of thinking or behavior. Rather, the capacity to *become* a subject is what distinguishes the human being from its animal substructure. The process of claiming fidelity to an event is, accordingly, irreducible to the human animality of the individual, which is itself devoid of ethical content. There are likewise no natural, a priori, or consensual ethical principles because such principles—which Badiou calls *truths*—are produced by the *decision* through which a subject pledges fidelity to an event.¹⁰²

Every event occurs within the context of a *situation*—defined by Badiou as the presentation of a multiplicity. The situation denotes "the place of taking-place, whatever the terms of the multiplicity in question."¹⁰³ That the situation presents a multiplicity is a corollary to the axiomatic decision, affirmed by Badiou, for the nonbeing of the one. According to this formulation, "the one *is not*."[104] What is countable belongs to a multiple as the member of a set; "oneness" is countable only as a mathematical operation, the "count-as-one."[105] Thus, unbound from the hegemonic power of the one, the situation presents pure multiplicity (the empty set) as the formal structure of being (*être*). As the place of pure presentation, the situation has the character of a thoroughly mathematized version of the Heideggerian clearing (*Lichtung*), understood as the appropriating event of being (*Ereignis*). What Badiou calls the event (*événement*), however, is not the opening of a temporal horizon, but a "hazardous, unpredictable supplement."[106] The event *supplements* the situation; the event is both *situated* and *supplementary*. It comes to pass within the context of a definite situation. Yet in making its appearance, it points retroactively to a *void* in the situation. The void must therefore be assumed as the structural possibility of an event.[107] Moreover, because the consequences of an event cannot be anticipated, it supplements the situation by introducing an element of chance which is fundamentally *undecidable* from the standpoint of the given situation.[108] The dualisms of being and event, the decided and the undecidable, thus constitute the fundamental dualisms of Badiou's thought.

Whereas ontology names the decision by which pure being is nothing but a multiple of multiples (a *multiple-sans-un*), ethics names the process by which the undecidable character of an event becomes decided by a subject within a determinate situation of being. In the process of becoming the subject of a truth, an event compels the subject to decide a new way of life within the altered conditions of the situation.[109] Thus, by the sole process of decision an individual exceeds its animal finitude, its being-for-death, and becomes—with all due qualification—*immortal*.[110] To live "as an immortal" is to live in accord with the immortality of a truth.

VI. THE AXIOM OF DECISION

Between being and event, the category of *décision* is at the center of Badiou's philosophic enterprise. It is also the source of some circularity in Badiou's treatment of the relation between ethics and ontology. On one hand, the ethic of truths is situated within the decision that ontology is mathematics, "the guardian of being qua being."[111] On the other hand, this same decision is the result of a decisive fidelity to the axioms that authorize post-Cantorian set theory: foremost the axiom of the empty set, which ensures that being qua being is pure multiplicity. Badiou's theory of ontology therefore presupposes the theory of ethics it is intended to support. However, this circularity is not self-affirming. It points, rather, to a question about the situation of analysis within the context of ordinary experience.

By starting from the axioms of set theory, Badiou begins with a decision for abstraction—in his language: *subtraction*. But subtraction is already a form of analysis—and because analysis is capable only of articulating the whole of experience into its constituent parts, it cannot account for the preanalytic context of experience. This is also to say that a procedure of analysis cannot account for its own beginning. As Stanley Rosen once observed: "Analysis is never merely the application of rules. It is also at once a seeing of which rules to apply and how to apply them."[112] Guiding any analysis is therefore some form of prudence, what the Greeks called *phronēsis*, which must take its bearings from a preanalytic perception of the continuum of experience.[113] There may well be a plurality of contexts and experiences. But the differences between experiential forms can be evaluated only subsequent to their apprehension which allows for the discursive comparison of their distinctive parts.

Specific to Badiou, but common across schools of analytic philosophy, the inability of analysis to account for its preanalytic context results in discarding the domain of preanalytic experience as a legitimate topic of investigation. As Badiou writes in *Being and Event:* "My discourse is never epistemological, nor is it a philosophy *of* mathematics. If that were the case, I would have discussed the great modern schools of epistemology (formalism, intuitionism, finitism, etc.). Mathematics is cited here to let its ontological essence become manifest."[114]

What Badiou specifies as "epistemology" points to a series of debates concerning whether mathematical praxis results from either the purely intellectual construction of forms or the discovery of fundamental principles that govern an independently existing objective reality. Whatever side one takes, if we choose to take a side, my point is only that this debate cannot be resolved from within the perspective of mathematics. We require an account of the human relation to the pretheoretical context of mathematical activity. Badiou therefore leaves us to begin with the axiomatic decision for set theory ontology. But as this decision identifies ontology with a formal system of mathematical signs, Badiou risks committing us to a purely formal system of rules for the manipulation of signs which are themselves subtracted from any consideration for their reference.[115] As Socrates says in the *Republic*, mathematicians only "dream about being" because in dreaming we take the likeness of something to be not a likeness, but rather the thing itself to which it is like.[116] If the decision to entrench ethics in ontology is likewise a matter of simply drawing out the ethical consequences of the ontology of truths, as Badiou states in the Preface to the English edition of *L'éthique* (1993),[117] what is there to distinguish this decision from anything other than an arbitrary act of will? Otherwise stated, is Badiou's ethics but a dream within a dream?

Badiou has responded to the related charges of "decisionism," famously leveled by Jean-François Lyotard, by emphasizing the manifest priority of the event to any possible decision.[118] More specifically, because the appearance of an event is unprecedented from the standpoint of the situation it creates not only new possibilities for profound transformation, but by necessity it *forces* a decision: to claim or not to claim fidelity to an event. In the language of Badiou: "The event is not the result of a decision." Rather: "The decision is to be uniquely faithful to the transformation."[119]

To give a simple example, when the music pioneer Robert Moog introduced the first commercially available electronic sound synthesizer in 1965, this was the result of a truth process owing to an event in the field of music. The event itself—the scientific opening of technological possibilities for the invention of a purely electronic musical instrument—first achieved a measure of truth in 1920 when Léon Theremin invented the etherophone that bears his name. It could be said, in the language of Badiou, that Moog and Theremin shared in their fidelity to the singular event that forced, through their decisions, the production of new truths in the musical field. What Moog advanced through his own technological innovation was a new way of manifesting this truth through the invention of his modular sound synthesizer. This in turn opened up new possibilities for musical expression. The audience and musicians who claimed fidelity to the evental opening secured by Theremin and Moog were then compelled to invent radically new ways of making and experiencing music. In more formulaic terms, the *event* "brings to pass 'something other' than the situation"; the act of *fidelity* sustains the break with existing opinions or "instituted knowledges"; and the *truth* produced by this fidelity then *forces* new knowledge into the existing situation.[120] In the present case, Moog's modular synthesizer created new sound possibilities for psychedelic music, progressive rock, krautrock, jazz fusion, electro, and so on. But crucially, these inventions were only subsequent to Moog's act of fidelity, as a matter of *choice*. In Badiou's words: "The interventional conception of truth permits the complete refusal of its effects. The avant-garde, by its existence alone, imposes choice, but not *its* choice."[121]

The imposition of choice serves to draw out the force of history in the determination of any decision or truth procedure. Events force decisions.[122] Decisions crystallize the "aleatoric historicity" of truths.[123] The decision is therefore the intended mastery of chance or what Machiavelli called *fortuna*, "which demonstrates her power where virtue (*virtù*) has not been put into order to resist her."[124] Along these lines, Badiou does not simply initiate "one more step" in the tradition of Descartes. Rather, he belongs with Descartes to the tradition of modern philosophy inaugurated by Machiavelli and Bacon, the paramount aim of which is mastery: in the case of Machiavelli, the mastery of political order; in Bacon and Descartes, the mastery of nature for the "relief of man's estate."[125] But specific to the tie between Badiou and Machiavelli, they both take their bearings from extreme situations; and they both conclude that daring trumps caution in unsettled times. As Machiavelli so unkindly put it: "Fortune is a woman; and it is necessary, if one wants to hold her down, to beat her and strike her down. And one sees that she lets herself be won more by the impetuous than by those who proceed coldly. And so always, like a woman, she is the friend of the young because they are less cautious, more ferocious, and command her with more audacity."[126]

VII. RECKLESS DECISIONS

We are now in a position to appreciate Badiou's statement that "philosophy, when it truly appears, is either *reckless* or it is nothing."[127] Within the lineage of Machiavelli, Badiou's starting point (the axiomatic decision for the nonbeing of the one) signals a new epoch of philosophical daring certified by the historical forcing of the decision that mathematics is ontology—and, more specifically, that being qua being is a multiple of multiples extending to an infinity of infinities. Indeed, we may go so far as to say that philosophy is either reckless or it is nothing precisely because philosophy is understood by Badiou as the bold mastery of its conditions in the areas of science, politics, art, and love. In the style of Machiavelli, philosophy is the risk of a decision for mastery, or else it is nothing. Now, if we are permitted this connection to historical antecedents, is it not the consequence that Badiou's decisionistic rationalism is itself sutured to a decision for daring in the domain of politics? At the very least, Badiou's axiomatic decision to found his entire discourse on the nonbeing of the one is consistent with a suture to the condition of politics in Machiavelli—namely, the intention to master *fortuna* by force, to make the human being the master of its destiny.[128]

If these observations do not alleviate concerns about a reckless decisionism at the core of Badiou's thought, it is because truths on Badiou's account are produced as a function of *virtù*, in the sense given by Machiavelli. Here virtue is not concerned with *aretē* or "excellence" in the classical Greek sense. Nor is it opposed to a traditional or commonsense notion of vice. The virtue of the decision is rather that which gives the subject its *strength* to master the trials of fortune: the chance effects of an event. When Badiou states his wish "to rediscover a foundational style, a decided style, a style in the school of a Descartes,"[129] he affirms the view that human life is fundamentally the mastery of fortune in union with the Cartesian decision that philosophy must be placed under the condition of mathematics. This combination of mastery and mathematical certainty gives birth to the distinctly modern belief that human beings possess the capacity to become the masters of their destiny. Yet the spontaneous mastery of the event is prompted only by the unpredictable machinations of history. If Badiou has not simply replaced the god of Heidegger with the saving power of the event, he replicates the wish of Machiavelli to preserve free will so that fortune may be the arbiter of only half of our actions.[130] Still, this does not remove the question about how to decide among competing events, which is to say, competing truths. How does one decide among decisions? By what criteria or criterion does one commit to one truth and not another?[131]

According to Nietzsche in the *Gay Science,* the "one thing needful" is "to 'give style'" to one's life.[132] Badiou's similar emphasis on a "decided style" (*Stil, style*) alludes to a close alignment with Nietzsche on the decidability of truth, in the precise sense that Badiou says: "Nietzsche constructs his own category of truth."[133] As Badiou reads Nietzsche, truth is reconceived as an act: the revaluation of all values. Because the process of revaluation is "subtracted from all evaluation," it "does not itself have a value."[134] It is rather "beyond good and evil," which leads Badiou to call the act of revaluation an "event."[135]

From these remarks, it is evident that Badiou wants to associate his own doctrine of truth with the Nietzschean act. In the aforementioned section of the *Gay Science*, this act is called a "great and rare art." Likewise, Badiou calls the existence of a truth-process "rare";[136] and in *Being and Event* he writes: "the trajectory of the true is practical [. . .] it *forces decision.*"[137] The generic procedure of a truth consists, therefore, in a rare act from the standpoint of the situation. Here, it should come as no surprise to see the trace of Nietzschean perspectivism, with respect to what is rare relative to the situation. But even more important, the Nietzschean act is an event in Badiou's parlance because it is an "act without a concept or program."[138] This is to say, the act or event is not projected into the future, but can be discerned only retroactively as a consequence of the "will to power, which is the interpretive capacity of the decision."[139] Thus, it is only by a pure act of will that an event can be recognized retroactively as a truth. This retroactive discernibility of an event also explains why the process of a truth requires a vow of faith. Because the decision is itself the act of valuation, there can be no independent standard by which to judge it. As Badiou confirms in the dictionary at the end of *Being and Event:* "there is therefore no contrary to the true."[140] Insofar as the decision marks a break from the existing situation, it is necessarily beyond valuation. Truth, according to Badiou, is for this reason "inevaluable."[141]

The inevaluable character of a truth makes it is impossible to rank one truth higher than another. There can likewise be no rank-ordering of decisions. In this sense, Badiou's style is that of Nietzsche's doctrine of the will to power subtracted from the rhetoric of rank order. The upshot, if that is the right word, is that Badiou liberates the will to power from the exclusive nobility of the aristocratic spirit. But in its place, one finds a revolutionary egalitarianism that cannot distinguish up from down. "The generic [truth] is egalitarian, and every subject, ultimately, is ordained to equality."[142] Hence, in *Logics of Worlds* (2006): "For us it is impossible to rank worlds hierarchically."[143] Sundered from the rhetoric of nobility or goodness, we are released into the aleatory flux of events and decisions. Nietzschean chaos may be stabilized by the mathematical dream of being, on the one hand, and the *virtù* of decision, on the other. But there are as many subjects as there are truths, with the result that Badiou's ethic of truths can expound only a schizophrenic perspectivism where each perspective awakens to a truth for which every other truth is an arbitrary dream of wakefulness. Put in slightly different terms, the decision to entrench ethics in a doctrine of ontological change—the *multiple-sans-un* understood as a "process of limitless self-differentiation"[144]—forces Badiou to privilege the new for the sake of the new. But this is because his ethics cannot distinguish what is new from what is better.[145]

In this same register, it is implicit within the ethic of truths that philosophy aims to think the unity of its conditions rather than orders of rank. Badiou tells us that philosophy is the act of "seizing" truths, and that this act "testifies to the unity of thought."[146] Under this assertion—and it is simply an assertion built upon the axiomatic foundation of the ontology of truths—philosophy appears as a descendant of the transcendental ego, which in Kant supplies unity to cognition. However, there is no equivalent to the power of apperception in Badiou. There is the mathematical operation of the count-as-one, which guarantees "there is oneness"; and in his critique of Kant, Badiou exposes the operational necessity of the count-as-one by subtracting it from the "transcendental unity of self-consciousness."[147] But philosophy itself is not self-conscious. (At least Badiou does not explain how it could be.) Nor is the unity of thought supplied by the cognizing activities of the human *psyche* or *cogito*. Instead, the unity of thought is supplied simply by the definition of philosophy as that which thinks the possible compatibility of truths within a given epoch.

By founding philosophy on the "ungrounded ground" of its conditions, Badiou therefore repeats in a different key the "deception of the beginning" decried by Adorno—and thus he returns us to the controversial purview of Rorty, for whom the meaning of philosophy can be changed simply by its being redescribed. What follows is no less a provocation than a fact. The subtraction of the cognitive faculty from philosophy renders philosophy the thoughtless unity of truths. Philosophy purified of the human soul becomes an epiphenomenon of the historicity of decisions—and as we have seen in the examples of Heidegger and Adorno, the subordination of thought to decision yields the negation of prudence by history.

Philosophy in Crisis 39

VIII. CARTESIAN NIHILISM

To return now to the question of the "better," Badiou's determination to collapse goodness into truth is nowhere more evident than in his creative rewriting of Plato's *Republic*. There one finds in a signature passage that it is not the Idea of the Good but the Idea of the True that is "beyond being." Or, as Badiou also has it, beyond "the order of that which is exposed to thought."[148] In *L'éthique*, Badiou pursues this same strategy by which an idea of the good is collapsed into the affirmation of a truth. The Good is here defined as "the internal norm of a prolonged disorganization of life." And further: "What provokes the emergence of the Good—and, by simple consequence, Evil— exclusively concerns the rare existence of truth-processes."[149] Just as an event breaks into human life as a radical disruption, the Good nominates the norm that measures the distance between our mere mortality and the truth-process by which an individual is converted into a subject.

By contrast, Evil—or, in *Being and Event*, what Badiou calls the "false" (*faux*)—is irreducible to the question of whether the human being is naturally dangerous. Instead, Evil arises as an obstacle to the Good.[150] Evil is therefore "not a category of the human animal, but of the subject."[151] Fidelity to a truth—captured by the maxim: "Keep going!" (*"Continuer!"*)—"is what tries to ward off the Evil that every singular truth makes possible."[152] The Good, as Badiou conceives it, is consequently not the Good at which all things aim. Rather, the Good is relative to whatever truth it signifies. History understood as the serial genesis of "Goods" is, accordingly, an expression of the ontological *multiple-sans-un* as a "process of limitless self-differentiation."[153]

This is a clever solution to the problem of knowing or identifying the human good, especially as this problem has dogged philosophical ethics in the tradition stretching from Descartes to Heidegger. By this I mean the tradition that Badiou identifies with—namely, the tradition that endeavors to assess the possibility of philosophy on the basis of the ontological question. The method of inquiry characteristic of this tradition is one that begins with the subordination of ethics to ontology under the assumption that whatever we may think about the human good must be regulated by an answer to the question of being.

There are, accordingly, two opposing yet closely related responses to the question concerning the possibility of philosophy.[154] These responses consist in the attempt to found philosophy on some thoroughgoing insight into the meaning of being, on the one hand, and, on the other, a critique of this same attempt to reduce the foundations of philosophy to an interpretation of the meaning of being. In turn, there are two fundamental versions of the initial ontocentric response. First, the version exemplified by the method of Cartesian science, which models itself on the paradigm of mathematical certainty and which makes of the philosophical foundations an abstract theoretical artifact: in Descartes, the thing that thinks, the *res cogitans*. Second, the version that attempts to retain what is thought to be the high level of certainty produced by the Cartesian method, while at the same time radicalizing the end toward which that method aims. To plot the relevant trajectory across recent European thought, Husserl proposed the standpoint of transcendental subjectivity in its constitution of the lifeworld, whereas Heidegger gave us the ontological priority of being-here (*Dasein*), later formulated in terms of the clearing (*Lichtung*) and the appropriating event of historical being (*Ereignis*). Badiou then follows in this tradition with the proposal for a set-theory ontology adapted from Georg Cantor according to which mathematics "thinks" being qua being.[155]

It is significant that across these proposals, they each decide for the subordination of ethics to ontology (or being-thinking in a properly qualified sense). However, this decision has the consequence of stripping away any conception of the good—or the human relation to an idea of the good—from the foundations of philosophy. They are thus each tasked with having to retroactively build an account of the human relation to the good into their philosophical systems, or else they are compelled to concede the impossibility of philosophy to speak intelligibly about the good or the human relation to an idea of the good. Whereas Heidegger exemplifies the most extreme consequence of this failure to reattach philosophy to its human roots, Badiou builds a notion of the good back into his philosophical system—but he does so at the risk of suspending the good from the ontology of truths. Like a dream within a dream, the "Good" is a fantasy of truth. It expresses, in Freudian language, the fulfillment of a wish that human beings are, or may become, the masters of their fortunes.

Such is the concise legacy of Cartesian rationalism in recent and contemporary European thought. It is, moreover, this legacy that I want to call into question—here in a preliminary fashion; in detail as this question bears on the philosophical contribution of Rousseau. I take my bearings from a singular passage in Rousseau's posthumously published *Moral Letters*, written around 1757/1758: "It is necessary to end where Descartes began: *I think therefore I exist*."[156] The project of turning Descartes' legacy on its head remains an untapped and underappreciated philosophical imperative. In the present context, this imperative is made all the more exigent by Badiou's explicit Cartesianism, which presents itself simultaneously as the historical continuation and refutation of Heidegger.

Distilled to its essence, the problem at hand concerns an elective affinity between two important features of the Cartesian legacy. The first concerns the subordination of ethics to ontology at the foundation of philosophy. The second concerns the way in which the subordination of ethics to ontology follows directly from the attempt to respond systematically to an immediate moral crisis. In every cited instance, we find that the effort to put philosophy on new foundations is oriented around a perception of moral *inquiétude*, which in turn results in the radical exclusion of ethical questioning from the very foundations upon which the solution is proposed. Thus, having "compared the moral writings of the ancient pagans to very proud and magnificent palaces built only on sand and mud," Descartes resolved to replace their "many diverse opinions" with more solid foundations secured by the principles and methods of *mathesis universalis*.[157] For Heidegger, by contrast, the destitution of being in the epoch of technological nihilism served as the moral crisis that required the thinking of being, whereas today the epochal reign of global capitalism is, for Badiou, the enemy that must be confronted by a philosophy competent to think "in level terms with capital."[158]

I do not doubt the severity of either problem. Yet if we concentrate on the seminal example of Descartes, it becomes evident that Cartesian method produces a radical disconnect between, on one hand, the perception of a moral crisis which serves to motivate his philosophical questioning in the direction of universal reason, and, on the other, the solid foundation of the *cogito sum* upon which he intends to rebuild the philosophical edifice. This dichotomy between moral insight and philosophical system-building is due to the fact that Descartes does not enter into the method of doubt from within the perspective of the *cogito*, meaning that neither the search for a scientific first principle nor its result in the *cogito sum* can account for the erotic character of Descartes' investigation. The source of philosophical eros is rather excluded from the foundation of philosophy or science. Yet we require precisely this account of the genesis of philosophical eros, which is to say, we require an account of how the "natural desire to know," so called by Aristotle, is transformed into the pursuit of rigorous science. In sum, we require an account of the possibility of philosophy itself, by which I mean the genesis of philosophical experience. But this is what Descartes and his epigones render impossible. Instead, philosophy appears as if by a pure act of will, a bold decision made by the philosopher—and so, it cannot account for its own possibility.

To push this point further, we may note how Cartesian thought is founded upon a *crisis*. In the sense given by the Greek noun, the word κρίσις indicates a decision: a power of distinguishing, separating, judging, or selecting. What has been selected in the case of Descartes is the idea that health is "unquestionably the first good and the foundation of all the other worldly goods."[159] It follows that a practical philosophy aimed at enhancing and prolonging physical life is valuable; and that in order for it to be effective, it must be secured by a first principle to provide certainty for the sake of utility.[160] Yet, "health" is not the first principle of Cartesian thought, which receives its legitimacy from the method of doubt and the deduction of the *cogito*—and as we know,

Cartesian method severs mind from body, thought from extension, and so the link to the vital object that Descartes wished to save.

Descartes therefore inaugurates a substance dualism which cannot produce apodictic knowledge about the living body it is supposed to benefit—and this is because the will to master nature by means of mathematical physics transforms both body and soul into purely formal, hence inert, substances. Moreover, this decision produces two incommensurable substances that—once analyzed or broken apart—cannot be brought back together again except by means of a mythical pineal gland. Thus, having been emptied of life—or the unity of body and soul that was once thought to sustain it—the "first good" becomes unintelligible or at best a fable.[161]

These results ensue directly from Descartes' founding of philosophy upon the paradigm of mathematical rationality, which produces not only a dualism of thought and extension, but more fundamentally a dualism between facts and values or formal structure and knowledge of the good. Again, the result is not only a philosophy or science that cannot account for its own possibility, but a method of inquiry that can neither justify itself nor tell us what is in fact "good" about modern science and its artifacts. In this way, Cartesian thought renders itself groundless, having sundered the very idea of the good that it hoped to secure.

IX. NIHILISM OR HAPPINESS

To bring all of this to a crucial point: at stake in the subordination of ethics to ontology is the question of whether an inquiry into the meaning of being can be assumed as the basis for a genuine "first philosophy." My thesis is that every endeavor to think the possibility of philosophy on the basis of being does not alleviate, but rather intensifies, the crisis of modern philosophical nihilism—the most severe consequence of the failure of philosophy to account for its own possibility.

If philosophy cannot account for its own possibility, then it must admit one of two fates. Either philosophy is impossible, or we require some nonphilosophical way of accounting for its possibility. If the former obtains, then what we mistake for philosophy can be only the arbitrary expression of the will to power. Nietzsche prevails, wisdom is chaos, and philosophy is transformed into the practice of mastery. If the latter obtains, then philosophy is not knowledge of itself, but knowledge of ignorance; and knowledge of ignorance cannot be the love of wisdom if it is not oriented by some notion of the good, in defiance of ignorance. Hence, we return to the original question concerning the subordination of ethics to ontology. If philosophy is more than knowledge of ignorance or the intermittent spasms of chaos, then it must legitimate itself though a confrontation with nihilism. It must demonstrate how the possibility of philosophy hangs on its capacity to give a reflexive account of its own possibility—and this requires some account of the good, or the human relation to an idea of the good, which is not subtracted from the foundations of philosophy itself.

In view of these observations, it is no accident that ever since Descartes modern philosophy—indeed, the entire situation of modernity—is rife with talk about alienation, anxiety, disenchantment, and death. In its essence, the modern crisis is one that leaves human happiness behind. No one understood this better than Nietzsche, for whom modernity takes hold by the radicalization of Cartesian decisionism and its final unmasking as the will to power. In the wake of Enlightenment, the will has become increasingly diseased. Every century becomes more decadent than the next, and life belongs to the "last men" who in their comfortable boredom prefer to will nothing if only to avoid having nothing to will. This is the passive nihilism that the last men call "happiness"—and they blink.

Nietzsche's Zarathustra offers the following aphorism in return: "I no longer strive for happiness. I strive for my work!"[162] As yet another instance of the modern disavowal of happiness, Badiou goes even further: "Every definition of Man based on happiness is nihilist."[163] "Between Man as the possible basis for the uncertainty of truths, or Man as being-for-death (or being-for-happiness [être-pour-le-bonheur], it is the same thing), you have to choose. It is the same choice that divides philosophy from 'ethics,' or the courage of truths from nihilism."[164] Is this not a repetition of Heidegger, for whom the goal of happiness was transformed into the "greatest nihilism?" After all, a truth is not a goal at which a subject can aim. For Badiou, a truth is *produced* through the act of fidelity to an event.

Whereas Socratic philosophy may be defined by its erotic attachment to happiness, in the sense that *eudaimonia* describes the active love of wisdom, the modern disavowal of happiness is a function of the Cartesian legacy as it passes from Nietzsche through Heidegger to Adorno and Badiou. In the case of Badiou, however, the nihilism of the contemporary epoch is owed not to the forgetting of being, but to the situation in which happiness as *jouissance* or "enjoyment" has taken hold—either as the pure and simple negation of the world, or as the empty imperative of consumer society.[165] According to the first formulation, there is passive nihilism, the will to will nothing, or our drugged releasement into oblivion. According to the second, our every move is plotted by the rituals of consumption and excretion. The synthesis of these two forms then yields the wasted production of waste, which Badiou identifies with the vapid "happiness" of humanistic capitalism.

At this point, the similarities between Badiou and Adorno will be obvious. Both invoke the Marxist critique of capitalist society, and both share

Nietzsche's contempt for the perverted attitudes of the last men. Yet Badiou resists the design of a melancholy science, which looks to engender a sense of critical responsibility by exposing reason to the concrete experience of its impotence. Instead, Badiou joins himself to what he calls Nietzsche's "personal entry into antiphilosophy" and the associated claim that because the ideology of Socratic asceticism excludes enjoyment as a topic of philosophical examination, it thereby drains the capacity of philosophy to think the contemporary situation.[166] From this it follows that the confrontation with nihilism requires a reversal of the heritage of Socratic asceticism in order to rethink the notion of enjoyment as a category of philosophical and cultural critique. More specifically, we are told, the philosophical reassertion of enjoyment will be instrumental to calling forth "the names with which logic will make the world to come." And further: "Philosophy has no other legitimate aim except to help find the new names that will bring into existence the unknown world that is only waiting for us because we are waiting for it."[167]

Against the vulgar enjoyments of consumer society, the reassertion of enjoyment as a philosophical imperative is rooted in Badiou's appropriation of *jouissance* from Lacan.[168] In order to avoid a long digression on Lacanian terminology, I note that for Lacan *jouissance* signifies the paradoxical mixture of pleasure and pain that a subject may derive from the transgressive impetus of its symptom. Within the symbolic arrangement of a world, *jouissance* also describes the point at which the order of a world may be transgressed by the striving for symptomal satisfaction. In confrontation with the legacy of Socratic ascetism, Badiou then adapts the notion of transgressive enjoyment to his formal ontology in order to indicate the "unnamable point," the "unforcible" remainder, "where a truth occurs as a hole in the sense-making of knowledge."[169] Put otherwise, *jouissance* occurs at the point of an eventual rupture. At the breach of an unmasterable excess, it cannot be captured by the Nietzschean act of nomination or the act by which a new symbolic order is forced into existence.

The impossible satisfaction of enjoyment thus constitutes the real object of ethical mastery. As Badiou puts the point in *L'éthique:*

> It is only by declaring that we want what conservatism decrees to be impossible, and by affirming truths against the desire for nothingness, that we tear ourselves away from nihilism. *The possibility of the impossible*, which is exposed by every loving encounter, every scientific re-foundation, every artistic invention and every sequence of emancipatory politics, *is the sole principle*—against the ethics of living-well whose real content is the deciding of death—*of an ethic of truths.*[170]

To repeat: "*The possibility of the impossible is the sole principle of an ethic of truths.*" Much like Adorno, for whom it is necessary to think the impossible for the sake of the possible, Badiou holds the impossible as higher than both possibility and actuality—but he does so because possibility and actuality are the controlling terms of the existing situation.[171] In contrast to Adorno, messianic impossibility is converted into perspectival impossibility; and against the doctrine of non-identity, Badiou offers the possibility of the event, which is only impossible from the standpoint of the existing situation. Again, with reference to *L'éthique:* "emancipatory politics always consists in making seem possible precisely that which, from within the situation, is declared to be impossible."[172] Flashing Marx, the aim is not simply to interpret the world, but to change it. The philosophical reassertion of enjoyment signifies the unique role of philosophy in bringing forth the world to come. Much like Nietzsche's philosopher of the future, Badiou's philosopher appears as the cheerful philosopher-legislator whose purpose is to name the events that will give rise to a future order of humanity.

Whether happiness belongs to our future is yet another question. In the line of reflection that concludes Badiou's plea for the philosophical reassertion of enjoyment, he quotes a passage from Jean Genet's great drama, *The Balcony*, in which a rebel insurgent praises "the future bearers of liberty."[173] Crucially, it is not happiness but *freedom* that identifies the final aim of a properly militant philosophy. Just as the transgressive aim of enjoyment consists in the generation of a future world, the anticipation of freedom reinforces the repression of happiness initiated by Descartes. In fact, it is only with the late addition of *Logics of Worlds* in 2006 that Badiou has endeavored to rehabilitate the category of happiness, not as the active principle of the philosophic life, but as an epiphenomenon of the ethical life, where every truth procedure is assigned a specific affect. Happiness (*bonheur*) names the affect of love; enthusiasm (*enthousiasme*), the affect of politics; pleasure (*plaisir*), the affect of art; joy (*joie*), the affect of science.[174]

Compelling as this arrangement may be, the correlation of truth to affect is entirely arbitrary. If these propositions hold any sense at all, their sensibility must be derived from the commonsense basis of the preanalytic situation—namely, the very domain from which Badiou subtracts the ontological schema upon which he builds his philosophical anthropology. Consistent with the terms of Badiou's axiomatic method, the assignment of a specific affect to a particular procedure of truth attests to no more and no less than Badiou's unwavering fidelity to the elegance of his system.

Nevertheless, it is not without philosophical significance that happiness returns in the thought of Badiou, as if by the vicissitudes of a return of the repressed. Still, more telling is Badiou's assignment of happiness to the affect of love, which appears in the Socratic register as the daimonic force which raises the potential philosopher into philosophy. If we take seriously the philosophical implications of Freudian drive theory, according to which human sexuality is expressed through the interaction of affects and ideas, then the attachment of happiness to the truth-process of love would appear as a return of the repressed which convenes the ancient love of wisdom. It follows that if we wish to investigate the possibility of philosophy, understood as the genesis of philosophical experience, then we shall have to investigate the enigmatic status of happiness in the genesis of philosophical eros.

Let us therefore express solidarity with Badiou's ethical imperative. It is time to take one more step. I began these remarks by considering the widely repeated claims about the end of philosophy. It is a corollary of each declaration that if philosophy has come to an end, then it makes no sense to speak about the responsibility of the philosopher. In the case of Hegel, one could speak about the responsibility granted to the champion of the Absolute, the scientist of wisdom. Otherwise, the responsibility of the philosopher may be converted into several stock examples: the revolutionary praxis of the proletariat in Marx; the creative domination of the *Übermensch* in Nietzsche; the therapeutic purification of ordinary language in Wittgenstein; the decisive leap into being in Heidegger. In response, Adorno attempted to mitigate the perils of postphilosophical thinking by invoking a melancholy science bent on exposing the impotence of reason to the masochistic punishment of ruthless self-criticism. In our own time, Badiou has responded that every declaration about the end of philosophy is most likely the rhetorical means to give philosophy itself a new aim. Badiou thus proposes a philosophy of the new, which begins by performing a resurrection of philosophy upon the corpse of ontology.

It is a further consequence of Badiou's thought that the orientation of ethics around definitions of the human as either a being-for-happiness or a being-for-death must all be abolished in exchange for a new doctrine of truth. For my part, I have tried to show how this new "ethic of truths" participates in a perpetuation of the Cartesian legacy and its characteristic subordination of ethics to ontology, which cannot help but exacerbate the problem of modern philosophical nihilism whereby philosophy is rendered mute by the demand to give a reflexive account of its own possibility. At bottom, this problem is a consequence of the Cartesian conversion of philosophy into method, which sunders the good from the foundations of philosophical questioning. In turn, philosophy is powerless to give an account of its own goodness, which makes it impossible to legitimate its theoretical or practical commitments, except by the powers of rhetoric or the pure force of will. What we require is therefore an account of happiness in its role as the founding question of philosophy. In the next chapter, I show how this account constitutes the exact point of intervention for Rousseau's contribution to a critique of Descartes.

As a final preparation, let us now perform an intervention of our own. In the spirit of fondness for a fellow traveler, Badiou gives special credence to one of Nietzsche's last letters—a note to Georg Brandes, postmarked Turin, January 4, 1889. The letter reads in total: "To my friend Georg. Once you discovered me, it was no great feat to find me: the difficulty now is to lose me . . . The Crucified." Badiou goes on to comment:

> Nietzsche is someone that one must at once discover, find, and lose. One must discover him in his truth, discover him in the desire of the act. One must find him, as he who provokes the theme of truth towards a new demand, as he who forces the philosophical stance to invent a new figure of truth, a new rupture with sense. And finally, of course, one must lose him, because anti-philosophy must, when all is said and done, be lost, or lost sight of, once philosophy has established its own space.[175]

In this same spirit, I wager the following proposition. If Badiou's decision for axiomatic certainty is forced by the process according to which a subject claims fidelity to a truth, then it must also be true that this same decision forecloses the zetetic spirit of Socratic ignorance through a polarization that recalls Max Weber's distinction between the ethics of conviction and the ethics of responsibility.[176] It is therefore in homage to Badiou's praise for Nietzsche that I say: Let us open ourselves again to ignorance. The time has come to lose Badiou.

NOTES

1. An extensive examination of this phenomenon can be found in part I of Thomas-Fogiel (2005) 2011. See also Castoriadis (1988) 1991, from which I draw inspiration. Whereas Castoriadis understands the "end of philosophy" to indicate the demise of individual and social autonomy, however, my analysis is guided by the etymology of the Greek *philosophia* and its connection to Socratic eudemonism.

2. Heidegger, BzP 206/161; 6/8.

3. Hegel, VPW 64–65/172: "In world history satisfaction cannot really be called happiness because it is a question of the satisfaction of universal purposes that transcend the sphere in which ordinary and particular inclinations can be satisfied. The object of world history is those purposes that have meaning in world history, purposes that are carried out with energy, by an abstract willing that is often directed against the happiness of individuals themselves and of other individuals. World-historical individuals have not sought happiness, yet they have found satisfaction." Cf. Hegel, PR §§124, 301; PhG §175: "Self-consciousness achieves its satisfaction only in another self-consciousness."

4. See Kant, GMS 396, 399, 437–40, 453. Cf. Hegel, E-I §54. Note how, in psychoanalytic terms, Kant's definition of *Glückseligkeit* as the satisfaction of base inclinations signifies a condensation and displacement of the Aristotelian distinction between *eudaimonia* (*Glück*, happiness) and *makariotēs* (*Seligkeit*, blessedness) (cf.

Aristotle, NE I.10.1101a1-13). This move is symptomatic of a protracted disavowal of the eudemonic end of classical philosophy, terminating in the destructive projects of Wittgenstein and Heidegger.

5. Wittgenstein, LoE 12.
6. Kierkegaard (1846) 1987, 80.
7. Kierkegaard (1846) 1987, 80. Kierkegaard's influence on Wittgenstein seems less well-known than his influence on Heidegger. For scholarship on the former, see Genia Schönbaumsfeld's *A Confusion of the Spheres: Kierkegaard and Wittgenstein on Philosophy and Religion* (New York: Oxford University Press, 2007). For the latter, see Heidegger, SZ 190n, 235n, 338n.
8. It bears emphasizing that whereas Hegel envisions the material actualization of wisdom as freedom in the ethical state, Heidegger requires the *Destruktion* of metaphysics as the first step toward a genuine thinking of being, or awaiting of its destiny, which Heidegger called *Gelassenheit*. On the Hegelian view, the end of philosophy is, accordingly, achieved by a progressive actualization of the dialectical unity of being and thinking, whereas, on the Heideggerian view, the end of philosophy is accomplished conversely, by dismantling the dialectical unity of being and thinking, which is said to express not only the highest philosophical standpoint, but the concealment of the primordial question of being by a metaphysical reduction of thinking to the determination of being as presence. With the publication of *Being and Time* in 1927, Heidegger set himself the task of destroying the history of ontology; and with this followed the abandonment of traditional philosophy as the love of wisdom, and its replacement by a purely phenomenological doctrine of thinking, that is, a *Denken des Seins* or a *Denken des Sinnes von Sein*. See Heidegger, EM 142–44. Cf. Heidegger, B 376–77 and Dahlstrom (2011) for additional comments.
9. Hawking and Mlodinow (2010), 5.
10. Bacon, AL 294.
11. Bacon, AL 475.
12. Adorno, AP 331/124.
13. Adorno, AP 331/124.
14. Adorno, AP 331/124.
15. Adorno, MM 55/50.
16. Adorno, AP 334/126.
17. Adorno, AP 334, 335/126, 126–27.
18. Adorno, AP 338–39/129.
19. Adorno, ND 15–16/3–4. Cf. Kant, KrV B21.
20. Adorno, ND 9/xix.
21. Adorno, ND 15/3.
22. Adorno, ND 50/40: "The confidence that from immediacy, from the solid and downright primary, an unbroken entirety will spring—this confidence is an idealistic chimera."
23. Adorno, ND 397–98/405–6. Cf. Foucault 1984, 42.
24. Adorno, AP 331/124.
25. Adorno, ND 359/366.
26. Adorno, ND 359/366.

27. Adorno, MM 283/247.
28. Adorno, MM 283/247.
29. Adorno, MM 283/247.
30. See Adorno, ND 149–51/146–48; 176–77/174–76, esp. 176/175: "Every concept, even that of being, reproduces the difference of thinking and the thought."
31. Adorno, MM 283/247.
32. Adorno, MM 283/247.
33. Adorno, MM 283/247.
34. Adorno, MM 283/247.
35. Heidegger, SZ 38: "Höher als die Wirklichkeit steht die *Möglichkeit*"; cf. SZ 42: "Dasein *ist* je seine Möglichkeit" (Heidegger's emphases).
36. Adorno, ND 73/65, 105/98; 75/67.
37. Adorno, ND 75/67.
38. Heidegger, SZ 308–10.
39. Heidegger, SZ 285.
40. Heidegger clarifies the ontological difference between decision (*Entscheidung*) and choice (*Wahl*) in BzP §§43–49. Cf. SZ 268.
41. Heidegger, SZ 12.
42. For related concerns regarding Heidegger's ontological neutralization of the Aristotelian virtues, see Gonzalez (2006), 145.
43. On "responsibility," see Heidegger, SZ 282–89, esp., 287.
44. Heidegger, SZ 288.
45. Critchley (2007), 36.
46. I adopt this formulation from Yovel (1998), 285.
47. I have addressed this issue in Fain (2018). The condensed account presented here may be appreciated within the context of recent efforts to show how Heidegger's existential analysis of conscience can explain Dasein's capacity to make itself responsible toward a set of moral norms. The problem is not that Heidegger leaves us without any devices to explain such phenomena. Rather, the problem is that Heidegger offers us no way to know whether one set of norms is any better than another, or whether one's commitment to a particular set of values can be anything more than an arbitrary leap or the creative expression of the will to power. For an example of the effort to rescue Heidegger from this moral vacuum, see Steven Crowell's (2008) examination of Heideggerian "kindness" (*Freundlichkeit*).
48. Cf. Adorno, ND 322/328: "This much should be granted to Hegel: not only particularity but the particular itself is unthinkable without the moment of the universal which differentiates the particular, puts its imprint on it, and in a sense is needed to make a particular of it."
49. Adorno, MM 283/247.
50. Adorno, ND 17/5.
51. Adorno, MM 283/247. Conversely, Adorno argues that the Kantian categorical imperative "simultaneously condemns the person to unfreedom in principle" (ND 253/256).
52. Adorno, ND 43/33 (emphasis added).
53. Adorno, ND 358/365.

54. Adorno, ND 354/362.

55. On Adorno's account, Heidegger's analytic of Dasein is a "metaphysics, which he does not want to be a metaphysics" (ND 277/281).

56. Adorno, ND 17/5.

57. Adorno, AT 461/311; 205/136.

58. According to his anti-idealist materialism, Adorno's idea of happiness (*Glück*) begins with sensual experience, often on a sexual model. Thus, one finds indexical expressions according to which happiness consists in "sexual union" (MM 248/217), "an after-image of the original shelter within the mother" (MM 126/112), or an "unrestricted openness [. . .] amounting to self-abandonment" (MM 228/200). This position is made even more explicit in *Negative Dialectics*, where Adorno writes, "all happiness aims at sensual fulfillment and obtains its objectivity in that fulfillment" (202/202). It is doubly revealing that Adorno remarked in conversation with Horkheimer that "Animals could teach us what happiness is" (DTP 40/16).

59. Adorno, AT 461/311.

60. Adorno, AT 461/311.

61. Adorno, AT 10/1.

62. Adorno, AT 7/12.

63. Adorno, MM 13/15.

64. Adorno, MM 13/15.

65. Adorno, MM 14/15.

66. Adorno, MM 14/15.

67. Adorno, MM 14/15.

68. Adorno, MM 20/19. From the Austrian author Ferdinand Kürnberger.

69. Adorno, MM 14/15.

70. Adorno, MM 43/39.

71. Hobbes, T vii, xxiv.

72. See Strauss (1935) 1996, 85–86.

73. Hobbes, EL II.10.8.

74. See Adorno, ND 29/17–18: "The need to lend a voice to suffering is a condition of all truth." See also ND 228/229: "In decisionism, which strikes out reason in the passage to the act, the act is delivered to the automatism of dominion. [. . .] But practice also needs something else, something physical which consciousness does not exhaust, something conveyed to reason and qualitatively different from it."

75. Rorty (2004), 11–16, esp. 13–14. Much again turns on Hegel: "The transition from a philosophical to a literary culture began shortly after Kant, about the time that Hegel warned us that philosophy paints its gray on gray only when a form of life has grown old" (Rorty, 2004, 9).

76. Adorno, ND 15/3.

77. Badiou, SM 69/71: "Par définition, la philosophie, quand elle apparaît vraiment, est *reckless* ou n'est rien." Badiou italicizes the English word "reckless" in the original.

78. Badiou, REPP 17–18/6.

79. Adorno, AP 343/132: "The productivity of thinking is able to prove itself only dialectically, in historical concreteness."

80. Adorno, AP 325/120.
81. Adorno, AP 339/130.
82. Adorno, ND 82/74.
83. Badiou, MP 11/31.
84. Badiou, MP 18/37. See Hegel, PR 26/21: "Philosophy is its own time raised to the level of thought."
85. See, for example, Badiou, "The (Re)turn of Philosophy Itself," CON 64/11.
86. Badiou, MP 46–48/66–67; Heidegger, FT 7/10.
87. Badiou, EE 7/2. On "disaster," see ETH 63, 76–77/71, 85–86.
88. Heidegger, ON 3/2.
89. Heidegger, N 2:458/"Sketches for a History of Being as Metaphysics," EoP 55.
90. Badiou, "The Question of Being Today," CT 26/TW 39. This essay also appears in the English translation of CT.
91. Badiou, "The Question of Being Today," CT 26/TW 40. See Heidegger, S-G 209/18.
92. Badiou, ETH 26/10.
93. In *L'éthique* and elsewhere, Badiou employs the terminology of Emmanuel Martineau's translation of *Sein und Zeit*, where *Sein zum Tode* is rendered as *être-pour-la-mort* (being-for-death), rather than the less controversial and more accurate *être-vers-la-mort* (being-toward-death). Badiou's choice of terminology, which was also used by Emmanuel Lévinas, is significant to the extent that the expression "*être-pour-la-mort*" signals an attunement that is not simply oriented "towards" death but is somehow "for" or "in favor" of death. An ethics that is "in-favor-of-death" is nihilistic for Badiou in the sense that it is directed at the avoidance of "evil" rather than the affirmation of a "good" or "goods" (ETH 48/30).
94. Adorno, ND 119/113.
95. Heidegger, BzP 417/330.
96. Badiou, EE 41/31.
97. Badiou, MP 59/79.
98. Badiou, "Philosophy and Desire," IT 37.
99. Badiou, EE 471/431. From Lacan (1966), 516.
100. Descartes, *Discours de la méthode*, A-T 6:7–8.
101. Badiou, EE 10/4.
102. Badiou, ETH 62–63/41–42.
103. Badiou, EE 32/24.
104. Badiou, EE 31–32/23–24.
105. Badiou, EE 32–34/24–26.
106. Badiou, ETH 91–92/67.
107. Badiou, EE 68–69/55–56, 203/182.
108. Badiou, EE 202/181.
109. Badiou, ETH 62–63/41–42.
110. Badiou, ETH 27–28/12; 131–32 (Appendix to the English edition).
111. Badiou, EE 22/15.
112. Rosen (1980), 9.

113. Cf. Lyotard's comment on *Being and Event:* "Je ne vois dans ton texte aucune place pour la receptivié" [I see no place in your text for receptivity] (1989, 243).

114. Badiou, EE 25/18.

115. Cf. Badiou, EE 14/8: "The thesis that I support does not in any way declare that being is mathematical, which is to say composed of mathematical objectivities. It is not a thesis about the world but about *discourse*" (emphasis added).

116. Plato, *Republic*, 476c5-7, 533b6f.

117. Badiou admits in the Preface to the English edition of *L'éthique:* "I had still not yet drawn all the practical consequences—and ethical consequences, for that matter—of the ontology of truths I had put forward five years earlier in *L'être et l'événement* (ETH liv).

118. See Lyotard (1989), 227–68.

119. Badiou, "Ontology and Politics: An Interview with Alain Badiou," IT 129, 130.

120. Badiou, ETH 91–95/67–70.

121. Badiou, EE 244/221.

122. Badiou, EE 470/430.

123. Badiou, EE 445/407.

124. Machiavelli, P §25.

125. Bacon, AL 294; NO 6: "so that the mind may exercise its right over nature." Descartes, *Discours de la méthode*, A-T 6:62: "and thus render ourselves, as it were, masters and possessors of nature."

126. Machiavelli, P §25.

127. Badiou, SM 69/71.

128. For the conditions of political mastery in Machiavelli, consider DL III, §35: "How dangerous a thing it is to make oneself the head of a new thing that pertains to many, and how difficult it is to treat it and to lead it, and, manage, to maintain it, would be too long and too high a matter to discuss." Cf. P §12: "The principal foundations that all states have, new ones as well as old or mixed, are good laws and good arms. And because there cannot be good laws where there are not good arms, and where there are good arms there must be good laws, I shall leave out the reasoning on laws and shall speak of arms." "Good arms," or instruments of force, are primary for imposing law upon the world and, hence, founding "new things." The link between the prince and the philosopher is not explicit in Machiavelli, but for Badiou the philosopher is a prince or a militant who masters fortune by force, and thus decides through danger the order of humanity. See Badiou, REPP 84/76: "Against the idea of normal desires we must sustain the militant idea of a desire that permanently affirms the existence of that which has no name."

129. Badiou, "Philosophy and Desire," IT 37.

130. See Machiavelli, P §25.

131. Simon Critchley has voiced similar concerns about the "heroism" of the decision. However, his concerns are directed toward the political consequences of Badiou's thought, whereas I am here concerned with its consequences for the understanding of philosophy itself. See Critchley (2007, 48, 77–78; 2000, 24–27). For Badiou's response to Critchley, see Badiou, CSC 14.

132. Nietzsche, FW §290.
133. Badiou, WN 2.
134. Badiou, WN 2.
135. Badiou, WN 3.
136. For example, Badiou, ETH 82/60; AM 26–27/17, 110/97.
137. Badiou, EE 469–70/430 (Badiou's emphasis).
138. Badiou, WN 3.
139. Badiou, EE 224/202.
140. Badiou, EE 561/525.
141. Badiou, WN 2; CD 9.
142. Badiou, EE 447/409.
143. Badiou, LM 155/143.
144. Badiou, "The Question of Being Today," CT 29/TW 42.

145. Cf. Badiou, EE 444/406: "A subject measures the *newness* of the situation to-come."

146. Badiou, "Definition of Philosophy," CON 79/23. English translations of this essay are also contained in IT and the English edition of MP.

147. Badiou, "Kant's Subtractive Ontology," CT 154–55/134–35. Adrian Johnston (2013, 116–19) has discussed this point in detail, but within the context of his own effort to vitalize a materialist philosophy in reference to the life sciences.

148. Badiou, RP 356–57/207; SM 99–101/105–7. Cf. Plato, *Republic*, 508e–509b.
149. Badiou, ETH 82/60.
150. Badiou, ETH 90–91/66–67.
151. Badiou, ETH 91/67. The same could be said for Rousseau.
152. Badiou, ETH 91/67.
153. Badiou, "The Question of Being Today," CT 29/TW 42.
154. This argument draws from Fain (2011), 556ff.
155. Badiou, "The Question of Being Today," CT 38/TW 48.

156. Rousseau, OC 4:1099/LM 189 (Rousseau's emphasis). For dating these letters, I refer to the editors of the Pléiade edition, Gagnebin and Raymond (OC 4:1786–7).

157. Descartes, *Discours de la méthode*, A-T 6:7–8.

158. Badiou, MP 39/58. Cf., for example, ETH 16–17/2–3, 18–19/4–5; 105–6 (Appendix to the English edition).

159. Descartes, *Discours de la méthode*, A-T 6:62.
160. See Kennington (2004, 108–9).

161. Not unlike the suggestive character of Descartes' autobiography. See Descartes, *Discours de la méthode*, A-T 6:4. For life as the unity of body and soul, see Aristotle, *De Anima*, II.1.412a14-20; II.4.415b8-b32.

162. Nietzsche, KSA 4:295/Z 237: "ich trachte lange nicht mehr nach *Glücke*, ich trachte nach meinem *Werke*" (emphasis added). See also Z 408/327. Consistent with the protracted disavowal of Socratic eudemonism, note how the death of God is inflected in Zarathustra's choice of *Glück*, a standard term for "happiness," but one that drops *Seligkeit* or "blessedness" from Kant's anti-eudemian notion of *Glückseligkeit* (cf. note 4). The happiness of the last men is, accordingly, replaced by the gaiety of creative work.

163. Badiou, ETH 57/37.
164. Badiou, ETH 54/35.
165. Badiou, "The Caesura of Nihilism," AFP 55–57. This citation refers to a lecture delivered on May 25, 2002 at the University of Cardiff, four years after the publication of *L'être et l'événement*.
166. Badiou, "The Caesura of Nihilism," AFP 54.
167. Badiou, "The Caesura of Nihilism," AFP 65.
168. See, for example, Lacan (1986), 208/177.
169. Badiou, "Truth: Forcing and the Unnamable," CON 209/142, 208/140; "The Philosophical Recourse to the Poem," CON 103/44.
170. Badiou, ETH 59/38–39.
171. Badiou, ETH 59/39.
172. Badiou, ETH 121 (Appendix to the English edition).
173. Badiou, "The Caesura of Nihilism," AFP 66.
174. Badiou, LM 85–86/76–77. See also Alain Badiou, *Métaphysique du bonheur réel*. Paris: PUF, 2015. Translated by A. J. Bartlett and Justin Clemens as *Happiness* (New York: Bloomsbury Academic, 2019).
175. Badiou, WN 10. See Nietzsche, eKGWB/BVN-1889, 1243.
176. See Weber (1919) 1996, 359–60.

Chapter 3

Rousseau's Intervention

I. TOWARD A NEW FIRST PHILOSOPHY

That Rousseau has something of value to say about the foundational question of philosophy will likely come as a surprise to even his most seasoned readers. Today, he is most often recognized as an *époque des Lumières* political philosopher. His best-known work is a treatise on government that inspired, in part, both the American and French Revolutions; yet the breadth of his genius far exceeds the moving power of his political writings. He was a composer and a music critic, a playwright and a drama critic, a novelist and a botanist. He is credited with inventing the modern autobiography; and as a founding father of literary Romanticism, he spurred the eighteenth- and nineteenth-century fascinations with primitivist doctrine. It is symbolic of his profound importance to the history of philosophy, moreover, that Immanuel Kant hung no pictures on his walls apart from a solitary portrait of Rousseau, featured prominently over his writing desk.[1] Rousseau exerted enormous influence over the architects of German Idealism, and for this reason he requires to be acknowledged as a pivotal figure in the history of modern philosophy. Indeed, by tracing the history of the human species from its origin in the pure state of nature, Rousseau inspired the human sciences, which seek to understand human experience less according to categories fixed in nature than through the artifacts of history and culture. Despite all of this, however, Rousseau's thought on the possibility of philosophy remains obscure. Of course, Rousseau was also a master rhetorician who did not wish to be easily understood. The question is *"Why did he wish to be obscure on the topic of philosophy?"*

This question points directly to the political treatment of philosophy, and it requires insight into both Rousseau's conception of philosophy and his notion of the political responsibility of the philosopher: two questions inextricably linked for Rousseau, precisely because his account of the possibility of philosophy is so deeply entwined with his treatment of philosophy as a political problem. This includes both the danger to which the philosopher is exposed by confronting hegemonic notions of the common good with the powers of free and rational inquiry, but also the risk to philosophy itself when the popular expansion of free and rational inquiry degenerates into politics or ideology. In either case, philosophy becomes destructive. Either it destroys the common opinions at the basis of society, or it destroys itself by becoming a mere contest of opinions. In order to penetrate Rousseau's account of the possibility of philosophy, it is therefore necessary to pass through his rhetorical defenses. In turn, this requires not only a demonstration of Rousseau's rhetoric, but the separation of Rousseau's thought on the possibility of philosophy from its political veneer in order to consider its contemporary relevance to the foundational question of philosophy—especially as this question traverses the Cartesian legacy from Heidegger to Badiou.

Our point of entry and overall orientation is Rousseau's critique of Cartesian science.[2] As Rousseau states in the *Moral Letters* from 1757/1758: "It is necessary to end where Descartes began. *I think therefore I exist.*"[3] These words immediately pose a question about the beginning and the end of philosophic inquiry. If it is necessary to end where Descartes began, where ought one to begin? I take this question as Rousseau's legacy-as-task. There is unfinished business when it comes to understanding the philosophical importance of Rousseau's opposition to Descartes—but in order to unpack this, it will first be necessary to prepare the historical and philosophical context which sets the terms for this debate. More specifically, we require the proper context to examine the founding decision of Descartes' thought—that is, the subordination of ethics to ontology and the instauration of a distinctly modern first philosophy for which the *cogito sum* becomes the foundational principle of philosophic inquiry. Rousseau's alternative response to the foundational question of philosophy will turn precisely on his critique of this decision and the results that follow from Descartes' reduction of philosophy to a method of investigation modeled on the mathematical and experimental sciences.

To begin, let us review Descartes' intervention in the discourse of first philosophy going back to Aristotle. This account is necessary to appreciate the philosophical significance of Descartes' contribution, as well as the stakes of Rousseau's methodological imperative to invert the Cartesian order of inquiry. Foremost, this line of questioning will call attention to the fundamental role of human sociality in Rousseau's conception of the possibility of philosophy. Likewise, it will bring into view the philosophical consequences of Descartes' decision to found philosophy by means of an axiomatic method.

In reference to the foundational question of philosophy, I will then examine Rousseau's specific use of the terms "origin" and "foundations" as they appear in the full title of the *Second Discourse*, the *Discours sur l'origine et les fondements de l'inégalité parmi les hommes*.

To anticipate my argument: I will demonstrate, first, how Rousseau conceives the genuine "foundations" of philosophy as plural; and second, how it follows that philosophy has its "origin" in the singular genesis of *amour-propre*. Specifically, I will argue that the plural foundations of philosophy are discovered, first, in the pretheoretical dimension of ordinary experience, which Rousseau calls "the ordinary course of things"; and second, in the abstract "pure state of nature" out of which *amour-propre* is derived from *amour de soi*. It will follow that, on Rousseau's account, philosophy has its origin in a form of moral questioning that is born with the genesis of *amour-propre* as it breaks through the plural foundations of philosophy. Contrary to Descartes' intention to produce a science of morality on the basis of his method, as stated in Part One of the *Discours de la méthode*, I will argue that for Rousseau moral questioning is in fact coeval with and inseparable from the possibility of philosophy itself. These observations will then provide the basis upon which it becomes possible to expose Rousseau's subtle yet radical effort to redefine the meaning of first philosophy—not in terms of an inquiry into the meaning of being, but rather as the proper designation for the foundational question of philosophy understood in terms of the genesis of philosophical experience. This profound change in the meaning of first philosophy is what I propose to call, under the aegis of Rousseau, *primal philosophy: the study of the genesis of philosophy itself*. From this account, it will then be possible to assess the implications of Rousseau's philosophic legacy for the lasting influence of Descartes upon the tradition of philosophy that culminates, successively, in Heidegger and Badiou.

II. DEFINITIONS OF FIRST PHILOSOPHY

There are three basic movements in the history of first philosophy before this topic was renewed to great interest by Edmund Husserl in lectures on *Erste Philosophie* from 1923/1924.[4] These three movements or distinct orientations may be designated by the proper names: Aristotle, Descartes, Rousseau. Aristotle was the first to introduce a formal notion of *prōtē philosophia* in the assemblage of writings we now call *Metaphysics*. In Book Γ of this text, Aristotle writes: "There is a science that studies being qua being and what belongs to it essentially."[5] This science ranks first because it concerns that which comes first in the order of knowledge (*gnōsis*),[6] namely, the first principles (*archai*) or foremost causes (*aitiai*).[7] Because being is that which is most universal and most unchangeable with respect to the intelligible order of the cosmos, it is also prior to the process of making divisions into kinds.[8] Since what is prior to division is absolutely first with respect to either *archai* or *aitiai*, the study of being qua being is called "first philosophy."[9] Shortly stated: Aristotelian first philosophy concerns the attributes of the intelligible structure of being, as that which underlies the appearing of beings—and as such, it concerns what is prior to any subsequent theoretical or practical inquiry.

Since the more indivisible is always prior, it is a consequence of this reasoning that Aristotle's definition of priority is reducible to the principle of independent existence. Aristotle writes: "all things which can exist independently of other things, while the other things cannot exist without them," are called "prior" (*proteros*).[10] This definition applies equally to the several senses of the prior, which include questions of temporal sequence, position in relation to a fixed point, the order of relation in knowledge, relations with respect to nature or essence, causal genesis, and the hierarchy of values.[11] Concerning the last which appears in the *Categories* as fourth in a list of five, Aristotle says: "prior" means "the best and most honorable."[12] While he expresses some reservation about this definition given its status as a colloquial saying of the *hoi polloi*, this definition not only echoes the ancient principle cited by Aristotle in the *Metaphysics* that "the older is better,"[13] but it also serves to affirm Aristotle's rank-ordering of the speculative sciences, where the priority of first philosophy is said to make it the "most honorable" (*timiōtaton*) in relation to physics and mathematics.[14]

Because the object of first philosophy is ordinally prior to that of the second sciences like physics and mathematics, it is likewise first in value and highest in rank, as the second sciences would be impossible without their dependence upon the intelligible structure of being. By contrast, Descartes appropriates the Aristotelian doctrine of priority, but to the reverse effect whereby what was highest for Aristotle becomes methodologically lowest and most foundational. This determination is conveyed poetically in the Preface to the *Principles of Philosophy* where Descartes describes his plan to reverse the Aristotelian order of knowledge by placing metaphysics at the root of the philosophical tree. This reversal is the product of Descartes' effort to carry Aristotle's principles to their logical end, which is why in this same text Descartes describes the disciples of Aristotle as walking down the right road, but in the wrong direction.[15] In sum, Descartes agrees with Aristotle that metaphysics, understood as the science of first principles and highest causes, must be first in the order of knowledge. But because ordinal priority terminates in the principle of independent existence, beyond which Parmenides warns against pronouncing "the altogether not," Descartes concluded that what was highest for Aristotle must serve as the foundation for a systematic approach to the achievement of "perfect knowledge."[16]

This difference between Descartes and Aristotle is put into sharp relief by the observation that, for Aristotle, we do not require metaphysics in order to undertake studies in ethics or politics—let alone rhetoric, poetics, or the parts of animals. For Descartes, however, the opposite is the case. To fulfil the promise of an entirely systematic scientific philosophy, to "deal in general with all the first things that can be known by philosophizing in an orderly way,"[17] Descartes invented a theory of evidence along with the method of doubt, which allowed him to deduce that most needful principle—the clear and distinct *cogito*—upon which the whole of certain knowledge could rest. Again, in reference to the philosophical tree: growing out of the metaphysical roots are the trunk which denotes physics, followed by the branches of which medicine, mechanics, and morals are most prominent. Or to put the point less metaphorically, the method of doubt produces the axiomatic principle of the *cogito*, which serves as the sole basis upon which Descartes hoped to ground "perfect knowledge" for the preservation of health, the procurement of skills, and the proper conduct of one's life.[18]

To the extent that Descartes was successful in producing a moral philosophy, however, it is incapable of legitimating its own goodness on its own terms. At bottom: because Descartes founds philosophy on the bias of mathematical form, he establishes a fundamental dualism between formal structure and knowledge of the good. In the domain of metaphysics, there is a further split between two formal substances, thought and extension, which the system alone cannot redeem except by the employment of a mythical salve such as the one secreted by the infamous pineal gland. In the domain of ethics, by comparison, the sundering of moral questioning from the scientific foundation of philosophy yields a provisional code of conduct, on one hand, and, on the other, a praxical project that cannot comprehend the human good as anything but the expression of *générosité*—the Cartesian forerunner of the Nietzschean will to power according to which Descartes' ambition to make us the "masters and possessors of nature"[19] is determined by a pure resolution of the will: "The freedom to dispose our volitions" while "never lacking the will to undertake and carry out whatever we judge to be the best."[20]

From this reduction of the human good to the mastery of nature, Cartesian science reduces human virtue to the virtually infinite progress of scientific and technological mastery. Moreover, because our notions of the human good are provisionally determined by the injunction to rule oneself in accordance with the most sensible opinions of the day,[21] there can be no transhistorical understanding of the human good. This also means that the highest human good, classically determined by the happiness of the philosophic life, is thereby sundered from the practical task of scientific mastery. Finally, the reduction of virtue to mastery yields a certain freedom—but a freedom from the ancient love of wisdom in favor of its replacement by the free pursuit of rigorous science.

Rousseau's critique of Descartes stems from observations such as these, beginning as early as 1739 in a poem published anonymously to honor his "Maman," Madame Françoise-Louise de Warens. This date is significant, as it shows Rousseau was already critical of the methods of Cartesian science eleven years prior to the publication of the *First Discourse* in 1750, and at least five years prior to his 1744 encounter with the Parisian intellectual milieu of Diderot, d'Alembert, and Condillac, et al. Titled "The Orchard of Les Charmettes" in reference to the house in Chambéry where Rousseau lived with Madame de Warens, the essential lines read:

> Sometimes applying my problems to Physics,
> I give free rein to the systematic spirit:
> I tentatively follow Descartes and his wanderings
> Sublime, it is true, but frivolous Novels.
> I soon abandon the unfaithful Hypothesis,
> Content to study natural History.[22]

These sentiments clearly voice Rousseau's early preference for the empirical methods of observation and experiment associated with *l'histoire naturelle*, in opposition to Descartes' *esprit de système* with its "unfaithful Hypothesis," which produces only "sublime" but "frivolous Novels." Yet this criticism grows progressively more detailed in Rousseau's mature work where it received its most direct expression seventeen years later in the *Moral Letters* of 1757/58. Unpublished in Rousseau's lifetime, but chronologically continuous with the *Second Discourse* of 1755, it is perhaps more than a happy accident that these letters were composed to "Sophie," the young Comtesse d'Houdetot, whose marriage to the Comte d'Houdetot made Rousseau's muse, the nominal figure of nascent wisdom, effectively unattainable. I cite from the Third Letter:

> With what distrust should we abandon ourselves to our weak intelligence, when we see the most methodical of Philosophers, the one who has best established his principles, and reasoned most consistently, going astray from the first steps and plunging from errors to errors in absurd systems. Wishing to cut the root of all prejudices, Descartes began by calling everything into question, subjecting everything to the scrutiny of reason; departing from this unique and incontestable principle: *I think, therefore I exist,* and proceeding with the greatest precautions, he believed he was going toward the truth and did not find anything but lies (*mensonges*).[23]

Let us examine this passage in detail. First, Rousseau's sense of "our weak intelligence" is formulated in opposition to the classical doctrine of rational strength. Second, this weakness is said to account for the "errors" and "absurd systems" produced by "the most methodical of Philosophers." Descartes' method of cutting to "the root of all prejudices" is therefore deficient—and a symptom of its weakness is expressed by Descartes' decision to found his system on the "unique and incontestable principle: *I think, therefore I exist.*" Rousseau does not question the axiomatic truth of Descartes' principle; just its value as the founding principle of an absurd system that terminates in "lies." Among the most prominent of these errors is the Cartesian doctrine of substance dualism. Rousseau continues:

> Based on this first principle he began examining himself, then finding in himself very distinct properties which also seemed to belong to two different substances, he first applied himself to knowing these two different substances well and, setting aside everything that was not clearly and necessarily contained in the idea, he defined one as extended substance and the other as the substance that thinks. Definitions all the more wise since they left the obscure question of the two substances as it were undecided, and since it did not absolutely follow that extension and thought were not able to unite and penetrate into an identical substance.[24]

This mention of the "obscure question of the two substances" likely draws from the substance monism of Spinoza, as a challenge to Descartes who is said to leave undecided whether thought and extension do not unite in a single substance. However, Rousseau remains content to leave this question undecided. At issue is not the true nature or intelligible structure of substance, but the method that *produces* substance as an object of analysis or philosophic inquiry. In other words, at issue is the method according to which questions are produced. If we wish to know the real basis of philosophic questioning, we require an investigation into the possibility of philosophy itself. Rousseau therefore concludes with a dismissal of Descartes:

> Very well, these definitions that seemed incontestable were destroyed in less than one generation. Newton caused it to be seen that the essence of matter did not at all consist in extension, Locke caused it to be seen that the essence of the soul did not at all consist in thought. Farewell to all the philosophy of the wise and methodical Descartes.[25]

For Rousseau, disagreements among metaphysicians and natural scientists are all symptoms of a failure—principally, in the methods and presuppositions of *first philosophy*. This argument receives even more penetrating treatment, albeit with a higher degree of subtlety, with the publication in 1762 of *Émile, ou De l'éducation*. Here, the discussion turns on the utility of modern medicine: one of three main branches on the Cartesian tree of philosophy.

Let us recall Descartes' assertion in the *Discours de la méthode* that "health" (*santé*) is "unquestionably the first good and the foundation of all the other goods of this life."[26] It is a consequence of this conviction that the human good becomes progressively attainable by the material achievements of medical science. In Book I of *Émile*, by contrast, Rousseau states in reference to the selection of his ideal student: "I am not able to teach living to one who thinks of nothing but how to keep himself from dying."[27] Rousseau appears to be in agreement with Descartes' defense of bodily health, insofar as "the body must be vigorous in order to obey the soul." However, Rousseau immediately calls modern medicine a "lying art" (*art mensonger*) which is "more pernicious to men than all the ills it claims to cure."[28]

It is worth pausing to note the verbal link between this description of modern medicine as a "lying art" and Rousseau's claim in the *Moral Letters* that Descartes "believed he was going toward the truth and did not find anything but lies."[29] If medicine is a lying art, its branch on the Cartesian tree must be the bearer of false fruit. Rousseau adds:

> Medicine is the fashion among us. It ought to be. It is the entertainment of idle people without occupation who, not knowing what to do with their time, pass it in preserving themselves. If they had had the bad luck to be born immortal, they would be the most miserable of beings. A life they would never fear losing would be worthless for them. These people need doctors who threaten them in order to cater to them and who give them every day the only pleasure of which they are susceptible—that of not being dead.[30]

Rousseau's acerbic wit to one side, this statement is important for the way it invokes the Socratic question concerning the right or best life. With reference to the quarrel between the ancients and the moderns, it is a perverse condition of bourgeois nihilism when modern medicine is treated as a source of entertainment and the only pleasure one takes in life is that of "not being dead." If one were unfortunate enough to have been born immortal, such a life would be miserable and worthless, as the value of life is reduced to the simple fear of losing it.

In short, a life reduced to mere preservation is not worth living. The example of modern medicine therefore serves to link Cartesian science with the teaching of false life. Rousseau admits: "I have no intention of enlarging on the vanity of medicine here. My object is only to consider it from the moral point of view."[31] This attack on modern medicine is thus a proxy for a much deeper challenge to the tenets of Cartesian science. Rousseau says: "I do not, therefore, dispute that medicine is useful to some men, but I say that it is fatal to humankind."[32] Put in terms familiar to Badiou, modern medicine is harmful to humankind for the way it makes the human being into a being-for-death. Under this conviction, the human being is defined essentially as a mortal victim—and mastery of death becomes the priority of life.

The teaching of Cartesian science is likewise false, according to Rousseau, because by lowering the human good to the preservation of health, it instills the fear of death over and against the courage for life. Cartesian science is thus a lying art because it reduces the meaning of life to fear and the conquest of fear. So, Rousseau writes: "I do not know of what illness the doctors cure us; but I do know that they give us quite fatal ones: cowardice, pusillanimity, credulousness, terror of death. [. . .] It less cures us of our maladies than impresses us with the terror of them. It less puts off death than makes it felt ahead of time."[33] Beginning with Descartes, it is only a short step from making death felt ahead of time to the futural anxiety of being-toward-death—that is, the Heideggerian doctrine of *Eigentlichkeit*.

It is a paradox that Cartesian daring in defense of modern science should result in the spiritual weakening of the human species. But Rousseau's purpose is not to supplant Cartesian metaphysics with a more perfect scientific system. It is, rather, Descartes' rationalist method and the ensuing ideology of technological mastery that Rousseau wishes to reject. At issue is the relation of Descartes' scientific method to knowledge of the human good. Descartes argues that philosophy or science will promote the human good by rendering nature useful to human ends. Health is the first of human goods because the mastery of nature requires an exercise of human will, which in turn requires health of soul and body. Yet there is nothing uniquely human about the goodness of health. As the basic good of all living things, it is the lowest human good.

Still more important is the fact that scientific and mathematical reasoning are incompetent to answer the question of the good itself. Let us reconstruct Descartes' method of universal doubt.[34] Consistent with the ambition of Socrates, Descartes wished to find true knowledge that transcends the always changing and contingent character of opinion. Yet as Bacon said, "the stars give little light because they are so high." The Socratic vision of Ideas is therefore insufficient to the task. Moreover, our perceptions sometimes deceive us—and if we can no longer trust what we see, we can no longer know by the mere act of looking. The act of seeing (or discovery) must therefore be replaced by making (or construction), and this requires a new method to abstract from history and opinion in order to found indubitable axioms on clear and distinct principles. Cartesian science thus replaces the old hermeneutic enterprise with a new scientific method. It aims to analyze the cosmos into clear and distinct formal categories, laws, or ratios on the model of geometry—and to reconstruct the whole based on these simple axioms.

Strictly speaking, Cartesian science is not concerned with origins or essences. It is concerned with how things work, not with what things are in themselves.[35] Nature is subsequently mastered by reconstituting it as mathematical structure: the "pure and simple" objects of arithmetic and geometry.[36] Mathematical certainty is likewise the standard of accuracy in the production of human understanding—and the mastery of nature by mathematical structure means the replacement of nature by theoretical artifice. In sum, it is by a pure act of will guided by the bold desire for mastery that Cartesian science understands the "formation of the world" as a theoretical artifact—that is, an abstraction.[37] However, the method cannot verify the goodness of its own abstractions, as it remains impossible to distinguish a good scientific analysis from one that is defective if we are not already acquainted with some sense of what a good analysis consists in—and hence some preanalytic, prescientific, or pretheoretical understanding of the good. In short, the tools of analysis are themselves unfit for judging good from bad, right from wrong, since the analysis of analysis may produce only another analysis *ad infinitum*. This is also to say that scientific certainty is no guarantee of prudence—and without prudential knowledge of the good, it is impossible to know if our analysis is worthwhile or complete. In fact, this point did not escape Descartes.

By his own admission, Descartes aims "not to teach a method which everyone must follow in order to direct his reason correctly."[38] Moreover, Descartes admits that his method may be harmful if it is not properly understood. As he put the point, "I hope it will be useful for some without being harmful to any."[39] It is important to acknowledge this distinction between the method as a formal set of procedures and the prudent application of the method. In itself, the method supplies no instructions for distinguishing those who may or may not be harmed by engaging in its application. Instead, Descartes can present only the pattern of his reasoning in search of self-sufficient truth. The method can provide us with analytic-synthetic tools, but it cannot teach us the prudent way to use them. This is precisely why the very first lines of the *Discours de la méthode* warn: "Good sense is the best distributed thing in the world: for everyone thinks himself so well endowed with it that even those who are the hardest to please in everything else do not usually desire more of it than they possess."[40]

Rousseau would surely agree. Satisfaction with a minimum of prudence is no prudence whatsoever. The problem is that Descartes' method cannot account for prudence, as knowledge of the good lies beyond the reaches of the method. Moreover, once we enter into universal doubt, we are barred from explaining the conditions that initially inspired us toward philosophy. Rousseau's intention is, accordingly, not to fight technical philosophy with another version of technical philosophy, but rather to submit the more salient claim that technical philosophy in general—and Cartesian science in particular—is insufficient to answer the most fundamental Socratic question: the question of human happiness, which Rousseau calls in the *Moral Letters* the "object of human life" (*l'objet de la vie humaine*).[41]

By invoking happiness as the "object" of human life, Rousseau sets the terms according to which Cartesian science may be evaluated from the standpoint of classical philosophy. To put this point in somewhat different terms, Rousseau's opposition to the Cartesian subordination of ethics to ontology stages a version of the quarrel between the ancients and the moderns, which serves as the starting point to rethink the meaning of "first philosophy." In the context of *Émile*, this version of "the quarrel" appears (with certain irony) through an oblique reference to Socrates' teaching in the *Phaedo*—namely, that the highest happiness of the philosophic life may be understood as the practice of dying or being dead.[42] To resume with the passage from *Émile*, Rousseau takes his bearings from the human being of pure nature, untouched by society or convention:

> Do you want to find men of a true courage? Look for them in the places where there are no doctors, where they are ignorant of the consequences of illnesses, where they hardly think of death. Naturally man knows how to suffer with constancy and dies in peace. It is doctors with their prescriptions, *philosophes* with their precepts, and priests with their exhortations, who debase his heart and make him unlearn how to die (*qui l'avilissent de coeur, et lui font désapprendre à mourir*).[43]

Not only does modern medicine—and by extension, Cartesian science—produce cowardice and fear of death, but "philosophers with their precepts" and "priests with their exhortations" are included with the doctors who debase the human heart and make us "unlearn how to die." It is worth noting that "priests" are linked with the *philosophes* and doctors as teachers of false lives. I shall return to this observation in chapter 4, section VI, as it bears special relevance to the teaching of the Savoyard Vicar. For now, let us concentrate on how Rousseau links "doctors with their prescriptions" and "*philosophes* with their precepts" to forgetting "how to die."

As we know, Socratic philosophy may be characterized by the practice of dying or being dead. To say that modern medicine has caused epochal unlearning of how to die is thus to claim that Cartesian science is fatal to humankind in direct proportion to the degree it forces the forgetting of Socratic philosophy. This correlation also calls attention to an important association between Socratic philosophy and the "natural human" who knows how to suffer and die in peace. This is not to say the human being of pure nature is a philosopher. But in order to correctly correlate this association between Socratic philosophy and the "true courage" of the natural human, we shall have to examine the details of this passage in relation to the *Second Discourse* where Rousseau introduces the human being of pure nature, abstracted from society.

As a preface to this examination, I note that Rousseau's rhetorical technique will permit us to distinguish a categorical "natural state" from the "pure state of nature." This is significant, as this distinction will correspond to a guiding thesis of my interpretation of Rousseau: that in all the works produced after the 1749 illumination at Vincennes, Rousseau is concerned to address the virtues and vices of various kinds of lives—much like he admits in the *Confessions* to his youthful admiration for the studies collected in Plutarch's *Lives*.[44] To note one important consequence of this observation, whereas Descartes' method fails to account for its relation to the human good, Rousseau makes the question of human happiness the guiding question of philosophy. But since questioning about happiness presupposes questioning about the good, a genuine "first philosophy" must be able to account for the "origin and foundations" of philosophy in a manner that explains its capacity to question about the good. Questioning about human happiness therefore serves as the entry point to examine the foundational question of philosophy itself. In fact, this correlation of a genuine "first philosophy" with questioning about the good makes it possible to explain the philosophic basis of Rousseau's entire effort to consider the various kinds of happiness that are available to various kinds of lives.

Thus, framed by the question of human happiness, Rousseau's analogy between medicine and philosophy grows in significance, as it points to how the rise of Cartesian science coincides with the abolition of philosophy in the Socratic-Platonic sense. Indeed, this version of "the quarrel" begins from the Socratic thesis that the possibility of human happiness is tied directly to the possibility of philosophy. Let us be reminded that whereas Aristotle distinguished two distinct senses of happiness, each corresponding to the difference between theoretical and practical virtue, no such distinction appears in Plato.[45] Rather, in Plato happiness is reserved for the philosopher who aspires to a life of reason achieved through the intellectual vision of Ideas. As the unity of happiness and philosophy works through a perfection of the intellectual capacity of *logos* to say what it has seen, the possibility of human happiness is moderated by the possibility of philosophy itself.

However, the interpretation of reason undergoes an important change at the beginning of the modern epoch. Starting prominently with Descartes and the antecedent influence of Francis Bacon, the life of reason is redefined on the model of mathematics and the experimental sciences. The human being retains its essence as a rational being, as in the Cartesian *res cogitans*. But in accord with the aim of building a comprehensive *mathesis universalis* as the foundation of the human sciences, the classical understanding of reason as *logos* is narrowed and redefined as *logismos* or *ratio*—that is, calculation. Philosophy in the old sense is accordingly replaced by the calculative techniques of scientific investigation—and this is precisely where Rousseau intervenes. By telling us that modern medicine makes the natural human "unlearn how to die," Rousseau indicates how—by converting philosophy in the old sense into science in the new sense—the life of reason is actualized as a kind of *pharmakon* that does not invigorate, but rather poisons the ancient link between philosophy and happiness.[46]

In what may be the most incisive line in the section of *Émile* now under investigation, Rousseau confirms this point with a second allusion to Socrates. He states: "If we knew how to be ignorant of the truth, we would never be the dupe of lies."[47] This line reads as a direct inversion of Badiou's ethical imperative to resolve oneself to the process of a "truth." But more expressly, it calls for an ethics of Socratic ignorance. In order not to be the "dupe of lies," "it is necessary to end where Descartes began." What appears as either first or foundational in the Cartesian doctrine can be neither "first" nor "foundational" for philosophy as Rousseau understands it. Instead, we are required to rethink the meaning of "first philosophy," and for Rousseau this means returning to the figure of Socrates and the fundamental question of human happiness understood as the "object of human life."

III. THE INTERIOR DOCTRINE OF FIRST PHILOSOPHY

To this point, we have seen that the question concerning the possibility of philosophy enters as the question of whether Descartes' foundational decision in favor of the mathematical paradigm can bear the weight of his arboreal model of philosophy. Put otherwise, for Descartes everything hangs on whether the decision in favor of the mathematical paradigm is self-legitimating. So far, we have seen that Descartes runs into serious difficulty when he is tasked with legitimating a philosophic or scientific account of the human good. Even if we affirm the ethos of mastery and the resolute conditions under which Descartes offers a provisional moral code, at the very least Descartes' method cannot account for the moral impetus to replace the ancient foundations of "sand and mud" that initially inspired his philosophic questioning.[48] As a result, the method cannot itself account for either its own goodness or its own possibility; and as we have seen, if philosophy cannot account for its own possibility, the result is what Nietzsche called "nihilism" when "the question 'Why?' finds no answer."[49] In the case of Descartes and those who follow him, this problem is a result of the purely willful decision to found philosophy on the "solid and firm foundations" of mathematics.[50] Such a decision may very well validate the logical results of a mathematically styled inquiry. But it does nothing to tell us about the difference between mathematics and philosophy.

Very much at stake in Rousseau's assertion "It is necessary to end where Descartes began" is therefore a question of method—especially, as this concerns the method that is proper to a genuine first philosophy. While the *Moral Letters* may contain Rousseau's most explicit challenge to Descartes, however, it is the similarly posthumous "Preface of a Second Letter to Bordes," written in 1753, that contains an essential key to Rousseau's critical intention. There, writing in defense of his 1750 *Discours sur les sciences et les arts*, Rousseau remarked:

> With so many interests to combat, so many prejudices to overcome and so many harsh things to proclaim, I thought that in my Readers' own interest I should, as it were, make some allowance for their pusillanimity, and only successively let them perceive what I had to tell them. [. . .] I therefore had to take some precautions at first, and I did not want to say everything in order to make sure that everything got a hearing. I developed my ideas only successively and always to but a small number of Readers. I spared not myself, but the truth, in order to have it get through more readily and to make it more useful. Often I went to great trouble to try and condense into a single Sentence, a single line, a single word tossed off as if by chance, the result of a long chain of reflections (*Souvent je me suis donné beaucoup de peine pour tâcher de renfermer dans une Phrase, dans une ligne, dans un mot jetté comme au hassard, le résultat d'une longue suitte de réflexions*). The majority of my Readers must often have found my discourses poorly structured and almost entirely disjointed, for want of perceiving the trunk of which I showed them only the branches (*faute d'appercevoir le tronc dont je ne leur montrois que les rameaux*). But that was enough for those capable of understanding, and I never wanted to speak to the others.[51]

This is a dense passage. It speaks not only to Rousseau's rhetorical intention, but also to his attitude about metaphysics or *prōtē philosophia*. In referring to the majority of his readers, he says: "For want of perceiving the trunk [. . .] I showed them only the branches." In the art of writing, he took great trouble to condense a long chain of reflections "into a single Sentence, a single line, a single word tossed off as if by chance." As any reader of Descartes will recognize, these lines demonstrate Rousseau's rhetorical technique through his effort to explain it. As the present passage indicates, we are asked to recall Descartes' philosophic tree by a "single word tossed off as if by chance." With respect to the *First Discourse*, Rousseau showed only the branches, merely named the trunk, and said nothing about the roots. The same may be said of the passage from *Émile* in which Rousseau cut to the root of Cartesian science but showed only the branch of medicine. "With so many interests to combat, so many prejudices to overcome and so many harsh things to proclaim," Rousseau resolved to keep the roots buried. He adds: "I did not want to say everything in order to make sure that everything got a hearing"; and he developed his ideas "successively," but only to "a small number of Readers." When addressing "pusillanimous" readers, Rousseau evidently judged it necessary to begin with the branches without revealing the roots. Hence, despite the "disjointed" appearance of his writing, this "was enough for those capable of understanding," and he "never wanted to speak to the others."[52]

These lines are enough to suggest that Rousseau perceived something dangerous about his thoughts on metaphysics or first philosophy. Beginning from his intention to reverse the order of Cartesian thought, we may infer that this danger concerns a link between moral theorizing, on the one hand, and first philosophy, on the other. The question is how to access this link, which is visible to "those capable of understanding," but deliberately hidden from the "others" to whom Rousseau "never wanted to speak." Today such divisions may seem untoward, but within Rousseau's intellectual context there was nothing unusual about the notion of maintaining what he called a *doctrine intérieur*, an internal or esoteric doctrine.[53] Even the famous *Encyclopédie* of the *philosophes* contains an entry called *Exotérique & Ésotérique*, which begins: "The ancient philosophers had a double doctrine; one external, public or *exotérique*; the other internal, secret, or *ésotérique*."[54] Provided this observation, it should come as no surprise to discover that Rousseau professed a manifestly negative attitude toward the *doctrine intérieur* while, at the same time, daring to harbor a secret teaching.

To give this point some context, in the second part of the *Confessions*, published posthumously in 1789, Rousseau identifies the internal doctrine with a "single article; namely that the sole duty of man is to follow the inclinations of his heart in everything." Rousseau then adds: "this morality gave me terrible matter for thought," and he calls it "the interior doctrine which Diderot talked so much about, but which he never explained to me."[55] In the *Reveries* of 1782, Rousseau would also reference the interior doctrine of his enemies, which he called a "secret and cruel morality," concealed behind a "mask," "purely offensive," "of no use for defense," and "good only for aggression."[56] And in the *Dialogues* from 1776, the character Rousseau remarks: "Our philosophers have what they call their interior doctrine, but they teach it to the public only while concealing themselves, and to their friends only in secret."[57] Taken together, these lines recall the damage to Rousseau's personal reputation when Voltaire twice succeeded in making the public believe that some of his anonymously published antireligious writings were authored by Rousseau.[58]

From these observations we may infer that Rousseau closely associated the *doctrine intérieur* with a certain license afforded by the widespread practice of anonymous publication in the eighteenth century. But while the episodes with Voltaire date to circumstances following the censure of *Émile* in 1762, Rousseau first addressed the *doctrine intérieur*, including his distaste for it, in an October 1751 reply to a critic of the *First Discourse*.[59] There, in a footnote dedicated to excoriating the ancient practice "embraced by all Philosophers," Rousseau condemned the teaching of "secret sentiments that were the opposite of those which they expressed in public." The issue was not, however, the practice of dissimulation, but the secret teaching of "some dangerous error." "The Epicureans denied all providence, the Academics doubted the existence of the Divinity, and the Stoics the immortality of the soul." Pythagoras, whom Rousseau calls "the first to resort to the internal doctrine," is also criticized for giving "secret lessons in Atheism while solemnly offering Sacrifices to Jupiter." The problem is not simply the irreligious nature of these doctrines, but the arrogance that leads "philosophers" to error.

Rousseau says the internal doctrine was "born together with Philosophy," and that "Philosophy will always defy reason, truth, and time itself, because it has its source in human pride, stronger than all these things."[60] Pride leads to the arrogance of thought; the conviction that one knows what is impossible to know—namely, in the present case, truth about the divine. At the same time, it is imperative to see how this footnote speaks only to the "impious dogmas" of various philosophic "Sects." Pythagoras is mentioned as the first to employ the internal doctrine, but Rousseau does not name the founders of the other schools. (Plato is not named as the founder of the Academics; Theodorus is cited to exemplify "one of the two branches of the Cyrenaics.") Most significantly, in contrast to these sectarian deviations, the name of Socrates appears nowhere in this footnote, which cites several instances of philosophic pride. This suggests that the "philosophy" Rousseau associates with the secret teaching of dangerous errors cannot itself be the genuine philosophy of Socratic ignorance. By a turn of irony, Rousseau condemns an exoteric interpretation of the internal doctrine while maintaining his own, more artful, literary practice.

This insight is crucial to accurately capture Rousseau's understanding of genuine philosophy in contrast to the degenerate philosophy of decadent philosophers. The latter "will always defy reason, truth, and time itself, because it has its source in human pride." Dangerous lies are not so easily expunged. However, it does not follow that all philosophy has its source in pride. Instead, we are required to distinguish degenerate philosophy from the genuine philosophy of Socrates. While it may be true that philosophy must inoculate itself against prideful excess after it is born, we now face a lacuna in Rousseau's account of the genesis of philosophy itself.[61] Going forward, we shall have to examine how Rousseau's literary practice involves his own interpretation of the *doctrine intérieur*—as well as why this doctrine is connected to his thoughts about metaphysics or first philosophy, on the one hand, and human inequality, on the other.

IV. INEQUALITY AND THE ART OF WRITING

When it comes to the topic of human inequality, Rousseau makes clear throughout his writings that he distinguishes between at least two fundamental types of human being. In the *First Discourse*, this distinction appears as the difference between the "Preceptors of Humankind" and "ourselves, ordinary men (*hommes vulgaires*), to whom Heaven has not vouchsafed such great talents." Rousseau's humility to one side, among these "learned men of the first rank" he includes such modern lights as Bacon, Descartes, and Newton.[62] Given Rousseau's criticism of Descartes, this statement may reek of contradiction; but Rousseau never leveled an outright rejection of the modern sciences. "To end where Descartes began" is to abolish neither the end nor the beginning. Even in the previously examined section of *Émile*, Rousseau writes: "Science which instructs and medicine which cures are doubtless very good. But science which deceives and medicine which kills are bad."[63] At issue is their proper application and utility for humankind.

Where the practitioners of science are concerned, Rousseau says they should find "honorable asylum" in the courts of kings. "Only then will it be possible to see what virtue, science and authority, animated by noble emulation and working in concert for the felicity of Humankind, can do."[64] Whatever Rousseau's criticisms, a talent like Descartes belongs with those "whom nature intended as her disciples," and who therefore "had no need of masters."[65] In *Émile*, this same distinction appears between "ordinary men" who "need to be raised" (*a besoin d'élever*) and the "others" who "raise themselves in spite of what one does" (*s'élèvent malgré qu'on en ait*).[66] Likewise, in the *Dialogues*, Rousseau puts a similar division into dramatic form through the conversation between two characters, Rousseau and the Frenchman, who debate the work of a famous (or infamous) author named Jean-Jacques. Whereas the Frenchman knows only the public discord about Jean-Jacques' controversial reputation, but lacks direct familiarity with his writings, the character Rousseau declares at the very beginning of the work: "About things I can judge by myself, I will never take the public's judgments as rules for my own."[67] The character Rousseau is thus a paradigm of self-sufficient judging, whereas the Frenchman represents a member of Jean-Jacques' popular audience—and his opinion changes only through the course of conversation.

As for the *Second Discourse*, Rousseau writes in his *Confessions* that it "found only a few readers who understood it in all of Europe, and none of them wanted to talk about it."[68] He also calls the preface to this *Discourse* "one of my good writings," and he notes in this connection that "I began to put my principles in view a little more than I had done until then."[69] Whereas the *First Discourse* kept the root buried, the *Second Discourse* promises more. Those "few readers who understood it," but wished not to talk about it, rightly adds to the intrigue. Rousseau's principles must contain something dangerous—at least from the standpoint of the few in their consideration of the many. The question is How shall we access these principles?

V. ROUSSEAU'S SYSTEM

Despite accusations that he was, in his own words, "a man of paradoxes, who made a game of proving what he did not think," Rousseau insisted that all his writings conform to "the same principles: always the same morality, the same belief, the same maxims," and even "the same opinions."[70] In the Third Dialogue, signaling his improved opinion of Jean-Jacques, the Frenchman similarly calls this "a coherent system which might not be true, but which offered nothing contradictory."[71] In fact, Rousseau insisted on the coherence of his system from the very start of his mature career. Beginning with the *Preface to "Narcissus,"* written in the winter of 1752/53, he contrasts *"mon système"* with a series of faulty interpretations of the *First Discourse*—and in the "Preface of a Second Letter to Bordes," dating from September 1753, he refers overtly to his "sad and great System," "the system of truth and virtue."[72]

Now, this line of interpretation becomes somewhat complicated in Book II of *Émile* when the narrator Jean-Jacques urges his readers to "always remember that he who speaks to you is neither a scholar nor a philosopher, but a simple man, a friend of the truth, without party, *without system*; a solitary who, living little among men, has less occasion to contract their prejudices and more time to reflect on what strikes him when he has commerce with them."[73] If it is not out of bounds to identify Rousseau with his narrator—at least in part, as Rousseau applies these appellations to himself—then Jean-Jacques' claim to be "a simple man without system" would seem to throw Rousseau's insistence on coherence to the wind. It is therefore pertinent to note that at an earlier point in this same book of *Émile*, Jean-Jacques submits a mindful warning: "Common readers, pardon me my paradoxes. When one reflects, they are necessary and, whatever you may say, I prefer to be a paradoxical man than a prejudiced one."[74]

Rousseau could certainly be less playful about his intention, but this passage opens up the possibility that he may be operating with two different senses of the word "system." In this connection, in the 1751 *Preliminary Discourse* to the first edition of the *Encyclopédie*—a text with which

Rousseau would have certainly been familiar—Jean le Rond d'Alembert reprised a related distinction between two notions of "system" made initially by Condillac. This distinction concerns the pernicious *esprit de système* of Descartes, described as the love of system for its own sake, in contrast to the *esprit systématique*, which does not rest upon "vague and arbitrary hypotheses," but rather seeks "the art of reducing so far as possible a large number of phenomena to a single one that may be regarded as their principle." About the latter, d'Alembert continues: "This reduction [. . .] constitutes the true 'systematic spirit' (*esprit systématique*)," which is not to be confused with "the 'spirit of systems' (*esprit de système*), with which it does not always agree."[75]

There is little doubt that Rousseau benefited from his conversations with Condillac and d'Alembert as a collaborator on the *Encyclopédie*.[76] In addition, the early "Orchard" poem to Madame de Warens had already given voice to skepticism regarding the *esprit de système* of Descartes. In the present context of *Émile*, it follows that Rousseau's claim to be "a simple man without system" must be a paradoxical expression of his adherence to the Encyclopedists' distinction between Descartes' *esprit de système* and the "true" *esprit systématique*. To be sure, this paradox would look like a contradiction to "common readers." But its meaning becomes evident to those capable of nuance—and Rousseau did not care to speak to the "others." If this assessment is correct, then the way into Rousseau's system must be through the principles and paradoxes that bind his works into a systematic whole.

Now, with regard to the point of entry, in the latter part of the *Dialogues* it is the Frenchman who identifies Jean-Jacques' "great principle that nature made man happy and good, but that society depraves him and makes him miserable."[77] This line effectively repeats the first sentence of the first book of *Émile:* "Everything is good as it leaves the hands of the Author of things; everything degenerates in the hands of man."[78] While these assertions may problematize our hope for a moral or political solution to the fact of human misery, for the Frenchman it is a corollary of Jean-Jacques' great principle that "human nature does not go backward and it is never possible to return to the times of innocence and equality once they have been left behind."[79] A similar statement is also found in the Preface to the *Second Discourse*, where Rousseau indicates that any hope of returning to the pure state of nature would have to be the stuff of fantasy. However, for the Frenchman, these observations yield instructions for entering Jean-Jacques' system. "From my first reading," he says, "I had felt that these writings proceeded in a certain order which it was necessary to find in order to follow the chain of their contents. I believed I saw that this order was the reverse of their order of publication, and that going backward from one principle to the next, the Author reached the first ones only in his final writings."[80]

According to the Frenchman, Jean-Jacques' system includes only the published writings from 1750 to 1762, beginning with the *First Discourse* and ending with the *Social Contract* and *Émile*. The 1762 *Letter to Beaumont* and the 1764 *Letters Written from the Mountain* are explicitly excluded as personal defenses of Jean-Jacques' honor and homeland.[81] Nevertheless, when considering the hermeneutic utility of the Frenchman's advice, it is necessary to remember that he speaks for Jean-Jacques' popular audience. While the *Dialogues* describe the process by which the character Rousseau succeeds in reversing the Frenchman's opinion about Jean-Jacques, the Frenchman is undeniably one of those ordinary men who do not raise themselves, but who need to be raised. We must therefore be on guard against any presumptions to the effect that the Frenchman ever penetrates the depth of Jean-Jacques' system.[82] Instead, the insights he obtains through the transformation of his opinion must reflect the substance of Jean-Jacques' teaching only insofar as it is directed to the public.

As if to bolster this point, we are warned earlier in the *Dialogues* that one should not mistake the opinions of an author's characters for the opinions of the author himself.[83] It also matters that, by the end of the *Dialogues*, the Frenchman is so convinced of Jean-Jacques' teaching that he declares to Rousseau: "It is odd that I am now more decided than you about the feelings you had such trouble making me adopt."[84] In the spirit of Socratic ignorance, we are now prepared to note how the character Rousseau maintains a distance with respect to the Frenchman's "more decided" interpretation of Jean-Jacques.

This observation calls for one further comment on the method of interpreting Rousseau's system. It is not insignificant that the Frenchman is portrayed specifically as proceeding "by synthesis."[85] Beginning with Jean-Jacques' "great principle that nature made man happy and good," he seeks an architecture of the whole. According to the Frenchman, this system may offer "nothing contradictory," but it also might not be "true." One simply cannot know if Rousseau's system is the true system as long as one proceeds by synthesis; foremost, because it is impossible to arrive by synthesis at a first principle, such as the principle concerning the natural goodness of man. The synthetic method may be useful in scientific or political matters, that is, for the purpose of building a coherent teaching founded upon a rationally deduced first principle. But the synthetic method cannot be the method of Rousseau's *philosophic* inquiry or the process according to which Jean-Jacques arrived at the "great principle" itself. The Frenchman's advice may be useful for educating ordinary people in the teachings of Jean-Jacques, but it is dispensable for those who are truly self-sufficient.[86] If we wish to penetrate the deepest or most hidden part of Rousseau's teaching, we shall therefore have to rely more on our own prudential powers of interpretation than on the

Frenchman's prescriptive advice. This is why the character Rousseau states to the Frenchman at the outset of the *Dialogues:* "Everything I will say to you can be understood only by those to whom there is no need to say it."[87]

VI. RHETORIC OF THE ROOT

Let us return to "a single Sentence, a single line, a single word tossed off as if by chance."[88] While the *First Discourse* showed only the branches, merely named the trunk, and was silent about the roots, in the *Confessions* Rousseau calls the *Second Discourse* "a work of the greatest importance"[89] in which his principles are developed "completely" and "with the greatest boldness, not to say audacity."[90] In what follows, we will find the roots buried in the *Second Discourse*. But we shall first have to penetrate Rousseau's rhetorical defenses.

In the *Confessions*, Rousseau notes that in contemplating the ideas that formed the *Second Discourse*, his "soul *raised itself (s'élevoit)* close to the divinity."[91] Thus, replicating the language used in *Émile* to distinguish between those who raise themselves and those who need to be raised, Rousseau put himself implicitly in the category belonging to minds of the highest rank, while the motion of raising himself up to the divinity recalls the Platonic doctrine of philosophical ascent. Whereas the *First Discourse* opened up an inquiry into "one of the grand and finest questions ever raised" concerning "one of those truths that affect the happiness of humankind," the *Second Discourse* looks higher (or comparatively deeper) to investigate the "most useful and the least advanced of all human knowledge," namely, "that of human being."[92] Rousseau also bolsters his Socratic *bona fides* by adding: "I dare say that the inscription on the Temple at Delphi alone contained a more important and more difficult Precept than all the big Books of the Moralists." And: "I therefore consider the subject of this Discourse to be one of the most interesting questions Philosophy might raise, and unfortunately for us one of the thorniest Philosophers might have to resolve: For how can the source of inequality among men be known unless one begins by knowing men themselves?"[93]

Gnōthi seauton, "know thyself." This is, of course, the Socratic imperative inscribed on the Temple at Delphi. To find the roots we seek, we shall have to pursue an inquiry into self-knowledge, not with respect to ourselves as individuals, but in view of the higher question concerning the nature of our species. In seeking to know ourselves through an inquiry into human nature, Rousseau proposes to uncover the origin and foundations of human inequality. Yet, to this point, Rousseau's silence about the philosophic roots also serves to intimate some danger in this inquiry. What could be so dangerous about the question of human nature that Rousseau felt the need to maintain silence about the "roots?" The answer to this question points directly to Rousseau's critique of Descartes and its significance for the meaning of a genuine first philosophy. To that end, Rousseau provides a clue in commenting on the method of his inquiry. He writes:

> If I have dwelt at such length on the assumption of this primitive condition, it is because, having ancient errors and inveterate prejudices to destroy, I believed I had to *dig to the root* (*creuser jusqu'à la racine*), and to show in the depiction of the genuine state of Nature (*veritable état de Nature*) how far inequality, even natural inequality, is from having as much reality and influence in that state as our Writers claim.[94]

By "digging to the root" Rousseau indicates—in reference to the Cartesian tree—that the *Second Discourse* contains his meditations on metaphysics or first philosophy. As such, the dirty work of excavation points to a quest for first principles (*archai*) or foremost causes (*aitiai*). This insight is reinforced by the observation that, in the *Discours de la méthode*, Descartes compared "the writings of the ancient pagans that deal with morals to very proud and magnificent palaces built on sand and mud (*sable et boue*)."[95] Rousseau likewise comments in the Preface to the *Second Discourse* that "human establishments seem at first founded on piles of Quicksand (*Sable mouvant*)" and that "it is [. . .] only after setting aside the dust and sand (*poussiére et sable*) that surround the Edifice, that one perceives the unshakeable base on which it is raised, and learns to respect its foundations."[96]

Whereas Descartes sought to correct ancient errors in moral reasoning by founding philosophy upon a new foundation modeled after mathematics, Rousseau proposes to interrogate the state of nature in order to correct "ancient errors and inveterate prejudices" concerning the "reality and influence" of human inequality. Crucially, both efforts involve a ground clearing effort, with the corresponding aim of discovering the genuine basis of philosophy. But whereas Descartes' *Discourse* begins with the perception of moral *inquiétude* and its immediate suppression by the analysis of the *cogito*, Rousseau identifies the inquiry into human inequality with digging to the philosophic root. To end where Descartes began, we must therefore overturn the Cartesian subordination of ethics to ontology (or being-thinking, broadly understood) in order to investigate the moral or political root of philosophic inquiry. It follows that the investigation of first philosophy, understood as an investigation of the first principles or foremost causes of philosophy itself, shall thus be led by questioning into the genesis of human inequality—its emergence from "the genuine state of Nature" where "even natural inequality" is very far "from having as much reality and influence as our Writers claim."

By intending to end where Descartes began, we can now see that Rousseau returns to the genuine beginning that was sundered decisively from the axiomatic foundation of Cartesian science. From the standpoint of Descartes, the task of philosophy is to build, retroactively, a doctrine of morality upon the scientific foundation of the philosophic edifice. If it fails, then philosophy is forced to admit that it no longer concerns wisdom about the whole, as it becomes impossible to speak about the human good as anything but the free expression of the will—that is, Cartesian *générosité*, the "firm and constant resolution [. . .] to carry out whatever one judges to be the best."[97] On this account, moral or political virtue is replaced by the pure resolution of the will, with the result that judgments about the good are decided purely in terms of the will to power. I submit that by turning to an investigation of the origin and foundations of human inequality—and the rootedness of moral or political questioning in a revised notion of first philosophy—it is precisely the decisionistic character of Cartesian *générosité* that Rousseau wished to challenge.

VII. ORIGIN AND FOUNDATIONS

We are now in a position to examine Rousseau's specific use of the terms "origin" and "foundations," as these words appear in the full title of the *Second Discourse*, the *Discours sur l'origine et les fondements de l'inégalité parmi les hommes*. The fact that Rousseau maintains a distinction between these terms is likely to have been obscured by the common abbreviation of this title as either the *Discourse on the Origin of Inequality* or more simply the *Discourse on Inequality*, as Rousseau himself occasionally referred to it.[98] Nevertheless, by distinguishing the terms "origin" and "foundations," Rousseau reveals a key to elaborating his philosophic method—specifically, vis-à-vis Descartes. In this regard, Rousseau's principal concern is Descartes' replacement of the genuine foundations of philosophy with a technical artifact. Or to put this point in terms familiar to Rousseau, the task is one of disentangling nature from artifice in order to set aside the dust and sand that has concealed the genuine origin and foundations of philosophy itself.

Much like Descartes, Rousseau's effort to distill the origin and foundations involves a method of abstraction. But instead of beginning with a purely willful decision to found philosophy on the model of mathematics, Rousseau begins from the unified stratum of ordinary experience, which he twice calls in the famous letter to Voltaire of August 18, 1756 "*le cours ordinaire des choses*," "the ordinary course of things."[99] This phrase was common to the Fathers of the Catholic Church who used it to denote what is ordinary or natural in contrast to miracles, which are extraordinary: "*above, contrary to,* and *outside* nature."[100] That Rousseau employed this language is a testament to his subtlety, especially as this phrase appears in the context of his polemic against Voltaire's appeal to the Leibnizian "best of all possible worlds" doctrine, which inspired the theological optimism of Voltaire's poem on the Lisbon earthquake of 1755.

At the same time, however, Part One of the *Second Discourse* contains another comparable expression, namely, "*le cours ordinaire de la vie*," "the ordinary course of life."[101] In contrast to "the ordinary course of things," Rousseau used this second expression to indicate the generally placid life of the human being in the pure state of nature, unperturbed by the distortions of society. Thus, whereas "the ordinary course of things" refers to the preanalytic or pretheoretical dimension of quotidian experience (ordinary everyday experience untouched by any attempt to understand it by theology or science), "the ordinary course of life" is abstracted from "the ordinary course of things" in order to expose an image of human life unadulterated by society. On this reading, it is therefore possible to assert that in the writings from 1755 to 1756 Rousseau was operating with two senses of the ordinary: one pertaining to average everyday experience; the other to a purely natural life abstracted from society. Provided that we are "digging to the root," I suggest that these two senses of the ordinary correspond directly to the plural "foundations" of philosophy.

To sharpen this point, I note that the word "foundations" (*fondements*) appears seven times in the *Second Discourse*, whereas the singular "foundation" (*fondement*) appears only twice. Similarly, the singular "origin" (*origine*) appears fifteen times in the *Second Discourse*, while the plural "origins" (*origines*) appears only twice. These observations align with the emphasis given by the full title of the *Second Discourse*. Moreover, where Rousseau writes of plural "origins," this reference is restricted to the genesis of multiplicity in languages or societies, and is always used in reference to how others have conjectured about these topics.[102] By contrast, when Rousseau uses the singular "foundation," it is always in the negative. For example, he claims that an "Arbitrary Power, being by its Nature illegitimate, cannot have served as the foundation for the Rights of Society."[103] Likewise, mirroring this usage: "Society no longer offers to the eyes of the wise man anything but an assemblage of artificial men and factitious passions which [. . .] have no true foundation in Nature."[104] The correlation between an "arbitrary power" and the worrisome absence of a "true foundation in Nature" should alert us, if only indirectly, to Rousseau's position against the decisionistic and therefore unfounded construction of theoretical artifacts, such as the principle of the *cogito sum* and its footing in the mathematical paradigm upon which Descartes intends to found his scientific edifice. What is required in response is, accordingly, an account of the foundational character of the pure state of nature and its significance for the possibility of philosophy itself.

To that end, it is the express aim of the *Second Discourse* "To mark, in the progress of things, the moment when, Right replacing Violence, Nature was subjected to Law; to explain by what chain of wonders (*enchaînement de prodiges*) the strong could resolve to serve the weak, and the people to purchase an idea of repose at the price of real felicity."[105] More succinctly, Rousseau's inquiry is fundamentally concerned with the chain of wonders through which genuine happiness was replaced by moral or political inequality. To the extent that the *Second Discourse* shows Rousseau digging to the root, his meditations on first philosophy must be contained in this line of questioning—that is, the question concerning the moment when human happiness becomes a moral or political problem. This is precisely the question of a singular "origin." For the moment, let us note only that insofar as Rousseau indicates a singular "origin" of inequality in the title of the *Second Discourse*, moral or political inequality cannot emerge *sui generis* from the pure state of nature, but only through the process by which the human being emerges from its presocial condition. The pure state of nature is, by definition, free from moral-political ideas. What we now require is an account of the significance of these insights for Rousseau's critique of Descartes, especially as this concerns the question of human happiness and its relation to the possibility of philosophy.

VIII. NATURE AND ARTIFICE

When it comes to thinking about the genesis of "human establishments," of which philosophy would be one, Rousseau's strategy is to begin from "the ordinary course things," the everyday condition of social life; presumably, the first foundation. However, the appearance of what is *first* is revealed retrospectively as the *second* foundation by virtue of a chiasmus effect achieved by abstracting the pure state of nature from the ordinary social state. On this reading, a genuine first philosophy must be concerned with the transition from the first foundation to the second, that is, the transition from the pure state of nature (*le cours ordinaire de la vie*) to the social state (*le cours ordinaire des choses*). Where the genesis of philosophical experience is concerned, this means showing how the love of wisdom has its *origin* in that chain of wonders according to which the idea of repose was purchased at the price of real felicity. In other words, a genuine first philosophy must be concerned with the genesis of philosophical experience and its rootedness in that most fundamental Socratic question: the question of human happiness, "How shall I live?" To anticipate: By showing how the possibility of philosophy is rooted in the mediation between two foundations, I shall argue that Rousseau shows how philosophy can give a reflexive account of its own possibility, provided that the genesis of ethical experience is coeval with the genesis of philosophy itself. If this account is correct, then philosophy will no longer face the Cartesian problem of having to build an account of the human relation to an idea of the good retroactively into the philosophic edifice. Instead, with Rousseau, it becomes possible to understand questioning about the good as intrinsic to the possibility of philosophy itself.

In order to see how the question of happiness motivates questioning about the good in Rousseau's account of the possibility of philosophy, it is necessary to examine his vision of the human being as it emerges out of the pure state of nature. Let us take our bearings from the epigraph to the *Second Discourse:* "What is natural has to be investigated not in beings that are depraved, but in those that are good according to nature." This line comes from Aristotle's *Politics*, specifically, in the context of Aristotle's discussion of the natural slave.[106] According to Aristotle's teleological cosmology, what is good according to nature must exemplify the perfection of a natural end. In the case of the human being, that end is the perfection of reason. Defined as a *zōon logon echon*, the animal that has speech, the naturally perfect human is one who speaks with perfect reason, to the extent possible for human beings. Because speech naturally expresses sociality, this also means that the human being must be a *zōon politikon phūsei*, a political animal by nature. It follows that those who live outside the strictures of politics must be either gods or beasts.[107] However, this paradigm is complicated by the life of *theōria* or contemplation, especially when measured against the life of practical virtue, which counts as second best. This is because Aristotle makes the life of contemplation separable from politics, which implies that a life constrained by politics may amount to Aristotle's version of a noble lie.[108] In the case of the natural slave, by contrast, we are dealing with a deficient human specimen; one deficient in *prohairesis* or the capacity for deliberative choice. In this case, the capacity to attain the natural human end is compromised or stunted—and because we cannot discern what is best by examining what is inferior, the attempt to investigate nature in what is depraved can produce only a depraved account of nature.

For his part, Rousseau's account of human corruption is an important key not only for revealing the principles of his system, but also for understanding how he positions his revised conception of first philosophy against the doctrines of both Aristotle and Descartes. As I will try to show, by inquiring into the historical emergence of the human being from its presocial beginnings, Rousseau will challenge the antecedent doctrines of first philosophy by showing how the corrosive effects of human sociality expose the question of human happiness as the foundational question of philosophy. Because this insight pertains to Rousseau's Socratism, the way into this argument will also prove significant, as Rousseau thinks the question of human happiness through the problem of knowing human nature—specifically, by mounting a critique of Aristotle, which turns on an altered image from Book Ten of Plato's *Republic*.

It should be clear by now that Rousseau is a profoundly subtle writer. After situating the problem of human inequality within the lineage of a Socratic pursuit of self-knowledge, as instructed by the inscription at Delphi, the *Second Discourse* recalls Plato's image of the Glaucus statue, "which time, sea, and storms had so disfigured that it less resembled a God than a ferocious Beast."[109] The myth remembers Glaucus as a fisherman who was transformed into an immortal deity after eating a divine herb with the power to bring dead fish back to life. In the *Republic*, this reference operates as an allegory about the nature of the human soul. Because the statue was planted in the sea, its "original nature" (*archaian phusin*) is no longer visible: "some of the old parts of his body have been broken off and the others have been ground down and thoroughly maimed by the waves." All the while shells and seaweed have grown upon him "so that he resembles more a beast than what he was by nature."

The problem identified by Plato is one of perceiving the original nature of the soul, independent of the destructive effects of nature, "not maimed by community with the body and other evils." The Glaucus allegory thus presents the puzzling image of an artifactual presentation of a mortal-turned-immortal soul, grossly disfigured by its exposure to nature. It is possible to read this in at least two ways: from the competing standpoints of theology or anthropology. In the theological (or broadly mythopoetic) sense, the eroded presentation of an immortal soul evokes an implicit challenge to the classical doctrine of immortality. In the anthropological and more immediately relevant sense, the Glaucus statue presents an image of the human soul corrupted by the natural inclinations of the body and "other evils." In Rousseau's version, however, it is not nature but *society* that functions as the source of human corruption. Thus, Rousseau laments "the human soul altered in the lap of society by a thousand forever recurring causes." Among such causes he includes "the acquisition of a mass of knowledge and errors," "changes that have taken place in the continuation of Bodies" (presumably an inertial effect of the progress of corruption), and "the continual impact of the passions," all of which have altered the human soul "in appearance to the point of being almost unrecognizable."[110]

On Rousseau's account, the Glaucus allegory performs two important functions. First, it shows Rousseau standing Aristotle on his head. With respect to the epigraph taken from the *Politics*, the investigation into what is good by nature cannot take its bearings from the natural human end so conceived by Aristotle. No doubt Rousseau follows Aristotle's injunction not to investigate what is natural in beings that are depraved—as indicated by the Frenchman's discovery of Jean-Jacques' "great principle" concerning the natural goodness of man. But contra Aristotle, human sociality does not express a natural human good. Instead, it designates the source of human ills. This calls into question the perfection of reason as the natural human end, which also brings us to the second function of the Glaucus statue: to show the difficulty of disentangling what is natural from what is not. This difficulty is indicated, first, because the apparently natural accretions on the statue are themselves artifacts of human sociality;[111] and second, because the project of excavating the original nature of the soul is obstructed by its conversion into a divine artifact, on the one hand, and a mythical divinity, on the other. All of this finally leads Rousseau to say: "In a sense it is by dint of studying man that we have made it impossible for us to know him."[112]

Rousseau therefore exposes a paradox. "Every progress of the human species removes it ever farther from its primitive state," with the result that "the more knowledge we accumulate, the more we deprive ourselves of the means to acquire the most important knowledge of all."[113] The problem of knowing human nature is consequently bound to fundamental restrictions imposed by our attachments to society, while the artifacts we use to understand ourselves are themselves the sources of distortion.

Accordingly, nature does not corrupt nature; the body and its inclinations do not alone corrupt the soul. Rather, the soul is so corrupted by its exposure to society as to make the difference between nature and artifice appear indistinguishable. At bottom, the problem of knowing human nature is a matter of method. Because human life is profoundly mediated by a tension between nature and society—indeed, the history of human sociality—the original of human nature is so thoroughly obscured by the forces of history that we can proceed only by *imagining* the human being stripped completely of social convention. Yet a work of the imagination cannot in principle bring us closer to nature because the imagined image is itself an artifact of human invention. The imaginary construction of the purely natural human being invariably exposes the idea of human nature as itself an artifact. We shall therefore have to separate, as far as possible, the constructed artifact of human nature from human nature itself—as nature could not be corrupted if it did not exist as such.

As for the Glaucus statue, its function is to show how the Delphic imperative requires a method of discovery though construction, where the construction of a theoretical artifact exposes the limit of philosophic knowledge while at the same time pointing beyond this limit to a darkly visible, though inaccessible, original position.[114] To that end, Rousseau writes:

> Let my Readers therefore not imagine that I dare flatter myself with having seen what seems so difficult to see. I have initiated some arguments; I have hazarded some conjectures, less in the hope of resolving the question than with the intention of elucidating it and reducing it to its genuine (*véritable*) state. Others will easily be able to go farther along the same road, though it will not be easy for anyone to reach the end. For it is no light undertaking to disentangle what is original from what is artificial in man's present Nature, and to know accurately a state which no longer exists, which perhaps never did exist, which probably never will exist, and about which it is nevertheless necessary to have exact Notions in order to accurately judge our present state.[115]

This passage contains several important features. First, Rousseau proposes a conjectural account of the pure state of nature. Second, the purpose of this account is not to posit some apodictic knowledge of an original nature, but rather to elucidate a question by "reducing it to its genuine state." Third, Rousseau admits that this original state "no longer exists," "perhaps never did exist," and "probably never will exist." It is, accordingly, not so much the conjectural account itself that should command our attention, but its function—to formulate a question by which "to accurately judge our present state." This formulation calls attention to the essential place of poetry in Rousseau's philosophic method. As in the Glaucus allegory, Rousseau formulates a question about the relation between nature and artifice in order discern the problem at stake in knowing human nature—the question of the human qua human, untouched by history or convention.

At the surface level of politics, we require an answer to this question in order to know whether human inequality is authorized by nature. However, this effort to "elucidate the nature of things" invariably transforms the idea of nature into a philosophic problem.[116] Nature is a problem to the precise degree that it is thoroughly and irrevocably saturated with history. Insofar as the idea of nature serves as the classical standard of the human good, the human good is subject to change insofar as nature is suffused with history. At the extreme end of this line of reasoning, the ever-changing character of human nature dissolves the meaning of the good into a periodic history of "goods," at which point we run dangerously close to relativism—if not chaos.

This is one expression of the problem we today call historicism. Succinctly stated, historicism reduces all attempts to know the truth (e.g., about nature or the good) to some contingent historical context. It follows that the power of human understanding is restricted by the progress of history, which is to say, historicism threatens the possibility of philosophy insofar as philosophy is thought to aim at a form of transhistorical understanding—in principle accessible at all times and places.[117] By hazarding some conjectures, "less in the hope of resolving the question than with the intention of elucidating it,"

Rousseau pursues a method of discovery through construction. There can be no unmediated vision of an original nature or ground of philosophic inquiry. Instead, the imagination is the condition of reflective thought, as we are required to construct an image in order to reflect upon the difference between the image and its original. Stated somewhat differently, the constructive character of the imagination is the means by which we attempt to say what we have seen. But poietic artifacts do more than this. They point back to the source of vision—to a source that regulates the possibility of accurately saying what we see. The essential function of poetry in philosophy is thus to open up a space for reflection: to expose a state of affairs that is not of our own making. This also means that poetry is the instrumental condition of self-knowledge, which Rousseau calls "the most useful and least advanced of all."[118] As a matter of method, the poietic artifact makes it possible for us to understand ourselves by extending our vision beyond the immediate situation, whatever it may be. Indeed, it is only by going beyond ourselves that we may return into ourselves through the effort to know ourselves. In this way, poetry serves philosophy as the instrumental means to formulate the most needful question "to accurately judge our present state."

IX. SETTING ASIDE THE FACTS

The task at hand is one of digging to the root in order to discover the chain of wonders that has caused us "to purchase an idea of repose at the price of real felicity."[119] At stake is a question concerning the original of human nature and its significance to answering the question of human happiness. The correct formulation of this question will open up the way to judge the present condition of humanity. The problem, Rousseau contends, is that philosophical conceptions of human nature have so far been mistaken about the meaning of "nature" in "human nature." He writes: "The Philosophers who have examined the foundations of society have all felt the necessity of going back as far as the state of Nature, but none of them has reached it." Indeed, "all of them, continually speaking of need, greed, oppression, desires, and pride transferred to the state of Nature ideas they had taken from society; They spoke of Savage Man and depicted Civil man."[120] To properly address the philosophical debate about the nature of human nature, it is therefore necessary to conceive the human being wholly abstracted from the source of its corruption by society.

Let us pause to note that Rousseau makes a point not to confuse this account of the pure state of nature with the biblical account of human life before the fall. Regarding the latter, the human being has already "received some lights and Precepts immediately from God."[121] By contrast, Rousseau proposes an entirely nontheological conjecture. In the pure state of nature, the human being will be stripped of any a priori knowledge or divine commandments such as the one given to Adam and Eve not to eat from the Tree of Knowledge. Rousseau continues:

> Let us therefore begin by setting aside all the facts, for they do not affect the question. The inquiries that may be pursued regarding this Subject ought not to be taken for historical truths, but only for hypothetical and conditional reasonings; better suited to elucidate the Nature of things than to show their genuine origin, and comparable to those our Physicists daily make regarding the formation of the world.[122]

Notice that Rousseau uses the same expression—that of setting aside: *écarter*—to indicate the methodological ground clearing activity that involves both "setting aside all the facts" (*écarter tous les faits*) and "setting aside the dust and sand" (*écarté la poussiére et le sable*).[123] As noted earlier, the latter expression points specifically to both Descartes' effort to replace the ancient foundations of "sand and mud" and Rousseau's subsequent critique of this effort by Descartes to put philosophy on new foundations akin to mathematics. To "begin by setting aside all the facts" is likewise a way to clear the ground in order to rethink the origin and foundations of philosophy, as it were, from the root.

That Rousseau's account of the pure state of nature is now "comparable to those our Physicists daily make" may therefore be read in two ways. Either the propositions of "our Physicists" (Galileo, Newton, Descartes, etc.) are no less conjectural than the "hypothetical and conditional reasonings" that Rousseau proposes to investigate. Or else this statement is another indication that Rousseau intends to position the substance of his thought against the prevailing influence of the scientific method in matters of human inquiry. In the latter case, one thinks primarily of Descartes and his epigones among whom Hobbes figures prominently. After all, Hobbes is one of Rousseau's major targets of reproach for importing features into human nature that could be acquired only in society.

To give one important example, in the Dedication to *De Cive* Hobbes allows that man may be a wolf to man, which is to say, the human being is by nature vicious and predisposed to run in packs.[124] On this point, Richard Tuck astutely notes that Hobbes was not concerned with the abstract question of human nature which interested Rousseau.[125] So, in this respect, Rousseau's complaint about Hobbes appears misplaced to the extent that Rousseau and Hobbes essentially agree that the passions of comparison and emulation— which Rousseau will trace to *amour-propre*—are at the source of war and misery.

Nevertheless, Rousseau wished to go beyond the likes of both Descartes and Hobbes in order to think anew the meaning of human being, not only to address questions of politics and political right, but also the radical question of first philosophy understood in terms of the origin and foundations of philosophy itself. If this inquiry is at all comparable to "those our Physicists daily make," its measure of truth or certainty will be contained in Rousseau's effort "to elucidate the Nature of things" after "setting aside all the facts." Projecting forward, we shall see that Rousseau's account of the solitary human in the pure state of nature is not simply conjectural, but that it holds a deeply human truth, which serves as the first principle or starting point for elucidating the possibility of philosophy itself. As Rousseau says, in defense of his method, "such conjectures become reasons when they are the most probable that can be derived from the nature of things and the only means available to discover the truth."[126]

X. IN THE LYCEUM OF ATHENS

We are now in position to see exactly how Rousseau's inquiry into the original of human nature operates on two levels simultaneously: one political, the other philosophical. On one hand, the confrontation with Hobbes motivates both the doctrine of natural human goodness and Rousseau's subsequent critique of authoritarian politics, which rests upon the possibility of educating human beings toward virtue (both individual and political). On the other hand, the conjectures concerning the pure state of nature serve as the strategy and method for challenging the antecedent conceptions of first philosophy that terminate in the question of being (being qua being in Aristotle, the being of the *cogito* in Descartes). We are also warned that this inquiry into the origin and foundations of philosophy may be dangerous, which is why Rousseau barely exposes the root. However, this is also the point at which the political and philosophic ends of Rousseau's inquiry converge—precisely where the investigation of nature intersects with the foundational question of happiness or the human good. There is thus a unity within the division of politics and philosophy which is mirrored, if not affirmed, by Rousseau's express intention to address the *Second Discourse* to both philosophic and nonphilosophic audiences simultaneously. In fact, it is within this same statement of Rousseau's rhetorical intention—at the end of the untitled Exordium, in preparation for the investigation of nature in Part One of the *Second Discourse*—that he expands the criticism of Cartesian science to include a critique of Aristotle from the standpoint of Plato. Rousseau writes, in a line of inspired subtlety:

Since my subject concerns man in general, I shall try to speak in a language suited to all Nations, or rather, forgetting times and Places, in order to think only about the Men to whom I am speaking, I shall suppose myself in the Lyceum of Athens, repeating the Lessons of my Masters, with the likes of Plato and Xenocrates as my Judges, and Humankind as my Audience.[127]

In the sentence immediately preceding these lines, Rousseau specifies his intention to investigate "what Humankind might have become if it had remained abandoned to itself." Again, at stake is the transhistorical question of human nature, the nature of the human species abstracted from society. By speaking in "a language suited to all Nations," on one hand, and "forgetting times and Places," on the other, Rousseau also states his intention to shift between the registers of history and eternity. This is another way of indicating a division between politics and philosophy, where politics is concerned with the always changing character of human social affairs, while philosophy is concerned, at least traditionally, with the eternal and unchanging order of truth and wisdom.

According to this same division, Rousseau's political message should be available to all, while his philosophic teaching aims at a much smaller audience. This becomes clear through the examination of Rousseau's rhetoric. By envisioning himself "in the Lyceum of Athens [. . .] with the likes of Plato and Xenocrates as my Judges," Rousseau invokes an opposition between the schools of Aristotle and Plato, along with a need to moderate his speech according to the demands of his Aristotelian confines.

In this connection, we have already seen Rousseau take a similar position with his treatment of Aristotle in the epigraph taken from the *Politics*. There, Rousseau made use of Aristotle in order to accept and simultaneously revise the Aristotelian doctrine concerning the investigation of what is good by nature. It bears noting that Aristotle was also the patron philosopher of the Scholastics, whom Rousseau liked to berate for wrapping Christian theology in the authority of philosophy.[128] Yet, by citing both Plato and Xenocrates as his judges, Rousseau reminds us that he wished not only to be held to the high moral standard of Xenocrates, but that he is also speaking to a hostile audience. To cite the master on this very point, in *Menexenus* 235d Socrates remarks that it is easy to praise Athenians before an audience of Athenians, but persuasive rhetoric is required to praise Athenians before an audience of Peloponnesians or Peloponnesians before an audience of Athenians. So, it seems the stakes concerning the origin and foundations of philosophy are quite the same for Rousseau. By investigating the origin and foundations of human inequality in the Lyceum of Athens, Rousseau directs us to a Platonic notion of the origin and foundations of philosophy itself.

XI. THE PURE STATE OF NATURE

a. Paradox of the Good

If Rousseau thought it was necessary to take precautions when digging to the root, it is because he perceived something dangerous about the investigation into metaphysics or first philosophy. As we shall see, this danger is revealed by a fundamental insight derived from Rousseau's effort to interrogate the pure state of nature and its fabled icon, the abstract human "abandoned to himself." At issue is a paradox concerning Rousseau's conception of the human good. On one hand, the pure state of nature will reveal the natural goodness of the human being unadulterated by society. On the other hand, Rousseau describes a "chain of wonders" by which "the strong could resolve to serve the weak, and the people to purchase an idea of repose at the price of real felicity."[129]

In the former case, the human being is good by nature because it has no knowledge of the moral-juridical good. Discursive notions of "good" and "right" are absent in the pure state of nature. In the latter case, the moral-juridical good emerges with the introduction of human sociality, from which follows the desire for happiness and the invention of political inequality. Concisely stated, the human being is good by nature; by nature, the human being is free from any notion of the moral-juridical good. Much therefore hinges on the problem of the good and its *absence* in the pure state of nature. On one hand, the *idea* of the good emerges as the source of human corruption; on the other, the teaching of natural freedom from the moral-juridical good is a dangerous public teaching. It is finally this paradox that Rousseau perceived as dangerous. It requires a salutary teaching to prevent vulgar readers from disregarding the public good, while at the same time it serves as the basis for Rousseau's revision of the tradition of first philosophy from Aristotle to Descartes.

These observations indicate why Rousseau would have wished to bury the roots of his philosophic enterprise. As we saw in section III of this chapter, Rousseau maintains a certain exoteric contempt for the *doctrine intérieur*, insofar as it had been used by the *philosophes* and various non-Socratic sects to proliferate the secret teaching of pernicious falsehoods. However, Rousseau also addressed himself to a tiered audience divided among those who either possess or lack the capacity (or determination) to penetrate the political veneer that overlays his philosophic teaching.

As if to underscore this point, the *Second Discourse* includes an *Avertissement* between the Preface and Exordium which alerts readers to both Rousseau's "lazy practice of working in fits and starts" and the importance of the notes that supplement his argument. These notes may "stray so wide of the subject that they are not good to read together with the text." But Rousseau tried to follow "the straightest road," and he urges those with "courage" to "start over again" and "amuse themselves the second time with beating the bushes." For those who lack the aptitude or patience, "little harm" will come from ignoring the notes completely. Stated with maximum concision, philosophy is for the few; political speech is for the many.[130]

With respect to Rousseau's political teaching, the *Second Discourse* was written in response to the question given by the 1754 Dijon Academy essay competition: "What is the origin of inequality among men, and is it authorized by the natural law?"[131] In the preface, Rousseau makes fast work of this question's basic premise. He observes that the natural law tradition from the ancients to the moderns is fraught with disagreements, and he ultimately contends that the notion of natural law itself is an inherent contradiction. First, the notion of law is entirely conventional. It is a "common utility" derived from the human need to govern the social state from which Rousseau abstracts the pure state of nature. Second, the force of law is experienced as such only by those who can "submit to it knowingly."[132] Since the man of pure nature is abstracted from society, he cannot knowingly submit to what lies beyond the scope of his experience. It is therefore "impossible to understand the Law of Nature and hence to obey it without being a very great reasoner and a profound Metaphysician. Which precisely means that in order to establish society men must have employed an enlightenment which develops only with difficulty and among very few people within society itself."[133]

In other words, the idea of natural law presupposes a form of social inequality that could inspire an enlightened few to rule the many. Rousseau consequently traces the source of social or political inequality to the advancement of enlightenment. The salient question is not whether human inequality is authorized by nature, but whether the advancement of enlightenment legitimates the regime of law—or more directly, the regime in which "the strong could resolve to serve the weak, and the people to purchase an idea of repose at the price of real felicity."

This question serves as the political veneer for Rousseau's philosophic teaching. But it also points to the beginning of philosophic questioning, as it springs from the moment when the issues of politics and philosophy converge on questions concerning the meaning of happiness and the right order of society. These questions both presuppose the fundamental question of the good and its introduction into human life. The story of the pure state of nature is accordingly designed to illuminate the good itself as a fundamental problem. To be sure, without knowledge of the good, it is impossible "to accurately judge our present state."

b. Wonder Not in Nature

Let us begin again by setting aside all the facts. "Hence disregarding all the scientific books that only teach us to see men as they have made themselves, and meditating on the first and simplest operations of the human Soul," we perceive "two principles anterior to reason (*antérieurs à la raison*)." One "interests us intensely in our well-being and our self-preservation, and the other inspires in us a natural repugnance to seeing any sentient Being, and especially any being like ourselves, perish or suffer."[134] Anterior to reason, before we are taught to see human beings as they have made themselves, we find the principles of self-preservation and pity (*pitié*), which Rousseau calls "the internal compulsion of commiseration" (*l'impulsion intérieure de la commisération*).[135] Without having to introduce the attributes of sociability, Rousseau claims that all the rules of natural right seem to flow from the combination of these principles in our minds. But since these principles operate independent of reason, the human being of pure nature does not possess a notion of what is "right." Such notions could only be established on "other foundations," after the successive developments of reason have "succeeded in stifling Nature."[136]

It is important to see that the anteriority of reason does not mean that the human being without society is devoid of rationality. Rousseau notes that even the animals have "ideas" (*idées*), meaning that human beings and the beasts excel in the use of reason only by a difference of degree.[137] In the same way that the human infant is not without a faculty of reason despite lacking the "art of speech," Rousseau likewise considers the instrumental capacity of reason as distinct from language. On this point, Rousseau agrees with the early moderns for whom reason is not defined as *logos*, but more narrowly as *ratio* or calculation.[138] In fact, the rational character of the purely natural human is evident from the opening lines in Part One of the *Second Discourse*, where Rousseau plainly states that he is not interested in telling a story about the evolution of the human being from some prehuman form:

> However important it may be, in order to judge soundly regarding Man's natural state, to consider him from his origin, and to examine him, so to speak, in the first Embryo of the species, I shall not follow his organization throughout its successive developments: I shall not pause to search in the animal System what he may have been at the beginning, if he was eventually to become what he now is; I shall not examine whether, as Aristotle thinks, his elongated nails were at first claws;[139] whether he was as hairy as a bear and whether, walking on all fours, his gaze directed to the Earth, and confined to a horizon of a few paces, determined both the character and the limits of his ideas. I could form only vague and almost imaginary conjectures on this subject. [Instead,] without taking into account the changes that must have occurred in man's internal and

external conformation, as he gradually put his limbs to new uses, and took up new foods, *I shall assume him always conformed as I see him today*, walking on two feet, using his hands as we do ours, *directing his gaze over the whole of Nature,* and *with his eyes surveying the vast expanse of Heaven.*[140]

I want to emphasize three observations as they pertain to the possibility of philosophy. First, the human being of pure nature is not subhuman. Rousseau does not begin from a condition completely lacking in all human traits.[141] Instead, the human being that Rousseau investigates is "always conformed" as we see him "today." Second, Rousseau envisions the human being in the pure state of nature directing his gaze to the whole of nature and heaven. This comprehensive vision demarcates the prereflective horizon of intelligibility that belongs to "the ordinary course of life" (*le cours ordinaire de la vie*). The basic structure of ordinary experience therefore includes the freedom to transcend the immediate situation, to look beyond the earthly realm of physical contingency. Moreover, because the Socratic-Platonic tradition conceives of philosophy as mediation between the human and the divine, it is also evident that the human being possesses a natural capacity for philosophy. However, Rousseau also indicates that simply looking at the whole of nature and heaven is insufficient to turn the human being into a philosopher. *Life in the pure state of nature is not a philosophic life.* Instead, after stripping the human being of its "supernatural gifts" and "all of the artificial faculties he could only have acquired by prolonged progress," Rousseau sees "an animal less strong than some, less agile than others, [. . .] the most advantageously organized of all, [. . .] sating his hunger beneath an oak, slaking his thirst at the first Stream, finding his bed at the foot of the same tree that supplied his meal, and with that his needs are satisfied."[142] The human being of pure nature consequently lacks all desires or inclinations beyond the immediate satisfaction of physical needs. This leads to a third observation. In keeping with Rousseau's anti-Aristotelian attitude, he subtly challenges Aristotle's thesis in the *Metaphysics*, which links the genesis of philosophic wonder to the pleasures of the senses—in particular, the sense of sight which naturally inspires the desire to understand.[143] For Aristotle, philosophic wonder emerges directly from the human being's innate capacity to experience awe or puzzlement at what it perceives through the senses. Where Rousseau disagrees with Aristotle is on this exact point concerning the process that actualizes the human capacity for wonder.

As Aristotle has it, the faculty of memory is required for the generation of experience (*empeiria*), which takes shape through our repeated encounters with things in the world. From the repeated perception of particular things, the faculty of memory retains abstract impressions that form the universal concepts upon which the accumulation of knowledge builds experience.[144]

For Aristotle, the desire to understand the world is then a natural extension of experience. Because knowledge of the universal is embedded in the particulars of the world, the human being is led by nature to explore the universal through experience of the particular. Such activity gives birth to the arts (*technai*) and sciences (*epistēmai*).[145] But more importantly, with respect to the possibility of philosophy, Aristotle posits an *endogenous* desire for knowledge, which he calls "wonder" (*thaumazein*).[146] It is because of wonder that we do not simply observe phenomena, but wish to know *how* or *why* they appear. As Aristotle says: "The actual course of events bears witness to this; for thoughtfulness (*phronēsis*) of this kind [pursued for the sake of knowledge, and not for any practical utility] began with a view to recreation (*rhastōnēn*) and pastime (*diagōgēn*), at a time when practically all the necessities of life were already supplied."[147]

In this context, Aristotle cites Egypt's ancient priests, whose leisure (*scholē*) made possible the invention of mathematics and the use of arts and sciences to satisfy natural needs and inclinations.[148] By contrast, for Rousseau, when all the necessities of life are supplied in the pure state of nature, there is no stimulus to philosophic thoughtfulness because there is no question of satisfying every demand of life. Whereas, for Aristotle, philosophy begins with wonder as an escape from ignorance or the absence of understanding,[149] for Rousseau, there is no natural human need for such escape as long as the needs of physical life are satisfied by nature.

In sum: for Aristotle, philosophic wonder is derived from our perception of the world, whereas for Rousseau, merely gazing at earth and heaven is insufficient to provoke the sense of wonder in which philosophy begins. Of course, Rousseau is speaking through a fable, but it has a philosophic purpose—and even Aristotle states in the section of the *Metaphysics* now under examination: "The myth-lover is in a sense a philosopher, since myths are composed of wonders."[150] In the case of Rousseau, we are after that "chain of wonders" which led the human being to "purchase an idea of repose at the price of real felicity."[151] At root, this question concerns the beginning of wonder. But just as Rousseau imagines himself in the Lyceum of Aristotle, we seek a philosophical account of the genesis of philosophy—an account that may be held to the standards of Plato and Xenocrates.

c. Metaphysical and Moral Sides

In order to see how Rousseau's challenge to Aristotle on the genesis of wonder is consistent with his intention to turn Aristotle on his head, it is necessary to complete his portrait of the human being wholly abstracted from society. Beginning from the premise that what is good by nature cannot be investigated in beings that are depraved, the subtraction of society as the source of human ills renders a solitary animal without morality or convention. The human being of pure nature is therefore "good" because neither good nor evil. In the absence of a life with values, existence is restricted to the purely physical plane. For this reason, Rousseau distinguishes between two kinds of inequality. The first he calls "natural or Physical" because it is "established by Nature" and "consists in the differences of age, health, strengths of Body, and qualities of Mind, or of Soul (*qualities de l'Esprit, ou de l'Ame*)." The second he calls "moral or political" because it depends upon convention and is authorized by human consent. He includes with the latter the various privileges and prejudices that coincide with the accumulation of wealth, honor, and power—especially the power to make others submit and obey.[152] In the solitary state, by contrast, human powers would not exceed the few merely physical needs for food, shelter, rest, and occasional procreation.[153] Such beings would be self-sufficient and therefore "free"—and without having to depend on others, they would be "equal," as equally free to satisfy every requirement of life. Insofar as "every animal has ideas," it is therefore "not so much the understanding (*entendement*) that constitutes the specific difference between man and the other animals," but the capacities of *freedom* understood as "the power of willing, or rather of choosing" and an "almost unlimited" faculty of *perfectibility*, which Rousseau calls "the source of all of man's miseries."[154]

Up to this point in the text, Rousseau has considered only "Physical man." He now turns to the "Metaphysical and Moral side." Yet the "metaphysical" and the "moral" are not mutually reducible. The former corresponds to freedom, the latter to perfectibility. Whereas the "operations" of the beasts are fixed, as they choose or reject "by instinct," the human being, "perhaps having none that belongs to him," "recognizes himself free to acquiesce or to resist." Rousseau adds: "Physics in a way explains the mechanism of the senses and the formation of ideas," but the "power of willing" and the "sentiment of this power" are "purely spiritual acts about which nothing is explained by the Laws of Mechanics." It follows that human freedom belongs to "meta-physics" in the proper, etymological, sense.

By contrast, it is only "with the aid of circumstances" that the "faculty of perfecting oneself" is activated. Perfectibility is the faculty that "successively develops all the others, and resides in us, in the species as well as in the individual."[155] However, freedom from instinct is the basis—indeed, the metaphysical "root"—of human perfectibility, understood as the faculty that makes possible the exit from the purely natural state. Concisely stated, human beings possess freedom from the first; but perfectibility, hence the beginning of moral life and misery, is activated only by the contingent effects of "circumstance."

In a way comparable to Haeckel's law, that is, the principle by which ontogenesis reproduces phylogenesis, Rousseau proposes an analogy by which psychogenesis reproduces phylogenesis. In the present context, the psychogenesis of the human individual is reproduced at the conjectural level of the species.[156] Rousseau indicates as much when it comes to contemplating the possibility of philosophy as a uniquely human psychical achievement. With reference to the human being of pure nature:

> His imagination depicts nothing to him; his heart asks nothing of him. His modest needs are so ready to hand (*si aisément sous sa main*), and he is so far from the degree of knowledge necessary to desire to acquire greater knowledge, that *he can have neither foresight nor curiosity*. The spectacle of Nature becomes so familiar to him that he becomes indifferent to it. Forever the same order, forever the same revolutions; *he lacks the wit to wonder at the greatest marvels* (*il n'a pas l'esprit de s'étonner des plus grandes merveilles*).[157]

I note that "wonder" (*étonnement*) serves as the middle term between nature and history, just as the absence of wonder corresponds to the absence of the historical sense of time. The human being of pure nature has neither foresight, nor curiosity; hence, no sense of having a future or a past. Without a productive imagination, experience is restricted to a kind of atemporal present, which recalls, in reverse effect, the sense in which classical philosophy aims at transhistorical or eternal wisdom.

It may be just a "single word tossed off as if by chance," but without "the wit to wonder," Rousseau again affirms that the human being of pure nature is not a philosopher. In fact, "the only evils he fears are pain, and hunger." Rousseau does not say *death*, "for an animal will never know what it is to die, and the knowledge of death, and of its terrors, is one of man's first acquisitions on moving away from the animal condition."[158] Provided our attunement to Rousseau's art of writing, we may be reminded that the practice of dying or being dead describes the Socratic practice of philosophy—and philosophy is impossible without the "aid of circumstances." The confrontation with Aristotle which elicits Rousseau's wish to be judged by "the likes of Plato and Xenocrates" is consequently framed by this precise question about whether philosophic wonder owes its genesis to an endogenous or exogenous source. Furthermore, Rousseau's appeal to *the likes* of Plato and Xenocrates has the rhetorical effect of putting the philosophic reader in a position to judge Rousseau from this specific standpoint. To perform our duty as careful readers, we must therefore exit the pure state of nature by following the "chain of wonders" according to which philosophy becomes possible for human beings.

XII. THE CHAIN OF WONDERS

a. From *Amour de soi* to *Amour-propre*

Part One of the *Second Discourse* aims to demonstrate that "Inequality is scarcely perceptible in the state of Nature and that its influence there is almost nil."[159] Part Two is concerned with the genesis of moral or political inequality: "its origin and its progress through the successive developments of the human Mind or Spirit (*l'Esprit humain*)."[160] Taken as a whole, the *Second Discourse* elaborates the "chain of wonders" according to which the human soul serves as the ground of moral or political inequality. Still more concretely, Rousseau's text does not treat the genesis of human inequality as a historical question, as much as it does a psychical one. However, this inquiry is itself underwritten by an inquiry into the possibility of philosophy that proceeds by way of poetic abstraction. Evidently, the question of first philosophy or the genesis of wonder is concealed by Rousseau's political intention, which is concerned with moderating the problematic genesis of human inequality at the level of the social state. This also means that the philosophical and political ends of the *Second Discourse* converge at the point where the genesis of extraphysical inequality intersects with the genesis of philosophic wonder—that is, the point at which "an idea of repose" is purchased "at the price of real felicity." Hence, we arrive at the point where the question of human happiness is found at the source of philosophic wonder. If it can be said that Rousseau understands psychology as first philosophy, it is because he understands the activation of the faculty of perfectibility as crucial to the moment that unites the foundational question of philosophy with the source of human misery.

Perfectibility is the faculty which, "by force of time" (*à force de tems*) draws the human being out of the "*condition originaire*" and "eventually makes him his own and Nature's tyrant."[161] With perfectibility comes innovation, mastery, and the enlargement of the passions. It is by the "activity" of the passions "that our reason perfects itself." And: "We seek to know only because we desire to enjoy. [. . .] The Passions, in turn, owe their origin to our needs, and their progress to our knowledge."[162] Yet the passions do not develop spontaneously from our needs, as human needs are completely satisfied in the pure state of nature—and Rousseau affirms that "perfectibility, the social virtues and the other faculties which natural man had received in potentiality could never develop by themselves."[163]

Among the "other faculties" received in "potentiality" are reason or understanding and imagination. Such faculties are activated only by "the fortuitous concatenation of several foreign causes (*causes étrangeres*)."[164] But this fundamental change is made inevitable by the "force of time." Again, Rousseau makes Aristotle the unstated target of his argument. For Aristotle, we seek to know by nature, owing to the pleasures of the senses; whereas for Rousseau, "We seek to know only because we desire to enjoy." Yet this desire is spurred only by the introduction of "foreign causes" from outside the condition of pure nature. The exit from pure nature therefore turns on the function of these "foreign causes" in deriving our "passions" from our "needs."

To that end, there is a single term which captures the restricted scope of natural human needs—namely, what Rousseau calls *amour de soi* in contrast to *amour-propre*. Whereas *amour de soi* expresses the natural sentiment of self-preservation, *amour-propre*—because it owes its origin to our needs, and its progress to our knowledge—has its ground in purely physical *amour de soi*.[165] Indeed, the exit from pure nature is explained entirely by the process through which *amour-propre* emerges from *amour de soi*—with the "aid of circumstances" and "foreign causes."

Now, *amour-propre* is a formidable and nearly untranslatable term in Rousseau's technical lexicon. Among scholars today it is commonly identified as a desire for recognition, which is to acknowledge that *amour-propre* is neither exclusively pernicious nor reducible to the source of human pride and everything that follows—from social alienation to the lust for domination.[166] Taken literally, *amour-propre* means something like the love of what is "properly" or "rightly" one's own. As a term of art, it has a rich history which I will not pursue in detail except to say its etymological roots are entrenched in seventeenth-century French translations of the ancient Greek *philautia*.[167] In Aristotle's account of friendship, for example, an individual's love for another derives from *philautia*, translated literally as "self-love." A virtuous self-love makes it possible to treat one's friend as "another self," in the sense that virtuous friends desire goods for each other in equal measure. The genuine "lover of self" is also said to be *spoudaios* or deserving of respect and serious worth because this person understands the beautiful and the good as something mutually beneficial. In this way, *philautia* in the highest sense expresses the completion of one's nature as a social animal.[168]

Somewhat closer to the conventional interpretation of self-love as "vulgar egoism" is the teaching of Diotima in Plato's *Symposium*. Although the word *philautia*, including its derivatives, is surprisingly absent from Plato's corpus,[169] the teaching of Diotima is remarkable for the specific reason that Blaise Pascal repeats the same metaphor in writing about *amour-propre* that Plato used in his dialogue on love—namely, that of a ladder. Within the context of Plato's dialogue, the notion of self-love is expressed as a desire for immortal virtue and famous reputation. This desire for immortality is also called the inspiration for all human action—or at least every pursuit undertaken by the lover of self. Self-love therefore indicates a wish to be revered for all eternity—specifically, for having given birth to beautiful lessons in prudence and other virtues such as those possessed by the poets and craftsmen who strive to acquire immortal fame by creating poetic or technological innovations.[170] In this sense, self-love—as a wish for immortality—expresses a desire to ascend from mortal finitude to the unchanging domain of truth and beauty. However, in the case of poets and craftsmen this desire is said to be imperfect because it attaches to a particular self, not to the universality of Ideas. The desire for ascent is also restricted by the imitative character of poetry and the infinitely changing character of technology, neither of which can produce the unchanging Idea of beauty, but only its representation in the arts, which are themselves transient. On the ladder of love, the poets and craftsmen are therefore stranded in the middle: above the lovers of beautiful bodies and beautiful speeches, but below the lovers of the beautiful itself, understood as the cause or principle that makes things lovable.

In the case of Pascal, by contrast, the relation between self-love and the desire for truth is reversed. Rather than appearing as an ascendant rung on the ladder of love, self-love is conceived as a rung on the ladder of fortune, which removes us ever further from the truth. This is because the very notion of self-love expresses a demand to be perceived as lovable; yet love from others is good fortune while the desire to be lovable easily becomes a source of self-deceit. Insofar as self-love cannot tolerate the imperfections that make us small and wretched, it becomes the source of disguise, falsehood, and hypocrisy. At worst, it provokes "a deadly hatred for the truth," which makes one care more about flattering the opinions of others than the truth of one's deficiencies. Pascal adds that people who are most favored by fortune are also the most vulnerable to the corrosive effects of self-love: "because people are more wary of offending those whose friendship is most useful and enmity most dangerous."[171] By ascending the ladder of fortune, the self-lover consequently falls deeper into falsehood.[172]

Rousseau very much agrees about the problems presented by *amour-propre*, but he views them as the vicissitudes of a highly plastic sentiment, irreducible to the expressions found in Plato, Aristotle, and Pascal. This is clearly stated in *Émile*, where Rousseau calls *amour-propre* "a useful but dangerous instrument."[173] As the source of love and friendship, it is useful.[174] As the source of social strife and misery, it is dangerous. Yet this fundamental plasticity allows it to be bent toward good or ill by a process of education.[175] Nevertheless, Rousseau tends to emphasize the destructive effects of *amour-propre* as part of his overall critique of Enlightenment modernity. In the *Second Discourse*, he calls it "only a relative sentiment, factitious, and born in society." To say that it is "factitious" is to indicate that with *amour-propre* comes artifice and convention. To say that it is "relative" and "born in society" is to acknowledge its source in interactions relative to other people.

It "inclines every individual to set greater store by himself than by anyone else, inspires men with all the evils they do one another, and is the true source of honor."[176] As such, *amour-propre* appears as a self-interested sentiment, but one that is infused with a reflective sense of value or self-worth—none of which exists in the pure state of nature.

For this reason, Rousseau is careful to warn his readers against confusing *amour-propre* with *amour de soi* (also called *amour de soi-même*), as the latter translates directly as "love of self" (or "love of oneself"). These "two passions" are "very different in their nature and their effects."[177] Whereas *amour-propre* is born only in society, *amour de soi* is a wholly natural sentiment of self-preservation, common to beasts and human beings. To this, Rousseau adds in *Émile* that *amour de soi* is "born with man"; and he calls it the "source of our passions," "a primitive, innate passion," "anterior to every other," and the "origin and principle" of which all the others are "in a sense only modifications." Rousseau also notes, as he does in the *Second Discourse*, that "most of these modifications have *alien causes* (*causes étrangeres*) without which they would never come to pass; and these modifications, far from being advantageous for us, are harmful." These new passions may be harmful because they "alter the primary goal" of *amour de soi*, as they engender interests in the human being that may exceed, and even contradict, our natural care for self-preservation.[178]

It is precisely this trajectory from *amour de soi* to *amour-propre* that explains the transition from the pure state of nature to the civil state. But between these ends Rousseau also identifies an intermediary condition, "the period of a first revolution," which slowly removes the human being from pure nature without precipitating the dangers immanent to the social state.[179] Such is the aforementioned difference between the natural human and the human being of pure nature. There are, accordingly, natural developments of the human soul which alone are insufficient to spur the derivation of *amour-propre* and hence the genesis of moral or political inequality.

b. Mechanical Prudence

To start again from the pure state of nature, Rousseau speaks of "nascent man" defined as "an animal at first restricted to pure sensations."[180] With "no idea of the future," nothing stirs his soul, which "yields itself to the sole sentiment of his present existence."[181] However, "the ordinary course of life" (*le cours ordinaire de la vie*) presents various "difficulties," and "it became necessary to learn to overcome them." Rousseau cites such natural difficulties as "the height of Trees" and the distance of their fruits, "competition from the animals trying to eat these fruits," and "the ferociousness of the animals that threatened his very life." This nascent human was thus "obliged" by nature to "attend to bodily exercise" in order to gain advantages in agility, speed, and fighting vigor.[182] Eventually, by the "force of time," increasing population density and strife induced by nature, along with "repeated interactions" of "various beings with himself as well as with one another," is enough to have "engendered" the perception of "certain relations" expressed by the words "great, small, strong, weak fast, slow, fearful, bold, and other such ideas."[183]

Everything contained in this list belongs to the purely physical domain.[184] There is nothing intrinsically "moral" or "political" about these terms, as they all express relations discovered through calculations concerning self-preservation. Nevertheless, the accidents of nature are enough to engender a restricted power of "*réflexion*"—further defined as "mechanical prudence"—which appears as a perfection of the natural capacity of reason defined as *ratio* or calculation. Stated more precisely, the natural sentiment of pity contains within itself a power of "identification," which precedes *réflexion* by putting us "in the place of him who suffers."[185] The interplay of calculative reason, care for self-preservation, and pity for the suffering other is spontaneously fashioned by the faculty of perfectibility into the powers of *réflexion* and mechanical prudence. These newly formed capacities allowed the nascent human to "look at himself," which, in turn, "aroused the first movement of pride (*orgueil*)." Rousseau explains: "this is how, while as yet *scarcely able to discriminate ranks*, and considering himself in the first rank as a species, he was from afar preparing to claim first rank as an individual."[186] In this way, the capacity for *réflexion* is foundational for the transition from nature to the social state. But mechanical prudence alone is "scarcely able to discriminate ranks," as it lacks any capacity to place moral or political value on purely physical forms of difference. Calculative reason therefore serves as the foundation of *amour-propre*. But with the addition of perfectibility and the beginning of *réflexion*, the faculty of reason functions only as a power of instrumental measure, which allows the nascent human to perceive its superior place in nature.[187] This likewise means that pride as such has nothing to do with moral or political valuation—or any notion of the good as such. Rather, it is limited to the calculation and exertion of power. At stake in the genesis of *amour-propre* is thus the question of the good and the process by which it enters human life.

c. Love and Wonder

We are now ready to see how the question of happiness or the human good, equally the source of philosophic wonder and human misery, intervenes as the particular *cause étrangère*, the "alien" or "foreign" cause, which—by the "aid of circumstances" in combination with the powers of *réflexion*—instigates the derivation of *amour-propre* from *amour de soi* and, hence, the possibility of philosophy itself. I note as a preface that while Rousseau treats the process by which *amour-propre* is engendered in the species as conjectural, these conjectures are allegorical of the same process in the human individual. According to this parallel, a hard realism permeates Rousseau's conjecture that life in the pure state of nature is "solitary." Just as every human infant is born alone and helpless, every one of us would perish without the interventions of a guardian. What is fundamentally at issue in Rousseau's account of the exit from pure nature is, accordingly, the inevitable yet wholly contingent effect of other people on the development of the human psyche, which Rousseau investigates at the twin levels of the individual and the species.[188]

This brings us to the most iconic moment in Rousseau's canon: in the epoch of the "first revolution," the image of nascent human beings at the cusp of society imbued with culture, gathered together "in front of Huts or around a large Tree," enjoying "song and dance," the "children of love and leisure (*enfans de l'amour et du loisir*)."[189] Rousseau calls this the "happiest and most lasting epoch [. . .] the least subject to revolutions, the best for man, one from which he would not have left but for some fatal accident (*funeste hazard*) which, for the sake of the common utility, should never have occurred."[190] Now, this statement requires an important qualification: it is the epoch "least subject to revolutions" until the time of the "first revolution." In the events that follow, "Everyone began to look at everyone else and to wish to be looked at himself, and public esteem acquired a price. The one who sang or danced best; the handsomest, the strongest, the most skillful, or the most eloquent came to be the most highly regarded, and this was the first step at once toward inequality and vice."[191]

Born from "love and leisure," a new category of experience is discovered: that of "public esteem." Along the chain of wonders, this signals the moment when "the strong could resolve to serve the weak, and the People to purchase an idea of repose at the price of real felicity."[192] I note that Rousseau's repeated use of the economic metaphor supplies a further hint that "the price of real felicity" is the artifice of "public esteem," the very opposite of "repose," as it preys upon the double desire to look at and be seen. This insight also serves as a subtle modification of Aristotle's thesis concerning the genesis of wonder. Much like Aristotle, Rousseau begins with an act of looking made possible by leisure broadly understood. But since the pleasures of sight and the other senses are insufficient to spur the genesis of wonder, Rousseau adds love as a condition in the context of acquiring esteem—and this induces the pleasures of sight and being seen.[193] These conditions on their own do not explain the genesis of philosophic wonder. But the taste for public esteem is discovered in the perceptions of "beauty" (*beauté*) or "merit" (*mérite*) that engender the "moral aspect of love" as a "factitious sentiment."[194]

Let us pause to consider the implications of these observations for Rousseau's challenge to the tradition of first philosophy. If we consider the literal meaning of the word, the genesis of "philosophy" as the "love of wisdom" indicates the genesis of a specific kind of love—namely, the kind of love that takes wisdom as its object. Understood this way, a genuine first philosophy cannot be concerned with discovering a scientific foundation of philosophy, as in Descartes. Nor does it concern an inquiry into the meaning of being, as the meaning of *prōtē philosophia* indicates for Aristotle. Instead, for Rousseau, a genuine first philosophy must explain the genesis of the love of wisdom as a specific kind of human experience or endeavor. With the introduction of the "moral aspect of love," distinguished from its purely physical expression as the "general desire that moves one sex to unite with the other," Rousseau challenges Aristotle on the crucial point concerning the endogenous source of philosophic wonder.[195]

If it can be said that philosophy begins in wonder for Rousseau, as it similarly does for Plato and Aristotle, then its source must be contained in the "chain of wonders" that explains the process by which the "moral aspect of love" takes wisdom as its object. Rousseau explains the beginning of this process by introducing beauty and merit as the *causes étrangeres* that seduce the human being into moral ways of loving. Stated more exactly, public esteem is identified with beauty in such talents as song, dance, strength, skill, and eloquence—and the perception of beauty transmits the idea of merit or the good as an object of desire. So much therefore turns on the moment when the promise of "repose" is purchased at the price of "real felicity," that is, the moment when the idea of the good enters human life as a question concerning happiness. I call "the good" a question because the sense of merit is contingent upon its perception as an object of esteem—and love from the other is never guaranteed.

With respect to morality or politics, the question of the good presents a problem, as it exposes differences of rank or inequality. Yet the question of the good alone cannot provide a standard for the rank ordering of merits. Such standards must be founded on "other foundations," which can be produced only in response to the question of the good as it breaks through the order of nature. In order to explain how love takes wisdom as an object, it is therefore necessary to explain how moral love is inspired to answer questions about the good. This in turn requires us to see how *amour-propre* is derived from *amour de soi*. For if the possibility of philosophy is founded with the moral aspect of love, then the process by which love takes wisdom as its object must follow the "chain of wonders" that lead through the genesis of *amour-propre*.

XIII. PRELUDE TO SEDUCTION

Rousseau does not employ the word *séduction* as a technical term, but the vocabulary of seduction appears throughout his works as a cause of great concern. In the *Discourse on Heroic Virtue* from 1751, Rousseau remarks that "unstable judgment and an easily seduced heart render men weak and petty."[196] In the *Preface to "Narcissus"* from 1752 to 1753, in a footnote concerning the dangers of *amour-propre*, he adds: "I have noticed that at present a great many petty maxims hold sway in the world which seduce simple minds with a false semblance of philosophy."[197] And in the magnum opus of 1762, it seems the entire education of Émile aims to protect him from seduction: "For against what seduction is he not on guard?"[198] Indeed, Jean-Jacques' first instruction to "tender and foresighted" mothers is to "form an enclosure around your child's soul at an early date."[199] It is easy to multiply examples.[200] But the case of Émile is paradigmatic of Rousseau's pedagogical imperative to secure the individual soul from the seductive "impact of human opinions," much like Epictetus taught: "It is not things, but opinions about things that disturb men."[201]

In the present context, the fundamental issue concerns the inflammation of *amour-propre* and its derivation from *amour de soi* by a process of seduction that has its source in the desire of the other—the font of public esteem. But while Rousseau cautions against seduction, on the one hand, it appears, on the other, that he simultaneously perpetrates a process of seduction in the soul of his most attentive readers. In the context of his critique of Cartesian science, in which it is necessary to end where Descartes began, I marked this as Rousseau's legacy-as-task. The reason stems from Rousseau's claim to show only the branches while concealing the root. For that matter, if the investigation into the possibility of philosophy reveals the human good as a fundamental problem, Rousseau would have had (or would have thought himself to have) good reason to keep this insight hidden from readers with "unstable judgment," as such readers are prone to "mistake unbridled license for freedom, which is its very opposite."[202]

With respect to the human good, it may be enigmatic, but this does not mean it is nonexistent. The same could be said of Rousseau's challenge to the tradition of first philosophy from Aristotle to Descartes. We have arrived at this point by picking up Rousseau's various guiding threads: where his comments on the *doctrine intérieur* point to his thought pertaining to the hidden root of a genuine first philosophy; in the way philosophic readers are distinguished from nonphilosophic ones, as those who raise themselves are distinguished from those who need to be raised; for the same reason Rousseau imagined himself in the Lyceum of Athens with humankind as his audience and the likes of Plato and Xenocrates as his judges; including his suggestion that courageous readers of the *Second Discourse* should "start over again and amuse themselves the second time with beating the bushes, and trying to peruse the notes."[203] These are all indications of Rousseau's intention to seduce attentive readers by the use of enigmatic statements that, if successfully implanted, are designed to pull the reader along obscure pathways to Rousseau's deepest or most hidden teaching. As Rousseau also wrote in the preface to the *Second Discourse:* "Others will easily be able to go farther along the same road, though it will not be easy for anyone to reach the end."[204] This comment is made in the context of remarks concerning the Glaucus allegory on the difficulty of separating nature from artifice or convention—that is, the very issue underlying the derivation of *amour-propre* from *amour de soi.* If the possibility of philosophy is founded with the genesis of *amour-propre*, the reader who has been seduced by Rousseau's enigmatic intonations must now endeavor one step farther to ascertain the process by which the genesis of *amour-propre* may engender the desire for philosophy.

NOTES

1. Kuehn (2001), 272.
2. The existing scholarship on this topic is surprisingly thin. The standard and still most significant commentary on Rousseau as a reader of Descartes is Gouhier (1970, esp. 49–83). Gouhier convincingly shows that Rousseau was not only a careful reader of Descartes' *Discourse on Method*, but that Descartes' method of doubt was instrumental to the method of Rousseau's ethical investigations as they appeared first in the *Moral Letters* and later, more fully formed, in the Savoyard Vicar's Profession of Faith in *Émile*. Several of Gouhier's observations are developed in Wilson (1983). Westmoreland (2013) also extends Gouhier's observations to argue that the Vicar's transformative "misuse" of Cartesian concepts points to a Rousseauian conception of first philosophy as practical philosophy. Additional, salient, observations about Rousseau as a reader of Descartes may be found in Strauss (1953, 264–65) and Velkley (2002, 39).
3. Rousseau, OC 4:1099/LM 189 (Rousseau's emphasis).
4. These lectures pursue a definition of first philosophy as phenomenology and represent the culmination of Husserl's project to renew the search for a genuine first philosophy, initiated in lectures from 1906 to 1907. These early lectures treat "first philosophy" as "the theory of knowledge" and "the critique of theoretical reason," defined as "the science of principles, namely the science of ultimate elucidation, of ultimate justification and bestowal of meaning, therefore, of ultimate clearing up, all that understood in the sense of universality on grounds of principle" ([1906/1907] 2008, 163). The neo-Cartesian spirit of Husserl's transcendental phenomenology is also evident from the title of his *Cartesian Meditations: An Introduction to Phenomenology*, published in 1931.
5. Aristotle, *Metaphysics*, Γ.1.1003a21-22.

6. Aristotle, *Metaphysics*, Δ.11.1018b32-4.
7. Aristotle, *Metaphysics*, Γ.1.1003a26-32.
8. Aristotle, *Metaphysics*, Γ.2.1004a2-9; Γ.1.1003a33.
9. Aristotle, *Metaphysics*, K.2.1060b4; K.2.1026a29-31.
10. Aristotle, *Metaphysics*, Δ.11.1019a4-5. Aristotle attributes this teaching to Plato, but Aubenque (2008, 44 n. 64) notes, following Ross and Trendelenburg, that this definition does not appear explicitly in Plato's written works.
11. This list is an abbreviation of the two lists that appear in *Metaphysics* Δ.11.1018b9-1019a14 and *Categories* 12.14a27-b24. Whereas the *Categories* lists five items, the list in the *Metaphysics* is divided into three parts: priority in relation to a fixed point, priority according to knowledge, and priority according to nature or essence. There are several entries under each heading, which makes the list from the *Metaphysics* more comprehensive, and likely a revision of the list in the *Categories*, though it notably omits the definition in the *Categories* of priority as a measure of value.
12. Aristotle, *Categories*, 12.14b3-5.
13. Aristotle, *Metaphysics*, A.3.984a1-5.
14. Aristotle, *Metaphysics*, E.1.1026a18-24.
15. See Descartes, *Principes de la philosophie*, A-T 9B:7–9.
16. Descartes, *Principes de la philosophie*, A-T 9B:2.
17. Descartes, Letter to Mersenne (11 November 1640), A-T 3:239.
18. Descartes, *Principes de la philosophie*, A-T 9B:2; 9.
19. Descartes, *Discours de la méthode*, A-T 6:62.
20. Cf. Descartes, *Les Passions de l'âme*, A-T 11:§153.
21. Descartes, *Discours de la méthode*, A-T 6:23.
22. Rousseau, OC 2:1128/OMdW 8. For Rousseau's introduction to Descartes, Malebranche, Locke, Leibniz, the *Logic* of Port-Royal, and so on, see OC 1:237/C 198–99.
23. Rousseau, OC 4:1095/ML 186.
24. Rousseau, OC 4:1095–96/ML 186.
25. Rousseau, OC 4:1096/ML 186.
26. Descartes, *Discours de la méthode*, A-T 6:62.
27. Rousseau, OC 4:269/E 53.
28. Rousseau, OC 4:269/E 54.
29. Rousseau, OC 4:1095/ML 186.
30. Rousseau, OC 4:269/E 54.
31. Rousseau, OC 4:269/E 54.
32. Rousseau, OC 4:270/E 54.
33. Rousseau, OC 4:270/E 54.
34. Descartes, *Regulae* 3, A-T 10:366: "Concerning objects proposed for study, we ought to investigate what we can clearly and evidently intuit or deduce with certainty, not what other people have thought or what we ourselves conjecture."
35. Descartes, *Regulae* 5, A-T 10:379: "The whole method consists entirely in the ordering and arranging of the objects [. . .]."
36. Descartes, *Regulae* 2, A-T 10:365.

37. Descartes, *Les Passions de l'âme*, A-T 11:§152: "I see only one thing in us which could give us good reason for esteeming ourselves, namely, the exercise of our free will and the control we have over our volitions. [. . .] It renders us in a certain way like God by making us masters of ourselves, provided we do not lose the rights it gives us by timidity."

38. Descartes, *Discours de la méthode*, A-T 6:4.
39. Descartes, *Discours de la méthode*, A-T 6:4.
40. Descartes, *Discours de la méthode*, A-T 6:1.
41. Rousseau, OC 4:1084–87/ML 179.
42. Plato, *Phaedo*, 64a4-6, 67d7-10.
43. Rousseau, OC 4:270/E 55.
44. Rousseau, OC 1:9/C 8.
45. With the possible exception of the *Philebus*. See Fain (2018), 75 n. 59.
46. Cf. Rousseau, OC 3:44-45n./OBS 40-41n. Rousseau here identifies an ancient "hatred and mutual contempt [. . .] that has at all times reigned between the Doctors and the Philosophers; that is to say between those who use their heads as a storehouse for other people's Science and those who lay claim to a head of their own."
47. Rousseau, OC 4:270/E 54.
48. Descartes, *Discours de la méthode*, A-T 6:8.
49. Nietzsche, NF 350/WP §2. See Chapter 1, Section IV.
50. Descartes, *Discours de la méthode*, A-T 6:7.
51. Rousseau, OC 3:106/Bordes, 109–10. This letter, unpublished in Rousseau's lifetime, was written sometime in May–November 1753, placing it squarely between the *First* and *Second Discourses*.
52. Rousseau, OC 3:106/Bordes, 109–10.
53. Kelly (2003, 142–48) provides detailed evidence to this point, along with several corroborating references.
54. Diderot & d'Alembert, ENC 6:273–74.
55. Rousseau, OC 1:468/C 393.
56. Rousseau, OC 1:1022/R 26.
57. Rousseau, OC 1:695/D 28.
58. The publications at issue are the *Oath of the Fifty* and *Catechism of the Honest Man*. For a detailed account of this episode and its aftermath, see Kelly (2003), 8–12.
59. Rousseau, OC 3:46/OBS 42.
60. Rousseau, OC 3:46/OBS 42.
61. Cf. Kelly (2003), 148–67. Kelly argues that for Rousseau the internal doctrine "in its traditional form [. . .] has not been interior enough" (154). In commenting on the beginning of philosophy, however, he maintains Rousseau's statement that philosophy has its origin in human pride without subjecting this to further examination. He argues only that the philosopher must purge philosophy of pride in order to safeguard it from errors affecting the public good (154–66).
62. Rousseau, OC 3:29–30/FD 26–27.
63. Rousseau, OC 4:270/E 54.
64. Rousseau, OC 3:30/FD 27.

65. Rousseau, OC 3:29/FD 26.
66. Rousseau, OC 4:266/E 52. Cf. OC 3:29/FD 26.
67. Rousseau, OC 682/D 19. Cf. OC 4:248/E 39; OC 3:44-45n/OBS 40-41n.
68. Rousseau, OC 1:389/C 326.
69. Rousseau, OC 1:388/C 326.
70. Rousseau, OC 4:928/LtB 22. Cf. OC 3:71/LR 63, OC 3:230-31/LtP 223, OC 4:323/E 93. For the criticism of Rousseau, see, for example, Edmond Burke's review of Rousseau's *Letter to d'Alembert*, where he quips: "A tendency to paradox, which is always the bane of solid learning [. . .] has prevented a great deal of the good effects which might be expected from such a genius" ([1759] 1963, 89). For additional commentary, see Salkever (1977–78), 204.
71. Rousseau, OC 1:930/D 209.
72. Rousseau, OC 3:105/Bordes, 108–9.
73. Rousseau, OC 4:348/E 110 (emphasis added).
74. Rousseau, OC 4:323/E 93.
75. d'Alembert, DP vi/22–23. For additional comment, see Cassirer (1951), 8–9. Cf. Condillac ([1746] 1973) on the two kinds of metaphysics: "everyone allows himself to be seduced by his own system" (100/4); "By tracing our errors to the origin I have indicated, we enclose them within a single cause of which we cannot deny that it has hitherto played a large role in our judgments. Perhaps we may oblige even the most prejudiced philosophers to admit that this unique cause is the foundation of their systems, provided we put the question the right way" (270/198).
76. Rousseau, OC 1:347/C 291.
77. Rousseau, OC 1:934/D 213.
78. Rousseau, OC 4:245/E 37.
79. Rousseau, OC 1:935/D 213.
80. Rousseau, OC 1:933/D 211.
81. Rousseau, OC 1:933/D 211.
82. By contrast, Kelly and Masters suggest that "he may end as a philosophic reader" (1989–90, 246).
83. Rousseau, OC 1:750–51/D 70–71.
84. Rousseau, OC 1:939/D 217.
85. Rousseau, OC 1:933/D 211.
86. Masters' (1968) classic study takes its direction from the Frenchman.
87. Rousseau, OC 1:668/D 9.
88. Rousseau, OC 3:106/Bordes 110.
89. Rousseau, OC 1:388/C 326.
90. Rousseau, OC 1:407/C 341.
91. Rousseau, OC 1.388/C 326 (my emphasis).
92. Rousseau, OC 3:3/FD 4; 3:122/SD 124.
93. Rousseau, OC 3:122/SD 124.
94. Rousseau, OC 3:160/SD 157 (my emphasis).
95. Descartes, *Discours de la méthode*, A-T 6:7–8.
96. Rousseau, OC 3:127/SD 128.
97. Descartes, *Les passions de l'âme* §153, A-T 11.445-46.

98. To my knowledge, the most explicit statement on the difference between Rousseau's use of the terms "origine" and "fondements" appears in Jean Starobinski's Introduction to the Pléiade edition of the *Second Discourse*. "Cessant (pendant quelques pages) de reconstruire les *origines* et d'explorer les profondeurs du temps, il établit les *fondements* que toute société saine devrait reconnaître. C'est là ce que Rousseau appelle 'creuser jusqu'à la racine.' Contrairement à beaucoup de ses prédécesseures, Rousseau sait distinguer ce qui est commencement dans l'ordre chronologique, et ce qui est principe dans l'ordre idéal" (OC 3:lxv–lxvi). According to Starobinski, Rousseau's procedure of "cutting to the root" is meant to reveal an ideal order that will transcend history, and therefore serve as the unshakeable foundation of his political doctrine. I press no argument on this point. However, I also contend that Rousseau's political project overlays a deeper philosophical project, which is concerned with the genuine basis of philosophy itself. In both the aforementioned Introduction and "Rousseau et la recherche des origines," Starobinski obscures Rousseau's use of the singular "origine," thus preventing him from exploring its interpretive implications. See Starobinski (1971), 319–29/271–80.

99. Rousseau, OC 4:1062, 1064/LtV 235, 236.

100. Driscoll (1911).

101. Rousseau, OC 3:148/SD 146.

102. Rousseau, OC 3:151, 179/SD 149, 174.

103. Rousseau, OC 3:184/SD 179.

104. Rousseau, OC 3:192/SD 186.

105. Rousseau, OC 3:132/SD 131.

106. Aristotle, *Politics*, 1254a36-38.

107. Aristotle, *Politics*, 1253a26-29.

108. I owe this insight to conversations with Stanley Rosen.

109. Rousseau, OC 3:122/SD 124. For citations to the myth, see Plato, *Republic*, 611b-d.

110. Rousseau, OC 3:122/SD, 124.

111. Cf. Rousseau, OC 3:135/SD 135: "each species has but its own instinct, while man perhaps having none that belongs to him, appropriates them all [. . .]."

112. Rousseau, OC 3:122/SD 124.

113. Rousseau, OC 3:122–23/SD 124.

114. For related commentary on the Glaucus passage, see Starobinski (1971, 27–33/15–18) and Velkley (2002, 36–40).

115. Rousseau, OC 3:123/SD 125.

116. Rousseau, OC 3:132–33/SD 132.

117. For the problem of philosophical historicism, see Page (1995). Seminal texts on this topic include Strauss (1959) and Rosen (1969).

118. Rousseau, OC 3:122/SD 124.

119. Rousseau, OC 3:132/SD 131.

120. Rousseau, OC 3:132/SD 132.

121. Rousseau, OC 3:132/SD 132.

122. Rousseau, OC 3:132–33/SD 132. This passage has been the subject of considerable debate among scholars. The main disagreement concerns whether Rousseau

intends to set aside only "the biblical facts," or whether he intends to categorically set aside *all* the facts, including all pretense to historical or scientific truth. Proponents of the first view, among whom Heinrich Meier is most prominent, tend not to accept on face value Rousseau's repeated statements about the entirely conjectural character of the pure state of nature. On this view, Rousseau's version of the pure state of nature is said to function as a kind of scientific hypothesis about the evolution of humanity from its animal origin: what Meier calls "the historical anthropogenesis of humankind" (die geschichtliche Menschwerdung des Menschen) (1984, liii). This view is directly opposite the view of Christian theology, which would seem to confirm the "philosophically radical and scientifically serious character" of its argument. For my part, the above argument in Section VIII shows how "setting aside all the facts" allows Rousseau to generate the mythopoetic condition of philosophic inquiry. I also side with Gourevitch, contra Meier, in that I see no reason to turn Rousseau into a kind of secret Darwin—a reading which stands in direct contradiction to Rousseau's opening statement in Part One of the *Discourse*. Cf. Meier (1984), 168f, n. 211; Gourevitch (1988), 43–46.

For a review of the literature on the "state of nature" in Rousseau, see chapter 1 of Marks (2005). Though Marks does not address the passage in question, he claims in a footnote to join Gourevitch and others in reading the state of nature as conjectural (163–64 n. 10). However, he also argues that "the conception of nature advanced in the Preface of the *Second Discourse* is incoherent," mainly because Rousseau fails to maintain a strict separation between nature and history as evidenced by the various physical causes that compel the natural man to adapt to nature (4, 15–53). I submit, to the contrary, that dismissing the account in the *Second Discourse* amounts to a distortion of the problem that Rousseau wished to introduce regarding the relation between nature and history. Moreover, I shall argue below that physical causes alone are insufficient, on Rousseau's account, to make the human being a historical (and therefore moral or political) creature. For his part, Marks suggests that we should favor the account of nature in the first chapter of *Émile* over and against that of the *Second Discourse*. However, in order to make a convincing case, Marks would have to show that all of Rousseau's writings are *not* written according to the same principles, despite Rousseau's explicit statements to the contrary. Marks, unfortunately, does not address his criticism to this guiding principle of Rousseau's system.

123. Rousseau, OC 3:132/SD 132, 3:127/SD 128.
124. Hobbes, DC 3.
125. Tuck (1999), 199–200.
126. Rousseau, OC 3:162/SD 159.
127. Rousseau, OC 3:133/SD 132–33.
128. For example, Rousseau, OC 3:47/OBS 43.
129. Rousseau, OC 3:132/SD 131.
130. Rousseau, OC 3:128/SD 129.
131. Announced in the November 1753 edition of the *Mercure de France*.
132. Rousseau, OC 3:125/SD 127.
133. Rousseau, OC 3:125/SD 126.

134. Rousseau, OC 3:125–26/SD 127.
135. Rousseau, OC 3:126/SD 127.
136. Rousseau, OC 3:126/SD 127.
137. Rousseau, OC 3:141, 149–50/SD 140, 148.
138. Rousseau, OC 3:147/SD 146: "If Men needed speech in order to learn how to think, they needed even more to know how to think in order to find the art of speech." Cf. Note 10, OC 3:210/SD 207: "Although the organ of speech is natural to man, speech itself is nevertheless not natural to him." Contra Strauss, NRH 270; cf. Gourevitch (2013), 154.
139. Aristotle does not make the evolutionary claim, but Rousseau is likely citing the *History of Animals*, 2.8.
140. Rousseau, OC 3:134/SD 134 (my emphasis).
141. Contra Strauss, NRH 271, 273, 274, 292, 293. For a similarly critical reading of Strauss, see Gourevitch (2013), esp., 151–57.
142. Rousseau, OC 3:134–35/SD 134.
143. Aristotle, *Metaphysics*, A.1.980a22-28.
144. Aristotle, *Metaphysics*, A.1.980a28-981a2.
145. Aristotle, *Metaphysics*, A.1.981a1-b10.
146. Aristotle, *Metaphysics*, A.2.982b12-17. Cf. Plato, *Theaetetus*, 155c8-d8.
147. Aristotle, *Metaphysics*, A.2.982b24-26; 982b20-23.
148. Aristotle, *Metaphysics*, A.1.981b14-26.
149. Aristotle, *Metaphysics*, A.2.982b18-23.
150. Aristotle, *Metaphysics*, A.2.982b18-20.
151. Rousseau, OC 3:132/SD 131.
152. Rousseau, OC 3:131/SD 131.
153. Rousseau, OC 3:143–44/SD 142–43.
154. Rousseau, OC 3:141–42/SD 140–41.
155. Rousseau, OC 3:141–42/SD 140–41; OC 3:135/SD 135.
156. On Haeckel's law, see Laplanche, "The Unfinished Copernican Revolution," RCI xxxiii–xxxiv/EO 81–82.
157. Rousseau, OC 3:143–44/SD 142–43 (my emphasis).
158. Rousseau, OC 3:143/SD 142.
159. Rousseau, OC 3:162/SD 159.
160. Rousseau, OC 3:162/SD 159.
161. Rousseau, OC 3:142/SD 141.
162. Rousseau, OC 3:143/SD 142.
163. Rousseau, OC 3:162/SD 159.
164. Rousseau, OC 3:162/SD 159; OC 3:140/SD 139.
165. Rousseau, OC 3:219/SD 218.
166. Neuhouser (2008, 59–70) is a major proponent of this view, which draws on the influential scholarship of Dent (1988).
167. For a discussion of the seventeenth-century French interpretation of *amour-propre*, including brief comments on its relation to the Greek *philautia*, see Force (2003) and Fuchs (1977).

168. Aristotle, *Nicomachean Ethics*, 1166a33; 1168a28-1169b27.

169. For example, Brandwood (1976) does not record a single instance of *philautia* (self-love) or *philautos* (the self-lover) in Plato's entire lexicon.

170. Plato, *Symposium*, 208d6-211d3.

171. Pascal, *Pensées*, 978.

172. In the French literary tradition, this notion of *amour-propre* was further developed by François de la Rochefoucauld, *Maximes* (1665/78) and Pierre Nicole, *Essais de morale* (1671).

173. Rousseau, OC 4:536/E 244.

174. For example, Rousseau, OC 4:520/E 233: "So long as he loved nothing, he depended only on himself and his needs. As soon as he loves, he depends on his attachments. Thus are formed the first bonds linking him to his species."

175. As in the point, described in *Émile*, where *amour de soi* "turns into" *amour-propre*: "But to decide whether among these passions the dominant ones in his character will be humane and gentle or cruel and malignant, whether they will be passions of beneficence and commiseration or of envy and covetousness, we must know what position he will feel he has among men, and what kinds of obstacles he may believe he has to overcome to reach the position he wants to occupy" (OC 4:523–24/E 235).

176. Rousseau, OC 3:219/SD 218.

177. Rousseau, OC 3:219/SD 218.

178. Rousseau, OC 4:491/E 212–13. Cf. OC 4:322/E 92.

179. Rousseau, OC 3:167/SD 164. Cf. OC 5:395, 406/EOL 267, 277.

180. Rousseau, OC 3:164/SD 161.

181. Rousseau, OC 3:144/SD 143; 3:164/SD 161.

182. Rousseau, OC 3:165/SD 161.

183. Rousseau, OC 3:165/SD 162.

184. Cf. Hobbes's (EL II.10.8) similar list, which serves to demonstrate how disagreements about mere facts may serve as the ground of war. On Rousseau's reading, this characterization of the state of nature is evidence that Hobbes has not gone back far enough.

185. Rousseau, OC 3:155–56/SD 153: "Indeed commiseration will be all the more energetic in proportion as the Onlooking animal identifies more intimately with the suffering animal: Now this identification must, clearly, have been infinitely closer in the state of Nature than in the state of reasoning."

186. Rousseau, OC 3:166/SD 162 (my emphasis).

187. Cf. Rousseau's statement: "C'est la raison qui engendre l'amour propre, et c'est la réflexion qui le fortifie" (OC 3:156/SD 153). I interpret this to mean that reason "engenders" *amour-propre* by providing the foundation of calculative measure. But *amour-propre* does not emerge spontaneously and of its own accord from the calculative capacity of reason. In addition, a confluence of circumstances and alien causes are required to complete the derivation of *amour-propre* from *amour de soi*. Then, only after its emergence, may *réflexion* "reinforce" its effects.

188. This analogy between the human infant and the conjectural human of pure nature is put to greater use in *Émile* on the topic of infantile experience and the formation of ideas: "Let us suppose that a child had at his birth the stature and the strength

of a grown man, that he emerged, so to speak, fully armed from his mother's womb as did Pallas from the brain of Jupiter. This man-child would be a perfect imbecile, an automaton, an immobile and almost insensible statue." Rousseau concludes: "He would have only a single idea, that is, of the *I* to which he would relate all his sensations; and this idea or, rather, this sentiment would be the only thing that he would have beyond what an ordinary baby has" (OC 4:280/E 61). Nb. The reference to "an immobile and almost insensible statue" has its likely source in the hypothetical "homme statue" of Condillac's *Traité des sensations* (1754), where it was used to address the "Molyneux problem" of Locke's *Essay on Human Understanding* (1689).

189. Rousseau, OC 3:167/SD 164; OC 3:169/SD 166.
190. Rousseau, OC 3:171/SD 167.
191. Rousseau, OC 3:169/SD 166.
192. Rousseau, OC 3:132/SD 131.
193. It is possible to argue that, for Aristotle, because the beauty of the unmoved mover serves as the object-cause of desire and motion, it is accordingly the beauty of nature that inspires the natural desire to understand (*Metaphysics*, Λ.7, 1072a26-b2). The point of disagreement concerns precisely the implantation of some "foreign cause," which initiates the genesis of philosophic eros as a *rupture* within the order of nature.
194. Rousseau, OC 3:158/SD 155.
195. Rousseau, OC 3:158/SD 155.
196. Rousseau, OC 2:1273/DHV 315.
197. Rousseau, OC 2:969n./PN 101n.
198. Rousseau, OC 4:659/E 331.
199. Rousseau, OC 4:246/E 37, 38.
200. Cf. Rousseau, OC 2:962/PN 94; OC 4:326, 525, 535, 604, 658–59, 701, 731, 757/E 95, 236, 244, 293, 330–32, 363, 383, 401; OC 3:102/LNR 90; OC 1:357/C 299; OC 1:662, 693, 697, 704, 940/D 4, 27, 30, 35, 217; OC 5:42/LtdA 45.
201. Rousseau, OC 4:246/E 38; Epictetus, *The Encheiridion*, §5.
202. Rousseau, OC 2:1273/DHV 315; OC 3:113/SD 115.
203. Rousseau, OC 3:128/SD 129.
204. Rousseau, OC 3:123/SD 125.

Chapter 4

Primal Philosophy

I. GOING FARTHER

It is a guiding thesis of this book that Rousseau's critique of the tradition of first philosophy from Aristotle to Descartes has continuing relevance for contemporary concerns about the fate of philosophy after Heidegger. It is a corollary of this thesis that Rousseau perceived the need to rethink the foundations of philosophy, not for the sake of fashion or invention, but because the degeneration of philosophy under the aegis of Enlightenment required a return to the "origin" and "foundations" of philosophy itself. This motion of return applies in a double sense. It first concerns Rousseau's defense of Socrates against the usurpation of Socratic practice by the modern *esprit de système*. Second, because this motion involves a return to the idea of Socratic practice, it must presuppose the possibility of philosophy as a distinct form of human experience or endeavor—one rooted in the genesis of philosophic wonder. We consequently face the following situation. If the genesis of philosophic wonder takes root in a process of seduction, then we require a theory of seduction to account for the possibility of philosophy. Yet Rousseau does not provide a formal theory of seduction, in which case it is tempting to recall his reply in the "Preface of a Second Letter to Bordes" that "for want of perceiving the trunk" he showed "only the branches" and "that was enough for those capable of understanding."[1] If this response is sufficient, it is not satisfactory—especially if we want to grasp the unspoken root of Rousseau's legacy-as-task: the need to account for the possibility of philosophy and its significance for the discourse of first philosophy after Aristotle. In the spirit of "going farther along the same road," we now require an account of the process of seduction that explains not only the derivation of *amour-propre* from *amour de soi*, but also the genesis of philosophic wonder. To that end, I turn to the psychoanalytic theory of seduction first elaborated by Freud and more recently developed by the late Jean Laplanche (1924–2012).

It should be emphasized that this appeal to psychoanalytic insight comes as neither a decision for an arbitrary hermeneutic method, nor does it require us to refashion Rousseau's thought according to an external paradigm. It is rather my contention that Rousseau's mature thought contains within itself a nascent doctrine of seduction; and as a consequence, Rousseau's account of the genesis of philosophic wonder can be rendered visible, without distortion, by the deep compatibility it shares with the psychoanalytic doctrine. Broadly speaking, this compatibility consists in the emphasis we find on the desire of the other, understood as the source of enigmatic messages that possess the power of seduction for the same reason they escape translation. Precisely because these messages escape translation, they *demand* translation. As we have already seen, albeit in a preliminary way, this was the exact case in Rousseau's account of the *causes étrangeres*, the "foreign causes" that engender *amour-propre* by enlivening the force of public esteem—the exigent expression of the "moral aspect of love." I note that in speaking about "enigmatic messages" and a process of "translation," I am already using terms made available by Laplanche, for whom the revival of Freud's original seduction theory—first formulated in the 1895 *Project for a Scientific Psychology*—was the cornerstone of his important and still underappreciated effort to put psychoanalysis on "new foundations" through a strenuous and highly critical return to Freud.

Freud's original theory was intended to explain pathological phenomena, principally, the aetiology of hysteria and the unconscious formation of its symptoms, as in the exemplary case of Emma who displayed a phobia of entering into shops alone.[2] As Freud had surmised, the alterity of the transference in the analytic situation recapitulates an originary scene of seduction. It was therefore thought the treatment should consist in a hermeneutic "return to the origin," as relief should come from confronting the reality of an experience lost to repression—in the case of Emma, a forgotten scene of childhood sexual trauma. What Freud discovered, however, was not a linear account of traumatic cause-and-effect,[3] but rather a temporal model of psychic causality, which explained how the hysterical symptom could be linked to the forgotten trauma according to the two-stage logic of *Nachträglichkeit* (*après-coup*, deferred action). As Freud put the point: "A memory is repressed which has only become a trauma by deferred action."[4] There is thus a latency period after which a second scene retroactively evokes the initial trauma now manifest as a return of the repressed in the form of a symptom: a "mnemic symbol" of the original scene.[5] As Laplanche would later write: "*It always takes two traumas to make a trauma.*"[6]

Nevertheless, Freud renounced his "neurotica" in a famous letter to Wilhelm Fliess, dated September 21, 1897.[7] Of course, there were several reasons for this. The treatment outcomes were less than satisfactory. The high incidence of hysteria required an equally high rate of sexual abuse—and Freud thought "such a distribution of perversion against children is very unlikely." Yet, even more important, Freud had come to realize that the unconscious is not capable of reality testing. He notes: "There are no indications of reality in the unconscious, so that one cannot distinguish between truth and fiction that has been cathected with affect." It was therefore impossible to know if his patients were reporting actual events of sexual trauma or fantasies of seduction expressing Oedipal wishes. Given the poor outcomes of the treatment (interminable analyses, premature terminations), Freud also considered whether "in the deepest psychoses the unconscious memory does not force its way through." In such cases, "the unconscious never overcomes the resistance of the conscious," and the treatment is destined to fail.

It is worth stressing that by abandoning the seduction theory, Freud did not abandon the reality of childhood sexual trauma, but only the theoretical exigency of actual seduction, which he soon replaced with a theory of infantile sexuality and its endogenous development according to the universality of the Oedipus complex. Important for the present context, this shift had the consequence of marginalizing the primacy of the adult other in Freud's account of the psychosexual development of the human individual. As a result, it effectively repressed the function of *communication*, not only in the formation of pathological disorders, but also in the psychical development of the human being who is, from infancy, confronted with messages from the adult world—messages that demand translation in order to be mastered.

Now, it would be possible to make extensive comparisons between the use of subject-centered notions of the human being in Aristotle, Descartes, and Freud—in contrast with the radical decentering of human subjectivity found in Laplanche, Rousseau, and Plato. However, this claim and its extension to Plato will require elaboration. To project my argument forward, Plato will belong on the side of decentered subjectivity for the same reason Rousseau wished to be judged by the likes of Plato and Xenocrates. This argument rests ultimately on the rejection of Aristotle's account of the endogenous source of philosophic wonder, in conjunction with the further observation that an encounter with the question of happiness—hence, the transmission of an enigmatic idea of the good—is foundational for the possibility of philosophy itself.

For the moment, let us narrow the scope of comparison to Rousseau and Laplanche. It is imperative to see the structural similarities that permit the alignment of Rousseau's account of the genesis of *amour-propre* with Laplanche's return to the psychoanalytic theory of seduction. In this connection, there are three principal areas of comparison. The first pertains to the inexorable fact of seduction and its grounding in what Laplanche calls "a situation from which no human being is exempt: 'the fundamental anthropological situation,'" defined as "the adult-*infans* relation."[8] In *Life and Death in Psychoanalysis* (1970), Laplanche additionally notes: "it is only through abstraction that we can suppose the existence of a small human 'before' that seduction."[9] The phrase "that seduction" refers to the "implantation of adult sexuality in the child," which I shall address in a moment. The immediate point is to see how Laplanche's reference to a process of "abstraction" reflects the exact method of Rousseau's investigation in the *Second Discourse*, while the iconic moment in the genesis of *amour-propre*—the eruption of dance around a large tree—is the structural equivalent of the fundamental anthropological situation, also found in the mother-child relation in *Émile*. The second area of comparison then concerns the mechanism of seduction. Whereas Rousseau identifies the function of *causes étrangeres* in the genesis of *amour-propre*, Laplanche identifies the seductive power of enigmatic messages—transmitted by the *étrangèreté* ("foreign-ness," "alien-ness," "stranger-ness") of the adult other—in the constitution of unconscious processes including the sexual drive. Finally, the third area of comparison concerns Rousseau's account of the derivation of *amour-propre* from *amour de soi* in association with Laplanche's account of the process by which the sexual drive (*Trieb*) "leans on" the self-preservative function of instinct (*Instinkt*). When all of this is put together, we will be in a position to see how Laplanche's reformulation of Freud's original theory of seduction can help us to understand the conditions that engender the possibility of philosophy itself: the genesis of philosophic wonder or the process by which a certain expression of the *drive* comes to take wisdom as its object.

II. ROUSSEAU WITH LAPLANCHE

a. The Fundamental Anthropological Situation, Primal Seduction

In the reading of *Émile*, we have already noted Jean-Jacques' advice to mothers: to "form an enclosure around your child's soul at an early date." As in the Glaucus allegory, Rousseau is here concerned with the risk at which the human soul is exposed to the influence of other people. Likewise, in Book I of *Émile* we read: "In the present state of things a man abandoned to himself in the midst of other men from birth would be the most disfigured of all. Prejudices, authority, necessity, example, all the social institutions in which we find ourselves submerged would stifle nature in him and put nothing in its place."¹⁰ The soul of "pure nature" is thus in danger of corruption by its inevitable exposure to the other.

It is, of course, a paradox of Rousseau's teaching that Émile's happiness depends upon his protection from the inevitability of seduction. However, Rousseau was under no illusions about the possibility of putting his advice into practice. In a footnote critical of his contemporaries, he addressed this very problem in connection to their philosophic teachings. "One no longer studies, one no longer observes, one dreams; and we are gravely presented with the dreams of some bad nights as philosophy. I will be told that I, too, dream. I agree; but I give my dreams as dreams, which others are not careful to do, leaving it to the reader to find out whether they contain something useful for people who are awake."¹¹

This message is consistent with Rousseau's intention in the *Second Discourse*. For the reader who is "awake," Rousseau pursues a conjectural method, which aims to formulate the most needful question "to accurately judge our present state." This is the question of human nature and the process of its corruption in the social state. As Rousseau put this point to a gentleman who claimed to raise his son according to principles discovered in *Émile:* "That's too bad, sir, too bad for you and your son. I did not intend to furnish a method; I wanted only to prevent the evils of education as it existed."¹² Rousseau therefore presents the encounter with the other—indeed, the encounter with the desire of the other—as a fundamental and permanent problem for both the individual and the species. The education presented in *Émile* is intended more to expose this problem as a problem; less to claim an operable solution.

For his part, Laplanche identifies *la situation anthropologique fondamentale*, "the fundamental anthropological situation," as the inexorable scene of "primal seduction." In a lecture from September 20, 2002, Laplanche explains: "The theory of seduction is not a metaphysical hypothesis. Throughout the length of its trajectory in Freud, it is supported by facts of observation."¹³ The fact of observation that cannot be dismissed is the asymmetrical structure of the adult-infant relation. In the earlier text of *New Foundations for Psychoanalysis* (1987), Laplanche called this "the primal situation" (*la situation originaire*). The "primal" is "neither an abstract category, a philosophical transcendental, nor a 'mythical' outside of time."¹⁴ Instead, the term is used to translate Freud's employment of the German prefix *ur-* and the adjective *ursprünglich*.¹⁵ Laplanche emphasizes: "We are dealing with real time," that is, *l'événementiel*, the time of an "event," which serves as "not only the background against which events stand out, but also that which allows an event to exist, that which gives it its psychoanalytic specificity."¹⁶ The "primal" is, accordingly, "that element in the initial situation which is *inevitable* (*inéluctable*), which is *beyond even the most general contingency*."¹⁷ To this we may add: the most general contingency is a matter of life and death, as the infant is defined by the condition Freud called *Hilflosigkeit*, "helplessness," the incapacity to provide for itself.[18]

In dealing with the *primal situation*, we are therefore dealing with the inevitable—necessarily *universal*—situation of every newborn child.[19] This is the situation in which the infant in the etymological sense of the word (from the Latin *infans*, meaning "speechless") is confronted with an adult world consisting of messages it cannot understand.[20] What results is then the action of *primal seduction*, which describes how the attentions of the adult are seductive precisely because they convey verbal, nonverbal, or behavioral messages that are enigmatic and loaded with unconscious residues obtained in part from the adult's own experience of nurture and development.[21] It is the infant's inevitable failure to translate these messages into something meaningful that invariably constitutes primal repression; the genesis of infantile sexuality; and the restless, "driven," domain of the unconscious.

b. Enigmatic Messages, Primal Repression, the Unconscious

It is important to recognize that the human being does not enter the world already in possession of an unconscious. What Freud called "infantile sexuality" is not present from birth, nor does the adult transmit unconscious processes in the same way liquid is poured from one vessel into another—to recall Socrates' old joke about the transfer of wisdom. Instead, the transmission of enigmatic messages from adult to infant explains the formation of the unconscious, the sexual drive, and the constitution of psychic topography itself. Whereas Freud's original seduction theory was meant to account for the pathogenic vicissitudes of psychical trauma, Laplanche's signature contribution consists in putting the temporal logic of seduction and its rootedness in the communication of the other at the foundation of an effort to explain both the objects of psychoanalytic treatment (dreams, fantasies, neuroses, psychoses, etc.) and the conditions of their possibility in the ordinary process of human psychogenesis. Thus, borrowing from Einstein's distinction between two theories of relativity, Laplanche distinguished Freud's *restricted or special theory of seduction*, which concerns only pathological phenomena, from his own *general theory of seduction*, which accounts for the formation of the psychosexual subject, "the structure of the psychic apparatus or the apparatus of the soul, in general," and its beginning in the primal situation.[22]

At this point, it is worth repeating Laplanche's emphasis with Freud that above all else psychoanalysis is a method, a practice of deconstruction, which is inseparable from observations obtained in the psychoanalytic situation between analyst and analysand. A generalization of the theory of seduction is therefore possible because the analytic situation "*repeats* the primal situation of the human being."[23] As Laplanche explains: "My project consists in bringing what is foundational in the *practice* of psychoanalysis into relation with the foundational process of the human being, insofar as this is characterized by the creation of an unconscious."[24]

The key to theorizing the unconscious is, accordingly, the process of repression resulting from the transmission of enigmatic messages in the primal situation. This is what Freud called *primal repression (Urverdrängung)*—the process Laplanche understands as the partial but necessary failure of translation that accounts for the creation of the unconscious "as a place."[25] In Freud's words: "*the essence of repression lies simply in turning something away, and keeping it at a distance, from the conscious.*"[26] This defensive capacity is not present from the beginning; rather, it presupposes a "sharp cleavage" between "conscious and unconscious mental activity."[27] Freud therefore recognized the need to account for "a first phase of repression, which consists in the psychical (ideational) representative of the drive *(Trieb)* being denied entrance into the conscious."[28] However, Freud's understanding of how this could happen was remarkably obscure. As Laplanche points out with Pontalis in their encyclopedic *Vocabulaire de la psychanalyse*, the closest Freud came to an explanation was "the assumption of an *anticathexis* [. . .] which represents the permanent expenditure of a primal repression, and which also guarantees the permanence of that repression" through the force of a "secondary repression," that is, "repression proper" as an "after-pressure" *(Nachdrängen).*[29] In order to explain the mystery of Freud's postulate concerning a necessary "anticathexis" at the deepest region of the unconscious, Laplanche therefore invokes a "translation" model of repression, which can be explained only on the basis of enigmatic messages transmitted through the process of primal seduction.

Concisely stated, messages transmitted from adult to *infans* are enigmatic for two principal reasons: (1) they are compromised by the adult's unconscious and (2) the infant lacks the capacity to fully understand them, however polysemous they may be. In a striking passage from Book I of *Émile*, Rousseau precisely captures what is at stake:

> A child cries at birth; the first part of his childhood is spent crying. At one time we bustle about, we caress him in order to pacify him; at another we threaten him, we strike him in order to make him keep quiet. Either we do what pleases him, or we extract from him what pleases us. Either we submit to his whims, or we submit him to ours. No middle ground; he must give orders or receive them. *Thus his first ideas are those of domination and servitude.* Before knowing how to speak, he commands; before being able to act, he obeys. *And sometimes he is chastised before he is able to know his offenses or, rather, to commit any. It is thus that we fill up his young heart at the outset with the passions which later we impute to nature* and that, after having taken efforts to make him wicked, we complain about finding him so.[30]

The crucial lines are in italics in order to highlight the stunning accuracy with which Rousseau describes the primal situation between infant and adult. Through efforts to pacify the crying child, his "first ideas" are formed, "those of domination and servitude." However, the infant is sometimes chastised "before he is able to know his offenses," and for this reason his "young heart" is filled up "with the passions which later we impute to nature." This confusion about passions later imputed to nature reflects a serious interpretive problem concerning the Freudian distinction between "instinct" and "drive." I will return to this point momentarily. But as we know, Rousseau addressed an analogous problem in the Glaucus allegory, which prepares the framework for understanding the derivation of *amour-propre* from *amour de soi*. In the present context, the psychoanalytic end of this comparison presupposes the account of primal repression, which explains the infant's fundamental failure to translate the stream of messages it receives from the parental other. Rousseau captures this exactly when he indicates how the infant "is chastised before he is able to know his offenses." Such chastising messages may be conveyed in any number of linguistic or nonlinguistic ways. But the messages are enigmatic, in this case, because the infant is without any normative notion of "offense" through which to decode the adult's intentions. The infant may, of course, learn the "first ideas" of "domination and servitude" through these interactions, but the point of emphasis for Laplanche concerns not the manifest content of the adult's intentions, but the way such intentions are themselves "*compromised by the unconscious* of the originator."[31] What may be lost in translation, for example, is the way that loving involves "chastisement" or discipline—and these complex interactions may be further compromised by unconscious fantasies rooted in the adult's own experience of nurture in childhood.

Laplanche's translational model of repression thus explains how the primal repressed consists in untranslated, unmetabolized, residues of messages emanating from the adult for whom these messages also bear enigmatic content. It follows that the unconscious must be understood "*not as a stored memory or representation, but as a sort of waste-product of certain processes of memorization.*"[32] In slightly different terms, primal repression is explained by the "implantation" of "designified-signifiers," which constitute the unconscious as a topographical element within the infant's developing psychical apparatus.[33] These untranslated residues then serve as the reservoir of source-objects for the sexual drive.

Before we enter that discussion, I want to make three further points. First, the little human is not simply a passive receptor. Although the *infans* is helpless to defend itself against the incursion of enigmatic messages from the adult world, these messages "ask the child questions it cannot yet understand but to which it must attribute meaning and give a response."[34] Second, it is worth noting that Laplanche recovers the translation model of repression—or at least its inspiration—directly from Freud. As Freud wrote to Fliess in the letter of December 6, 1896: "A failure of translation—this is what is clinically known as 'repression.'"[35] Freud did not elaborate on the notion of "translation" as a psychical process, but insofar as messages from the other retain their *étrangèreté*, they cannot be said to have determinate content. This leads to a third point. The notion that such messages could be "interpreted" in the hermeneutic sense aimed at uncovering a "true" or "original" meaning is inadequate to the task confronting the infant who can at best endeavor to "translate" the address coming from the other.

In the words of Laplanche, *translation* consists in "the child's first attempts to construct for itself an interhuman world."[36] Yet every attempt at translation is simultaneously a failure of translation. In fact, the very effort at translation is indicative of at least two indissociable phases of primal repression. First, the *passive phase* of implantation, which inscribes the enigmatic message upon the surface of the infant's undifferentiated psychical apparatus, the Freudian "body-ego," which demarcates the periphery of the whole individual. Second, the *active phase* concerning the endeavor to translate or "bind" the intruding enigma by the nascent "ego" as a psychical agency, topographically situated as a *part* of the psychical apparatus—namely, the part "made in the *image* of the whole."[37] The primal repressed is, accordingly, partitioned within the psyche as the "primordial unconscious which thereby *becomes* an id."[38] In all, this means there is no single scene of seduction; no singular event of primal repression. Instead, the formation of the primal repressed must be understood according to the temporal logic of *Nachträglichkeit*—the afterwardness of translation—in which successive scenes contribute to the formation of the primordial unconscious, itself constitutive of the first source-objects of the drive.

c. Drive and Instinct, *Amour-propre* and *Amour de soi*

In order to account for the constitution of the drive, it is necessary to examine the difference between *Trieb* and *Instinkt*, "drive" and "instinct," in the Freudian lexicon. A major component of Laplanche's endeavor to put psychoanalysis on "new foundations" has been the restoration of Freudian drive theory, in opposition to dominant trends toward desexualization in object relations theory (e.g., Klein and Winnicott), attachment theory (Bowlby), and Lacanian structuralist theory. Were we to examine what is really at issue in these movements for the psychoanalytic understanding of the human being, we would see, beginning with Laplanche's argument in *Life and Death*, that such theories express the vicissitudes of various conceptual tensions within Freud's technical vocabulary; most especially, the tension between sexuality and the vital order—to the point that the vital order continually threatens sexuality with repression.

This matter has been further complicated by the failure of Freud's French and English translators to distinguish the notions of *Trieb* and *Instinkt* by rendering both terms universally as *instinct*. On the contrary, the *Instinkt* of Latin origin indicates an innate biological tendency, whereas the *Trieb* of Germanic origin derives from the verb *treiben*, meaning "push," "impel," or "put into motion." Lacan evidently recognized Freud's distinction when he remarked in 1958: "what he calls *Trieb* [. . .] is altogether different from an instinct."[39] However, Lacan did not dwell on this observation; and up to that point, the Freudian "drive" was understood unanimously in biological terms. It is only with Laplanche's recovery of Freud's theory of "leaning-on" (*Anlehnung, étayage*), through his work with Pontalis on the *Vocabulaire* of 1967, that it became possible to fully see the explanatory exigency of the distinction between instinct and drive (*pulsion* in French). As I will explain, the exigency of this distinction consists not only in the difference between a hereditarily determined behavioral pattern and the sexual drive which expresses tremendous plasticity in its aims and objects, but also the manner in which the drive is derived from the instinct, not by some mysterious endogenous impulse, but as a consequence of nurturing activities that stimulate the infant's body and precipitate auto-erotic needs.

With this important distinction in mind, there are two facets of Laplanche's reconstruction that bear attention. The first concerns the process by which the sexual drive leans on and is derived from the instinctual functions of self-preservation; the second concerns the implantation of adult sexuality—the introduction into the child of an *internal foreign body*—by the process of primal seduction and repression which creates the libidinal source of the drive. For an explanation, I shall turn in the next section to the most paradigmatic of primal situations: the oral model of infantile sexuality consisting of the nursling infant and the breast.

It should be noted in advance that just as Rousseau attributes the splitting of *amour-propre* from *amour de soi* to the effect of "alien causes," Laplanche likewise argues that primal seduction "carries the truth of leaning-on," consisting in the implantation of enigmatic messages from the adult world.[40] Moreover, just as Rousseau separates *amour-propre* from *amour de soi* according to the cleavage of moral-political artifice from the domain of pure nature, Freud maintained a similar cleavage of drive from instinct according to the derivation of sexuality from the vital order of self-preservation.

In this connection, *amour-propre* may well be understood as either the conscious affect of the drive or a vicissitude of human sexuality on the order of the theory of narcissism. With respect to the latter, the ego—understood as an agency of the psychical apparatus—is constituted by a libidinal cathexis which defends against the internal excitation of enigmatic messages that have been implanted by the action of primal seduction. In the context of Rousseau, *amour-propre* would then correspond to the investment of narcissistic libido—the erotogenic form of self-love—which firms up the ego as a relatively stable psychical structure. From this point, it becomes possible to explain how *amour-propre*, as a vicissitude of the sexual drive, takes over the domain of *amour de soi*, much like sexuality, in all its plasticity, compensates for the deficiencies of human instinct to the point that sexuality may outstrip the aims of self-preservation—or take them up entirely as its own. (I am thinking, for example, of libidinal attachments to one's nation or religion; attachments that allow an individual to die in valor with the courage of conviction.) Nevertheless, this can be only a suggestion, since any effort to render *amour-propre* in psychoanalytic terms presupposes the process of seduction which derives infantile sexuality from the vital order of biological instincts. Within the scope of the present study, it is the inexorable fact of primal seduction and its role in the genesis of the drive that I propose as the basis for a psychoanalytic account of the possibility of philosophy consistent with Rousseau's principles.

III. GENESIS OF THE DRIVE

The most systematic presentation of Freud's first drive theory appears in the essay "Triebe und Triebschicksale" (1915), translated by James Strachey as "Instincts and their Vicissitudes." This title is more accurately rendered as "Drives and their Fates," which calls attention to the termination point of the drive in a way that Strachey's translation of *Schicksal* as "vicissitude" does not. Along these lines, Freud cites four basic fates of the drive: reversal into its opposite, turning round upon the self, repression, and sublimation.[41] Freud adds: "Bearing in mind that there are motive forces which counteract the direct continuation of a drive, we may also regard these fates as modes of *defense* against the drives."[42] Every fate is therefore a defense against the drive and its satisfaction.

The variability of fates is also symptomatic of the drive's plasticity in comparison to the fixed character of biological instincts, as in the infant's oral instinct to suck the breast. This led Freud to further analyze the drive into four component terms, each of which corresponds by analogy to the component of an instinct. These are "pressure" (*Drang*), "aim" (*Ziel*), "object" (*Objeckt*), and "source" (*Quelle*).[43] The *pressure* is the "motor factor" of the drive. In economic terms, it exerts a "demand for work." The *aim* consequently indicates the "act to which a drive is driven."[44] Whereas the aim is fixed in the case of an instinct, the aim of a drive is dialectically related to the infinite variability of its object and source. The *source* involves both a fantasy and a stimulus implanted upon the surface of the body by the adult. In the oral model, this includes fantasies about the breast, "good" or "bad," along with the satisfactions or refusals of sensual sucking. The *object* is finally whatever, by its attainment, procures satisfaction of the aim through the release of tension within the drive.

Now, to say with Laplanche that the truth of leaning-on is primal seduction is, thereby, to acknowledge a deficiency in Freud's initial drive theory—namely, Freud's failure to account for how the adult's nurturing activities bear sexual messages that are unconscious for the adult and unmasterable by the child. Without taking account of the category of the message and its transmission by the asymmetrical relation of primal seduction, one is left with the impression that sexuality emerges spontaneously, of its own accord, from the instinctual function—in some way analogous to the release of a genie by the rubbing of a magic lamp. Yet something very different is happening. The intrusion and subsequent repression of enigmatic messages sent from adult to infant stimulates, and brings into existence, a form of auto-erotic activity that "leans on" the self-preservative function of nursing at the breast.[45] On its own, the theory of leaning-on describes how sensual sucking emerges from the place of nourishment. The drive and instinct originate in relation to the same source, and "leaning-on" describes how the drive splits from the instinct when the aim and object begin to diverge. In the oral model, the stimulation of feeding leads to the auto-erotic activity of sensual sucking; and in correlation, the object diverges *metonymically* from milk to breast, while the aim diverges *metaphorically* from nourishment to alternate ends modeled on the activity of incorporation.[46] What is missing, however, is the function of primal seduction and repression in the process of derivation itself.

When messages suffused with unconscious meanings are transmitted from adult to infant, the result is primal repression: the formation of the infantile unconscious by the untranslated residues of enigmatic messages sent from the adult. These untranslated residues constitute what Laplanche calls the first "source-objects" of the drive.[47] The source of the drive is, accordingly, neither endogenous nor biological, but rather the "adult other" (*der Andere*) who transmits the "other thing" (*das Andere*) which forms an "internal foreign body" (*corps étranger interne*) according the temporal logic of *Nachträglichkeit* (*après-coup*, deferred action).[48]

On this model, there is first the passively received inscription of enigmatic signifiers upon the periphery of the ego, understood as an undifferentiated body-ego; followed by the active effort to bind, metabolize, or translate the unmasterable remainders of primal seduction. This *nachträglich* effort to master, retroactively, the internal attacks of the repressed other initiates the process of topographical structuring between the unconscious and the preconscious-conscious domains of the infantile psyche. Partial translations are split-off into preconscious-conscious memories, while the untranslated remainders constitute both the source of the drive and its object. The drive therefore aims at the mastery of an object that is also, retrospectively, the implanted source of the drive itself.

In this way, the primacy of the other explains why, at the fundamental level of human psychogenesis, the drive does not have its source in something innate or endogenous to the body. Because the erogenous zones of the body constitute the privileged zones of exchange between infant and adult, there is rather a convergence of enigmatic messages and the bodily zones that precipitate the primal fantasies around which the sexual drive is organized. As a result, the object of the drive is neither (in the present case) the vital object of milk nor the sexual object of the breast, but a fantasmatic object which may be subject to transformation by the primary process activities of condensation and displacement. This also means that the fantasmatic object displaces, and covers over, the originary source-objects of the drive: the always already compromised messages of the adult other that comprise a void in signification. The drive is consequently a drive to translate the untranslated, and untranslatable, residues of enigmatic messages that demand to be mastered for the very reason they escape translation.

This account is consistent with Freud's original insight in *Beyond the Pleasure Principle* (1920) that dreams associated with traumatic neuroses are themselves expressions of the mind's effort to master trauma retrospectively.[49] In such cases, the trauma consists in a failure of mastery—and every reminiscence of the trauma is in effect a compulsion to repeat the failure of translation.[50] Laplanche likewise argues that at the level of ordinary psychogenesis the pressure of the drive does not arise from some biological or endogenous "demand for work," but rather from "the measure of the difference or disequilibrium between what is symbolizable and what is not in the enigmatic messages supplied to the child." The constancy of pressure exerted by the drive is, accordingly, "the measure of the quantity of trauma" that requires to be mastered by translation.[51] In short, the drive is essentially a drive for meaning. It expresses the *après-coup* of a compulsion to assign significance to the enigma of a message—a message that becomes (or can become) traumatic precisely because it fails to be mastered by translation.

If we now look back to the account of *amour-propre* described by Rousseau, it is possible to draw some important parallels. Foremost, it is evident that for both Rousseau and Laplanche there is a process of psychogenesis that originates from the desire of the other. For this and associated reasons, Rousseau's account of the genesis of *amour-propre* deeply anticipates the general theory of seduction that explains, in Laplanche's terms, the derivation of the human sexual drive in relation to the instinctual functions of self-preservation. For both Rousseau and Laplanche, the derivation of psychical entities is initiated, not as a result of some endogenous biological spontaneity, but as a consequence of the *étrangèreté* of the other who transmits *causes étrangeres* (Rousseau) or *messages énigmatiques* (Laplanche), which spur the genesis of the drive and, in Rousseau, its manifestation as *amour-propre*.

In addition, we find that both Rousseau and Laplanche identify a chiasmus in the question concerning the real starting point for an investigation into the constitution of the human being. In Rousseau, this structure of inversion was expressed by the doctrine of plural foundations, which may be understood as the difference between two senses of the ordinary: *the ordinary course of life* belonging to the pure state of nature and *the ordinary course of things* belonging to the domain of ordinary experience in the social state. It is, of course, only through a process of abstraction that it becomes possible to suppose a condition of experience *before* "the ordinary course of things," meaning that the first foundation of ordinary experience is, retrospectively, *second* in relation to "the ordinary course of life" (pure nature unadulterated by social artifice).

By comparison, Laplanche similarly distinguishes the *ratio cognoscendi* of the analytic situation, that is, the method of gaining knowledge through clinical experience, from the *ratio essendi* of the fundamental anthropological situation, itself the "real point of departure" for the psychoanalytic investigation of the human subject.[52] Moreover, in phrasing that remarkably resembles that of Rousseau, Laplanche calls this real starting point "a conjecture to be confirmed, and possibly falsified," as well as "a historical conjecture, to be situated within the history of the individual, of any individual we call 'human.'"[53] We are thus correct to be reminded of Rousseau's conjectural strategy in the *Second Discourse*, together with his claim that "conjectures become reasons when they are the most probable that can be derived from the nature of things."[54] For his part, Laplanche is even more emphatic: the theory of seduction is not a "metaphysical hypothesis," but is rather "supported by facts of observation," namely, the observation that the analytic situation occasions the provocation of the transference, hence, the reactivation of the primal, insofar as the analyst maintains the alterity of the other through the offer of analysis.[55]

IV. THE POSSIBILITY OF PHILOSOPHY

a. The Double Movement of *Après-Coup*

It is the argument of this book that Laplanche's work on the psychoanalytic theory of seduction can help us to complete Rousseau's account of the possibility of philosophy—that is, Rousseau's legacy-as-task. It is a corollary of this thesis that the possibility of philosophy itself is rooted in a reactivation of the primal. To that end, the general theory of seduction explains how the *causes étrangeres* cited by Rousseau—specifically, those enigmatic messages that bear on questions of happiness and ideations of the good—serve as source-objects for the drive that takes (or fails to take) wisdom as its object. This claim will automatically raise a further question about why philosophy should have its source in enigmatic messages concerning happiness and the good. The answer, we shall see, is rooted in what Rousseau called "the moral aspect of love," which finds its psychoanalytic analog in the eruption of sexuality into the asexual natality of the *infans*.

It should be stressed that this relation between the moral and the sexual exceeds mere analogy. Let us say that psychoanalysis speaks about sexuality in the extended sense belonging to the drive, understood as a drive for meaning. In Rousseau, the moral aspect of love is extended in a similar way. This is because the moral aspect of love originates in messages received passively from the other; and these messages invoke a demand for translation, specifically, with respect to the desire of the other—the spur of *amour-propre*. To state the point with maximum concision: *morality originates in sexuality*. Insofar as morality has its origin in the structure of a demand, it is a demand that comes from the other in excess of mere self-preservation. In fact, this demand is twofold according to the temporal action of seduction. There is first the enigma of the desire of the other, which may be formulated by the question: "What does it want from me?" Then there is the implantation of this enigma as an internal foreign body, which yields the corresponding question: "What does it want from me, this other within me?" To say that morality originates in sexuality is therefore to indicate how the drive expresses the twofold structure of a demand that receives its exigency in relation to the *étrangereté* of the other. Succinctly, the drive is constituted by an external demand imposed by the other; but through the process of implantation and primal repression, it also exerts a pressure from within.

In making this point, my present aim is not to propose a comprehensive doctrine of morality within the framework of the general theory of seduction. This endeavor would lead us too far astray from our immediate concern with the primal source of philosophy. Insofar as it can be said that morality originates in sexuality, I wish only to consider this within the parameters of Rousseau's legacy-as-task to rethink the meaning of a genuine first philosophy beginning from the foundational question of human happiness and its rootedness in the enigma of the good. For this purpose, it is sufficient that the action of seduction imposes the pressure of a twofold demand, at once from the external other and from the other within. The key is to recognize the sense in which the twofold demand of the drive is constituted by the *après-coup* of seduction, understood as a trauma that requires at least two separate moments in time.

I refer again to the case of Emma from the *Project* of 1895. In Freud's effort to explain how repression works as a pathogenic defense, he states: "A memory only becomes a trauma *nachträglich (après-coup)*."[56] There is consequently a relationship between two scenes separated by time but linked by association; in the present case, both scenes take place in a retail shop. Freud labels these scenes in the chronological order of their discovery. Scene I describes the evental *coup* ("hit" or "blow") in which Emma, near puberty at the age of twelve, perceived that she was being teased about her clothes by two shop-assistants who were laughing at her. One attracted her sexually and she ran away in fright. Scene II is then discovered *après-coup* as the memory of a childhood scene of sexual assault, provoked retrospectively by the laughter of the two shop-assistants in Scene I. According to the temporal scheme that is by now familiar, Scene II is chronologically *first* in relation to Scene I.[57] Freud was, of course, looking for the scene of an actual assault in order to explain Emma's fear of entering shops alone. But he was led to abandon this theory after coming to realize that some of his patients were reporting fantasies of seduction with equally powerful traumatic effects.

I recall this example in order to underline the traumatic effect of fantasies that stem from the memory of events which are understood *après-coup*. In the case of Emma, regardless of whether the memory of Scene II points to a real or imagined event, her phobia was organized retroactively around repressed fantasies of sexual gratification in association with a forbidden wish to provoke her own molestation. Laplanche observes, on a related point, that in Freud's correspondence with Fliess this model of repression extends to both neurotic and non-neurotic (or quasi-neurotic) forms of *après-coup*. Laplanche first refers to the letter of April 6, 1897 where Freud writes: "What I have in mind are hysterical fantasies, which regularly [. . .] go back to things that children overhear at an early age and understand only *après-coup*."[58] Freud's concern is with hysterical neuroses, but what interests Laplanche is the phenomenon that has its origin in the *après-coup* between "hearing" and "understanding." He then notes the sentence immediately following in Freud's letter: "The age at which they take in information of this kind is, strangely enough, from six to seven months on!" Laplanche records this and three similar instances in Freud's correspondence as "a major indication of the first, the original 'to-be-translated.'"[59] In other words, between "hearing" and "understanding" one finds the realism of the enigmatic message as well as Freud's implicit recognition that the translational model of repression explains a normal and universal aspect of human mental functioning.

In a subsequent but related comment, Laplanche adds that meaning produced *après-coup* "is not purely retroactive: it is a response to a prior, latent attempt at communication."[60] Meaning produced *après-coup* is therefore not arrived at in a single backwards stroke, as in the model of Jungian *Zurückphantasieren* (the retrospective transfer of adult fantasies onto childhood).[61] It is rather constituted by an initial failure of translation in conjunction with a second, retroactive, attempt. This means, for Laplanche, that the signature of *après-coup* is its twofold temporal structure—the same structure that forms the twofold demand of the drive.

On the model of *après-coup*, the drive is essentially a compulsion toward translation. Its object is precisely its source—and the reversibility of source and object expresses the temporal structure of the drive, "the indivisible double movement of 'being carried forward' and 'referring back.'" Whereas "being carried forward" consists in the "demand to translate the message of the other," "referring back" indicates "the whole *retroactive* movement of translation: a search for the secret of the enigmatic message, which must always more or less escape comprehension."[62] It is, accordingly, the interpersonal phenomenon of *après-coup* (its foundation in the primal situation) that explains its ability to reverse the proverbial "arrow of time," at once moving forward toward the message of the other, and backward toward the implanted otherness within.

b. The Timeless and the Good

I will soon explain how the temporality of *après-coup* applies to the genesis of philosophic wonder through the split between the two foundations of the ordinary: *the ordinary course of things* belonging to quotidian experience in the social state and *the ordinary course of life* belonging to the pure state of nature. But first, let us note how the bidirectional movement of the drive is organized around the timeless character of the unconscious or what Freud called, in *New Introductory Lectures on Psychoanalysis* (1932), "the unalterability by time of the repressed."[63] We are now in a position to see how the untranslatable remainder of messages from the other constitutes the timeless core of the unconscious. As I will try to show, the timelessness of the primal repressed accounts for both the transhistorical character of philosophy and its permanence as a universal human possibility.

For context, let us note that over the course of his career Freud identified four fundamental senses of the timelessness of the unconscious. Three of these are contained in a single passage from the 1915 paper "The Unconscious," where Freud remarks: "The processes of the system *Ucs.* are *timeless*; i.e., they are not ordered temporally, are not altered by the passage of time; they have no reference to time at all. Reference to time is bound up, once again, with the work of the system *Cs.*"[64] Five years later in *Beyond the Pleasure Principle*, Freud made the same observation: "We have learnt that unconscious mental processes are in themselves 'timeless.' This means in the first place that they are not ordered temporally, that time does not change them in any way and that the idea of time cannot be applied to them."[65] Another twelve years later, in the text of *New Introductory Lectures*, Freud adds: "There is nothing in the id that corresponds to the idea of time; there is no recognition of the passage of time."[66]

Distilled into four discrete aspects, the timeless character of the unconscious consists in: (1) the absence of temporal order, (2) indifference to the passage of time, (3) unalterability by time, and (4) independence from the idea of time. Each sense of the timeless operates as a bar against the translation of the unconscious into the temporal order of conscious thought. Understood within the general theory of seduction, this immunity of the unconscious to the arrow of time is explained by the translational model of repression and the enigmatic character of messages implanted by the other. Specifically, the imperviousness of enigmatic messages to translation explains their unalterability by time, hence, their persistence through time. The immutability of the enigma thus serves as the source of a drive to translate, which makes the timelessness of the unconscious in effect the *unmoved mover* of the human subject as a self-translating, self-theorizing being.[67]

This same dynamic also applies to the foundational question of philosophy and its rootedness in the enigma of the good. First, let us note Freud's own comments on the primal introduction of the good through the genesis of oral sexuality. The relevant comments appear in a passage from the 1925 paper "Negation" (*Die Verneinung*), directly within the context of a discussion concerning the function of judgment, which Freud splits into judgments of attribution and judgments of existence. The former "affirms or disaffirms the possession of a thing by a particular attribute," whereas the latter decides if "a presentation has an existence in reality."[68] Freud then defines "negative judgment" (*Verurteilung*) as the "intellectual substitute of repression." It expresses the notion: "This is something which I should prefer to repress"; as in the statement: "Now you'll think I mean to say something insulting, but really I have no such intention."[69] In this instance, the negative judgment is supposed to point the way to the repressed. Freud further states with respect to judgments of attribution: "The attribute to be decided may originally have been good or bad, useful or harmful. Expressed in the language of the oldest drive, the oral drives, it would be translated as: 'I should like to eat this,' or 'I should like to spit it out'; and, pushing the translation further: 'I want this inside me and that outside.'"[70]

In commenting on these passages, Laplanche notes that Freud places judgments of attribution *before* judgments of existence;[71] an observation confirmed by Freud, who writes: "Experience has shown the subject that it is not only important whether a thing (an object of satisfaction) possesses the 'good' attribute and so deserves to be taken into the ego, but also whether it is there in the external world, so that it can be gotten ahold of whenever it is needed."[72] In other words, knowledge of the external world is a product of experience; thus, starting from the primacy of the other and its message, the question of external reality presupposes the object-source of the drive. The judgment of existence is consequently *second* in relation to the judgment of attribution. The libidinal attribution "good" or "bad" is *anterior* to deciding whether the thing can be "gotten ahold of" as an object existing in reality.

Laplanche does not elaborate further on this observation, except to stress that in Freud's example "there is something to be translated, a primal to-be-translated, originally the 'good or bad,' which is then translated into a language" (i.e., "the language of the oldest drive, the oral drives").[73] For the purpose of understanding the possibility of philosophy, these primal ideations of "good" and "bad" are essential to the genesis of philosophic wonder.

To make this connection, let us reflect on the scene of primal seduction in *Émile*. There we saw how "domination and servitude" constitute the infant's "first ideas." Rousseau adds that the infant is sometimes "chastised before he is able to know his offenses or, rather, to commit any. It is thus that we fill up his young heart at the outset with the passions which later we impute to nature."[74] The passions "which later we impute to nature" are those that emerge with *amour-propre* or the moral aspect of love. They have their source in actions attributed to the adult, before they can be comprehended by the infant. The sources of moral normativity are therefore enigmatic from the start.

In the analogous scene of the *Second Discourse*, the iconic dance around a large tree, the first ideas of merit and beauty are likewise transmitted as *causes étrangeres* by the desire of the other. Through this process of transmission, the idea of the good enters into human life as a timeless question concerning the desire of the other, the one desiring of merit or beauty; and as a consequence, the human being is seduced into moral ways of loving. What bears emphasis in these examples is not only the enigmatic character of the good, but its function as a source of rupture within the premoral-presexual natality of the infant and its analog in the pure state of nature. That the infant is "chastised before he is able to know his offenses" indicates precisely the condition in anticipation of the *après-coup* of the good. It is not the initial event that is traumatizing, but the way it reverberates from the past to find its echo in the future.

c. Enigma of the Good

Shifting now to the possibility of philosophy, let us look again at Part One of the *Second Discourse*. There we find the image of the human being abstracted entirely from the social state. In the crucial lines, Rousseau writes: "I shall assume him always conformed as I see him today, walking on two feet, using his hands as we do ours, directing his gaze over the whole of Nature, and with his eyes surveying the vast expanse of Heaven."[75] Insofar as philosophy is traditionally conceived as mediation between the human and the divine, Rousseau indicates a natural capacity for philosophy in the human gaze that extends from "the whole of Nature" to "the vast expanse of Heaven." However, we have seen that simply looking at the whole of nature and heaven is insufficient to spur the genesis of wonder. The possibility of philosophy rests, instead, on the seductive power of *causes étrangeres*, which form the source-objects of the sexual drive and its manifestation, in Rousseau's language, as *amour-propre*. Thus, on the surface, the *Second Discourse* accounts for the emergence of the human being from the pure state of nature through the derivation of *amour-propre* from *amour de soi*. But since Rousseau showed only the branches, merely named the trunk, and kept silent about the roots, it becomes the responsibility of philosophic readers to investigate the origin and foundations of philosophy—and the *doctrine intérieur* that explains Rousseau's silence on this topic.

Regarding the latter, if ideations of the good enter human life as enigmatic messages or questions, then the good itself becomes enigmatic or questionable. It is easy to see how Rousseau would have perceived this insight as dangerous within the context of his critique of Enlightenment modernity and the way it sacrifices virtue in the name of scientific mastery. It follows that treatment of the good as a fundamental question risks questioning the value of the good as an object of knowledge or desire. Rousseau's principled love of the public good would have made it impossible for him to expose this teaching to those same unphilosophic readers who—after the publication of *Émile* and the *Social Contract*—would set his books aflame in Geneva, Paris, and the Hague. For that matter, the scales had already fallen from his eyes when he prefaced the *First Discourse* with the prophetic line from Ovid: "Here I am the barbarian because they do not understand me" (*Tristia*, V.x.37).[76]

As for the origin and foundations of philosophy, the enigma of the good—the origin or "source-object" of *amour-propre*—is split *après-coup* between the two foundations of the ordinary: *the ordinary course of things* in the social state and *the ordinary course of life* in the pure state of nature. To press on the etymological significance of "the ordinary," from the Latin *ordo* meaning "row," "line," "series," "rank," and "order," the division between the two foundations of the ordinary signifies the difference between two orders of experience divided by the enigma of a message, which invariably escapes translation. Between these two foundations, the translational model of *après-coup* captures the double movement of "being carried forward" and "referring back," that is, the libidinal economy of the drive.

In "being carried forward," there is the initial demand to translate the message from the other, which has ruptured the order of pure nature by the implantation of its enigma. In "referring back," a subsequent event within the order of the social state recapitulates the primal rupture within the order of pure nature. This reactivates the enigma of the message, which retroactively compels the drive to translate, despite the inevitability of its failure.

Rousseau captures something of this fate when he calls the pure state of nature "a state which no longer exists, which perhaps never did exist, which probably never will exist, and about which it is nevertheless necessary to have exact Notions in order to accurately judge our present state."[77] This line communicates both the inevitable failure of any "return to origin," as well as the attendant need to fill the void by the construction of a primal scene. What activates this need is the event within the order of the social state that *reactivates* the enigma of the primal: the other thing within us that leads to the other person who is its origin. For Rousseau, this primal enigma is precisely the enigma of the good, *the question of rank*, which precipitates the moral aspect of love from its basis in the purely vital order of self-preservation. The event within the order of the social state that reactivates the enigma of the good is, accordingly, *the question of happiness, the highest human good*—the question which only becomes a question when, upon the exit from pure nature, "an idea of repose" is purchased at "the price of real felicity."[78]

In sum: philosophy has its origin and foundations—which is to say, its possibility—in the universal scene of primal seduction. The possibility of philosophy is subsequently actualized when the drive takes wisdom as its object. This brings us to the genesis of wonder, which both Plato and Aristotle identify as the beginning of philosophy.

Earlier, I suggested that Rousseau aligns with Plato against Aristotle because he rejects the thesis that philosophic wonder emerges from an endogenous source within the human being. Instead, Rousseau outlines the conditions of pure nature that provide the ground out of which the possibility of philosophy may emerge. These conditions include the natural capacities of freedom, perfectibility, and calculative rationality, along with the sentiments of pity and self-preservation. Recall, in particular, that freedom designates metaphysical freedom from the determinate order of nature, whereas moral experience is engendered only with the genesis of *amour-propre*—that is, with the contingent aid of *causes étrangeres*, effectively, other people. It is only after the rupture within the order of pure nature that the whole of nature and heaven can become an object of philosophic wonder—and this is possible only through the "chain of wonders" that disclose the question of happiness as a fundamental human problem.

In the *Second Discourse*, this problem is made visible through Rousseau's response to the Dijon Academy's 1753 essay competition on the origin of human inequality and whether it is authorized by natural law. To cite one example from the text, Rousseau writes in the first paragraph of the Dedicatory Letter to Geneva that he could not have meditated on "the equality nature established among men and the inequality they have instituted without thinking about the profound wisdom with which both, happily combined in this State, contribute [. . .] to the preservation of public order and to the happiness of individuals."[79] It is, accordingly, the question of human inequality and the way it bears on human happiness that points to further questions about the right order of society.

Ultimately, these are questions that cannot be asked without presupposing access to a more primordial notion of the good. What now requires to be addressed is how the question of human happiness engenders philosophic wonder, that is, the process by which the drive (the moral aspect of love) takes wisdom as its object. To that end, let us first examine how the genesis of philosophic wonder is rooted *après-coup* in the enigma of the good. We will then be in a position to judge Rousseau as he wished according to the likes of Plato and Xenocrates.

V. REACTIVATION OF THE PRIMAL

a. Starting Again

Taking my bearings from Rousseau's legacy-as-task to end where Descartes began, I have followed his critique of Cartesian science down to the root of first philosophy. Fundamentally at issue for Rousseau is Descartes' decision to found philosophy on the model of the mathematical and the experimental sciences; and hence, the consequence of this decision, which severs not only the human relation to the good from the foundations of philosophy, but the ability of philosophy to account reflexively for the goodness of its own foundations. Rousseau responds by pointing, however indirectly, to the opposite thesis that the source of moral questioning—the enigma of the good—is inseparable from the possibility of philosophy itself. To end where Descartes began, it is therefore necessary to rethink the meaning of first philosophy. I have argued that for Rousseau a genuine first philosophy can be neither the study of being qua being nor the study of the relation between being and thinking. Foremost, this is because questioning into the meaning of being presupposes wonder about being. The genesis of philosophic wonder is therefore anterior to the question of being. In short, the foundational question of philosophy concerns the possibility of philosophic questioning. It follows, for Rousseau, that a genuine first philosophy must concern itself with the possibility of philosophy. This is what I call—under the aegis of Rousseau and with inspiration from Laplanche—*primal philosophy: the study of the genesis of philosophy itself.*

I designate *primal philosophy* in reference to the sense given by Laplanche to the scene of *primal seduction*. This is to indicate that philosophy begins in a process of seduction—and this process of seduction points back to the fundamental anthropological situation between infant and adult. Since primal philosophy concerns both the meaning of a genuine first philosophy and the possibility of philosophy itself, it must also concern the beginning of philosophic questioning and its rootedness in the process of primal seduction to which it owes its name.

Now, according to the traditions of Plato and Aristotle, philosophy begins in wonder. The word in Greek is *thaumazein*, as in the expression *huperphuōs hōs thaumazō*, "hypernatural wonder," which Theaetetus invokes with Socrates in order to describe the feeling of an upward journey beyond nature, toward the heavens; the kind which makes his head spin (*huper* = above + *phuōs* = natural).[80] This expression of Theaetetus is also reminiscent of the myth of the soul as a winged charioteer who, in the *Phaedrus*, makes the rough ascent to the rotating roof of the cosmos in order to glimpse the hyperuranian beings—namely, the Ideas, which exist above the cosmos and thus beyond time. For his part, Socrates responds to Theaetetus by saying: "this feeling of wonder shows that you are a philosopher, since wonder is the only beginning of philosophy."[81]

For Plato's Socrates, as for Aristotle, wonder has its source in *aporia*—a word meaning difficulty or impossibility of passage. In the *Theaetetus*, this is evident when Socrates compares himself to a midwife who, through the use of dialogue, brings his associates into *aporiai* analogous to the pangs of labor.[82] One could say, on this account, that philosophy begins in wonder at the arrival of an impasse; but the feeling, however painful, is one of elevation rather than despair. Evidently, wonder is produced by the traumatic force of *aporiai*, which inspire perplexity at a rupture within the order of the ordinary—a rupture that points to something extraordinary, which transcends the time and place of rupture.

In Aristotle, by comparison, the capacity to wonder stems from the natural desire to know; hence, the capacity to feel awe or puzzlement in the *aporia* of understanding.[83] Whereas Socrates provokes wonder in his interlocutors with speeches, for Aristotle the simple act of looking is sufficient to induce the feeling of wonder. This difference is significant, as it supports two different conceptions of the possibility of philosophy. Either philosophy requires what Laplanche would call the human transmission of a "to-be-translated," or its possibility lies in an endogenous capacity to experience wonder at the productions of the senses.

From the standpoint of primal philosophy, however, Aristotle scotomizes the primacy of the other in the genesis of wonder; and in doing so, he implicitly rejects Socrates' "second sailing," that is, Socrates' proposal to "take refuge in *logoi*" so as not to suffer blindness by viewing the beings directly in the eclipsed light of the good.[84] By contrast, Aristotle looks to the objects of the senses, and consequently blinds himself to the primacy of the other in the formation of desire. Stated somewhat differently, Aristotle accounts for only the manifest activities of the individual, without considering how these activities are themselves secondary in relation to an originary process—namely, that of seduction. This is evident in the way Aristotle presupposes a natural desire to know, without inquiring into the source of this desire or the circumstances of its activation. In fact, for Aristotle, the desire to know is not initiated by the confrontation with *aporiai*. Rather, this desire is posited as a natural human power, which discovers *aporiai* through the revelation of ignorance.[85] From the natural desire to know, philosophy is then supposed to spring as the spontaneous unfolding of an endogenous human capacity.

It is often said that Aristotle replaces Platonic madness with a more sober doctrine. This could not be more true of Aristotle's account of the nonerotic genesis of philosophy. In Plato, *erōs* comes from above and raises the potential philosopher into philosophy. It takes possession of the soul and compels ascent from the mortal domain of generation and decay to the domain of being that exists forever (*tiēs aei ousēs*).[86] This pursuit of eternal or immortal knowledge is what defines the philosopher as a lover (*erastēs*) of being and truth.[87] The philosophic nature desires (*epithumētēn*) all of wisdom; it reaches out (*oregei*) for the whole and all of what is human and divine.[88] Thus driven by *erōs*, this desire for the truth about being and the whole ascends to a vision of the transtemporal Ideas culminating in the Idea of the good, which is beyond being (*epekeina tēs ousias*), exceeding it in rank and power (*presbeia kai dunamei huperekhontos*).[89]

In Aristotle, to the contrary, there is no mention of *erōs* in his account of the beginning of philosophy. Rather, he alludes to it briefly in *Metaphysics* Λ, at the height of theoretical contemplation, where "the object of love" (*hōs erōmenon*)—the actual activity of thinking—evokes the affect of "the beautiful" (*to kalon*), the unmoved mover of cosmological attraction, the final cause of thought thinking itself.[90] Suffice it to say, Aristotelian sobriety purges *erōs* from the beginning of philosophy, and so induces the madness of circular reasoning.[91] By contrast, Platonic madness consists in the *erōs* for philosophy itself. As Diotima teaches Socrates in the *Symposium*, Eros is a daimon who mediates between gods and mortals; and in the *Phaedrus*, Socrates asserts: "the greatest of goods comes to us through madness when it is sent as a gift from the gods."[92]

b. Illumination as Platonism

In the context of Rousseau, there are at least two ways of approaching his understanding of the beginning of philosophy. The first is through his more or less explicit references to Plato and Socrates—largely in association with themes from the account of philosophical ascent in *Republic* VII. The second is through the autobiographical account of his illumination on the road to Vincennes. Whereas the first can be discerned within the published writings of Rousseau's system (1750–1762), the second extends outside the system to include the *Confessions* (1782–1789) and the January 12, 1762 Letter to Malesherbes—the latter of which offers the most detailed report of his illumination, though it exceeds twelve years after the event.[93] In the text of the *Confessions*, Rousseau recounts the moment on his walk to visit the imprisoned Diderot when he stopped to rest and found the Dijon Academy's prize essay question in the October 1749 *Mercure de France*. "At the moment of that reading," Rousseau writes, "I saw another universe and became another man."[94]

Up to this point in his life, Rousseau had been consumed with study dating back at least as far as the period he called "the short happiness of my life" with Madam de Warens at Les Charmettes—beginning most likely in 1736 at the age of twenty-four when she was thirty-eight.[95] During this time he read voraciously in philosophy, including works by Descartes, Locke, Leibniz, Malebranche, and the *Logic* of Port Royal.[96] In 1741 he produced his own system of musical notation, and in 1743 he published his *Dissertation on Modern Music*. By 1744 he claims in the *Confessions* to have formed the plan for his unpublished *Political Institutions* while working in Venice as secretary to the French Ambassador, M. de Montaigu; and by 1749 he was contributing articles on music to the *Encyclopédie*.[97] This is to say, the moment of his illumination bears the trace of *après-coup*, as his reaction to the Dijon Academy's essay question hit upon themes in Rousseau's studies that were already underway.

In the *Confessions*, the illumination serves as the symbol of a break which propelled Rousseau from his status as a middling author to a thinker of the first rank. However, in the Letter to Malesherbes, he describes the illumination as a kind of rupture—less a rupture with the past, than a rupture within the present; rendered in terms that specifically reflect the Platonic genesis of wonder. He writes: "If anything has ever resembled a sudden inspiration (*inspiration subite*), it is the motion that was caused in me by that reading; suddenly I felt my mind dazzled by a thousand lights; crowds of lively ideas presented themselves at the same time with a strength and a confusion that threw me into an inexpressible perturbation; I feel my head seized by a dizziness similar to drunkenness."[98] The references to confusion, perturbation, dizziness, and drunkenness—together with a sudden surge of interior motion—all allude to Platonic descriptions of the genesis of wonder or the *erōs* for philosophy driven to the point of Dionysian madness. As Rousseau describes it, the illumination intensified into a "violent palpitation," which caused him to collapse under a tree, sick to his stomach and unable to breathe, with such terrible agitation that when he finally stood up the whole front of his coat was soaked in tears without feeling he had shed them.[99]

It is evident from these details that if the general theory of seduction is to offer the basis for an explanation of Rousseau's illumination, it must begin from the observation of a trauma in association with moral questioning, viewed in light of the Dijon Academy's essay question. In making this suggestion, my purpose is not to approach Rousseau's writings through a psychoanalysis of his personality, as Jean Starobinski did in the seminal study of *Jean-Jacques Rousseau: Transparency and Obstruction* (1971).[100] If Rousseau's insight into the possibility of philosophy is a function of his personality, it is because his personality participates in philosophy itself. For present purposes, it is enough to note the specific exigency of moral questioning in the opening of Rousseau's illumination.

As a point of contrast, let us look at Rousseau's comparatively obscure account of the "first man who attempted to philosophize."[101] This discussion appears in an undated, posthumously published, and originally untitled work that today is called "Fiction, or Allegorical Fragment on Revelation." In my opinion, this text deals less with either the historical beginning of philosophy or the beginning of philosophy in a specific individual than it does with the impulse to form a religion on the basis of philosophical speculation. As such, this text presents the eventual opening of philosophy, followed by a critique of the tensions that ensue between the demands of reason and revelation.[102] I note that there is nothing in this text which pertains to the human emergence from the pure state of nature or the birth of *amour-propre* from *amour de soi*. If moral questioning plays a role in this account of the beginning of philosophy, it does so only indirectly in reference to the familiar themes of Plato concerning the order and intelligibility of the cosmos in light of the particular power of the sun, described at one point by Rousseau as "the mysterious star" (*l'étoile mystérieuse*) around which the cosmic revolutions seem to be made.[103] Insofar as the sun retains its Platonic association with the Idea of the good, it will suffice to note Rousseau's comment about its enigmatic status.[104]

For the purpose of comparison, let us recall that in the writing he produced in the immediate aftermath of the illumination, Rousseau makes conspicuous use of the image of the sun in association with what he calls "genuine philosophy" (*la véritable philosophie*). The salient passages appear in the first and final paragraphs of the *First Discourse* (excluding the Preface and Exordium). Starting with strong reference to the allegory of the cave in *Republic* VII (514aff):

> It is a grand and a fine spectacle to see man go forth as it were out of nothing by his own efforts; to dispel by the lights of his reason the darkness in which nature had enveloped him; to raise himself above himself; to soar by the mind

to the celestial realms; to traverse the vast expanse of the Universe with Giant strides, like to the Sun; and, what is grander and more difficult still, to return into himself (*rentrer en soi*), there to study man and to know his nature, his duties, and his end. All these wonders (*merveilles*) have occurred anew in the past few Generations.[105]

This passage is easily mined for comparisons to Plato's text. "To see man go forth as it were out of nothing by his own efforts" mirrors the prisoner who is released from his chains by the spontaneity of his nature. "To dispel by the lights of his reason the darkness in which nature had enveloped him" reflects both the darkness of the cave as the condition of human ignorance and the life of reason as the mode of escape. "To soar by the mind to the celestial realms; to traverse the vast expanse of the Universe with Giant strides, like to the Sun" indicates a clear reference to the hyperuranian realm and the Idea of the good. "To raise himself above himself" signifies the reflexive power of those who "raise themselves" in the ascent from ignorance to the love of wisdom. "And, what is grander and more difficult still, to return into himself, there to study man and to know his nature, his duties, and his end." This "difficult return into oneself" recalls both the return of the philosopher into the cave and the Socratic imperative *know thyself*, which orients the subsequent project of the *Second Discourse*. Altogether, these lines may be reformulated to say: the possibility of philosophy turns on a perception of the Idea of the good, which inspires a difficult return into oneself; hence, a reflective confrontation with ignorance, which leads from a study of the individual to the nature of the human being, "its duties" and "its end." Still, the knowledge we require remains unsettled. "All these wonders have occurred anew in the past few Generations." Hence, events within the modern epoch have renewed the exigency of our inquiry into the enduring questions of philosophy.

The last lines of the final paragraph then bookend the *First Discourse* with an important rhetorical flourish, which suggests an end that retraces its beginning. In fact, the structure is not unlike the twofold demand of the drive in relation to its source-object. In the present case, the pattern of return is communicated at the level of the text by repeating the connection between the "return into oneself" as "genuine philosophy." Again, I quote the passage and then offer comment.

> O virtue! Sublime science of simple souls, are so many efforts and so much equipment really required to know you? Are not your principles engraved in all hearts, and is it not enough in order to learn your Laws to return into oneself (*rentrer en soi-même*) and to listen to the voice of one's conscience in the silence of the passions? That is genuine Philosophy (*la véritable Philosophie*), let us know how to rest content with it; and without envying the glory of those

famous men who render themselves immortal in the Republic of Letters, let us try to place between them and ourselves the glorious distinction formerly seen between two great Peoples; that the one knew how to speak well, and the other, to act well.[106]

Between "ourselves" and the immortal men of the Republic of Letters, Rousseau elevates a vocation to philosophic practice over and against elegant speech. This is not the methodological *esprit de système* characteristic of Enlightenment, but a call to the "sublime science of simple souls," which takes virtue as its object. Its principles are "engraved in all hearts," and to learn its laws, one must "return into oneself" and "listen to the voice of one's conscience in the silence of the passions." The life of reason is thereby attuned to practical ends, which is why it must presuppose exposure to the Idea of the good. What reads in the first paragraph as a return into oneself from the hyperuranian height of the good is thus transformed in the final paragraph as a return into oneself, which locates the good in the voice of one's conscience. In stride with the Delphic imperative, yet deviating from the Platonic paradigm (because the retracement has the structure of a spiral, not a circle), Rousseau's continuation of the Socratic-Platonic legacy is also implicit in his notion of the genuine philosopher as a "friend of the truth."[107] As this designation indicates, the art of turning inward achieves the conversion of bodily *erōs* into Socratic *philia* "in the silence of the passions." In *Émile*, Rousseau would also call conscience "the most enlightened of philosophers."[108]

c. The Art of Turning Souls

In order to grasp the possibility of philosophy itself, we now require an account of how the *erōs* for philosophy is activated. For this purpose, let us focus on the relation between Rousseau's allusion to the Platonic Idea of the good and the motion of return, which appears as the signature of genuine philosophy. I refer again to *Republic* VII on the allegory of the cave and the need for a certain *technē* to inspire the "turning around" of the soul toward the Ideas.[109]

The theme of the cave allegory is the education of the philosopher. This education turns on the ascent to the Idea of the good. In the realm of the knowable this is the last thing to be seen, and only with considerable effort. But once seen, "it must be concluded that this is in fact the cause of all that is right and beautiful in everything. In the visible domain, it produces light and light's sovereign [its singular power of illumination]; in the intelligible domain, it is itself sovereign, and provides truth and intelligence—and anyone who is going to act prudently (*emphronōs*) in private or in public must see it."[110]

Socrates adds that the education in philosophy is not analogous to putting knowledge into the soul as if one were putting sight into blind eyes.[111] Stated in a different register, one cannot become a philosopher simply by hearing stories about philosophy. Instead, there is a power (*dunamis*) of the soul "in each of us," which must be "turned around," the whole soul together with the whole body, away from the world of becoming until it is able to endure looking at "what is" and the brightest part of "what is," namely, the good itself.[112] Socrates further states that this art of "turning around the entire soul" (*periagogē holēs tēs psychēs*) takes as given that sight is already there. The problem consists in correctly orienting the power of sight toward the domain of Ideas. For just as sight cannot be given as a gift to blind eyes, the possibility of philosophy depends on the action of seduction—the intervention of one who is proficient in the art of turning souls toward the Idea of the good.

Socrates leaves it rather ambiguous as to how the art of *periagogē tēs psychēs* raises the potential philosopher into philosophy. The dialogue describes how the education that begins in music and gymnastics leads to the increasingly abstract study of mathematics as the necessary preparation for dialectic, defined initially as the ability to give and receive *logos*.[113] But Socrates breaks off this discussion, as he tells Glaucon: "You will no longer be able to follow me, although there would be no lack of readiness on my part. For you would no longer see an image of the things we are discussing, but the truth itself, at least as it looks to me. Whether it is genuine or not, it is no longer worth insisting. But that there is something to see, one must insist on."[114]

I suggest that Socrates interrupts the discussion of dialectic for at least two reasons. It may be that Glaucon's youth, and perhaps his level of intelligence, allows him to follow Socrates only up to this point in conversation about the nature of philosophy. It may also be the case that Socrates is intensifying his seduction of the precocious Glaucon—and Socrates cannot simply put sight into blind eyes. As in Rousseau's formulation, the ascent to philosophy requires a return into oneself through which one raises oneself above oneself in light of the good.

In connection to this point, let us keep in mind that the *First Discourse* characterizes the philosopher as one who "raises himself above himself." This description anticipates the guiding distinction of Rousseau's rhetoric between those who raise themselves and those who require to be raised. Precisely at stake in this distinction are the conditions that engender the possibility of philosophy.

In the case of Glaucon, he has shown that he can be led up to the point of dialectic; but he alone must raise himself to the level of *philosophy*—if only he is able. Provided that the good itself is "beyond being," and therefore beyond *logos*, Socrates' preservation of the enigma of the good would serve in principle to intensify the process of seduction aimed at inspiring Glaucon's *erōs* for philosophy. On the Idea of the good, however, there is an important difference between Plato and Rousseau. Whereas Plato locates the good itself in the hyperuranian domain beyond being, Rousseau finds it in conscience—within the domain of the human soul.

When Rousseau writes of the "natural goodness of man," this goodness consists in the innocence of moral-juridical notions of good and bad, better and worse. By the same token, the prisoners in the allegory of the cave can be said to exist under a condition of nihilism, defined as the complete absence of knowledge of the good. For this reason, the prisoners cannot be relativists, since relativism is the inability to rank order goods, whereas nihilism indicates the void of the good itself. Stated in poetic terms, the prisoners know only shadows of *things*, but nothing of *values*. From the standpoint of the uninitiated, speech about the good attacks their ignorance as something alien and hostile; or in terms familiar to Laplanche, the message comes from the other and attacks from within. This is why the philosopher who returns into the cave must endure ridicule and even threats of violence as he attempts to relate what is outside to the prisoners still enchained.[115] Because the Idea of the good enters into human life as a traumatizing message, it demands to be mastered by translation or a mechanism of defense.

It is likewise a feature of Rousseau's Socratism that the possibility of philosophy turns on the introduction of the good into human life—and this occurs ineluctably by a process of seduction. By founding the possibility of philosophy in the genesis of *amour-propre*, Rousseau makes it possible to identify the interpersonal source of wonder in the scene of primal seduction, insofar as it consists in the transmission of messages or *causes étrangeres* that bear the enigma of the good. As the enigma is unaltered by the passage of time, it holds as the enduring source-object of philosophic wonder. Indeed, its persistence is explained by the process of implantation and primal repression, which does not leave behind a meaning to be deciphered, but rather the residues of untranslated messages that are themselves excluded from the order of representation. For related reasons, I suspect this is why Socrates says: "Every soul pursues [the good] and does everything for its sake. It divines that the good is something, but falls into *aporia* and is unable to grasp sufficiently what it is, or to have a lasting trust about it, as it has about other things."[116]

In the lines preceding this statement, Socrates demonstrates that there is no noncircular definition of the good, as the good may be defined in terms of the useful and the beneficial, but the good itself cannot be defined in terms that do not already imply the sense of goodness.[117] My response, on the basis of Rousseau together with Laplanche, is that the Idea of the good enters into human life as an enigma or a question; abstractly, as the question of rank, received through the seduction of the other's message, which constitutes the unconscious and the drive.

Thus, when Socrates describes the Idea of the good as "beyond being," he distinguishes it from other Ideas such as beauty or justice which are retained within being (*ousia*). Socrates indicates that the Ideas are "thought but not seen,"[118] but there is some mystery about how the Idea of the good can be the "cause of knowledge and truth" (*aitian d' epistēmēs ousan kai alētheias*).[119]

The Ideas are said to be eternal, so they do not come into being or pass away. The Idea of the good cannot therefore be the cause of Ideas like beauty or justice, if "cause" is taken to mean "bring into being." Instead of thinking the relation of Ideas in ontogenetic or simply mythical terms, it is more sensible to say that the Ideas are themselves the expressions of enigmas that share in the timelessness of the primal repressed. As in the genesis of *amour-propre*, the perception of beauty or merit transmits the enigma of the good through the desire of the other; but beauty and merit take on moral or political significance only *après-coup*—after the implantation of the good as an enigma, the result of the intersubjective process called primal seduction. The Idea of the good is then distinguished from other Ideas by its power to reveal them as objects of wonder. This is why the good is "beyond being" and distinguished in "power" and "rank." It is only because the good itself is transmitted as a question through the desire of the other that enduring questions about the likes of beauty, justice, or the meaning of being qua being can be valued as desirable or good. Moreover, because such notions are themselves illuminated by the enigma of the good, they must also be eclipsed by its enigma.

From this it follows that the possibility of philosophy requires the primal seduction of the good. In Plato, the art of turning souls toward the good itself is the prototypical example, since it is through enigmatic speech about enigmatic Ideas that Socrates intends to inspire the *erōs* for philosophy.[120] In the *Theaetetus*, Socrates compares this art to that of a midwife who assists in helping others find "in themselves, from themselves" (*autoi par' hautōn*) the path to truth and wisdom.[121] This same art is of course on display in the *Republic*, when Socrates breaks off his discussion about the *aporia* of the good for reasons having to do, at least in part, with increasing Glaucon's philosophic wonder.

It may be said, in this regard, that the art of turning souls involves an attitude of refusal, which Plato reproduces for the reader through his use of dramatic dialogue. Rousseau then adopts this technique in his discussion of the *doctrine intérieur* and elsewhere, as when he claims to show only the branches without revealing the roots, or when he distinguishes between readers who raise themselves and those who must be raised. These are all ways of introducing wisdom as an object of desire, as something obscure and difficult to attain, if only accessible to an exclusive few. Indeed, the promise of wisdom in combination with its refusal is what makes the art of *periagogē tēs psychēs* an art of seduction—one that aims to compel the potential philosopher toward the independent practice of philosophy.

VI. GUARDIAN OF THE ENIGMA

There is, at this point, an important parallel to draw between the Socratic art of turning souls and the provocation of the transference in psychoanalytic practice. I shall not investigate this at length, but I want to mention a few salient observations for the purpose of explaining how the drive takes wisdom as its object. It is a principle of Plato's dialogues that in discourse about philosophy we are never shown a conversation between individuals of equal status. The relation is always asymmetrical in a way that recalls the analytic situation. Laplanche notes that the offer of analysis creates the essential dimension of the transference; not the whole of the transference, but the "driving force at its heart," that is, "the reopening of a relation, the originary relation, in which the other is primary for the subject."[122] There is, therefore, a dissymmetry in the analytic situation which replicates for the analysand (and perhaps reflexively for the analyst) the infantile condition of helplessness (*Hilflosigkeit*).

In Laplanche's terms, this asymmetrical relation makes the analyst the "guardian of the enigma," which is to say, the offer of analysis, to speak freely and free associate, reinstates the confrontation with the enigma of the other: the external other and the other within. Laplanche adds that the offer of analysis proposes "a certain path towards truth, supposed to lead towards the good, towards well-being." However, the benevolent neutrality of the analyst requires "a radical refusal to know the good of the patient, to know the truth about his good."[123]

As the guardian of the enigma, this radical refusal to know the good of the other reproduces, for the analysand, a situation that is in many ways akin to the adult-*infans* relation; and as a consequence, the analyst reopens for the analysand "the dimension of interior alterity which allows the instauration of alterity in the transference."[124] In other words, in functioning as the guardian of the enigma, the analyst provokes the transference of the primal situation—indeed, the situation of primal seduction—in which the enigma of the good is primordially at issue.

Things are very similar in the action of philosophical seduction. There is an asymmetrical relation between the philosopher and the potential philosopher which may be recreated or enacted at the level of the reader and the text. It should be emphasized that a text or experience which is not intended to be seductive may be seductive nonetheless. In the instance of Rousseau's illumination, for example, the Dijon Academy's prize essay question proved seductive for Rousseau, not because it was seductive by design in the sense belonging to the art of turning souls, but because it tapped into a chain of wonders that made it seductive for Rousseau on the model of *après-coup*. There is thus a sense in which, for each of us, philosophy is more or less already underway as part of our adult quotidian experience. But this should come as no surprise from the standpoint of the general theory of seduction. As a theory of the primacy of the other in the formation of human subjectivity, it locates the possibility of philosophy within the universal inevitability of primal seduction. What the general theory of seduction helps us to understand is not only why philosophy is a universal human possibility, rooted in the timelessness of the unconscious, but also why the multitude, whom Rousseau called *les hommes vulgaires*, tends to turn away from philosophic questioning.

On this point, let me briefly mention the Savoyard Vicar's profession of faith in *Émile*. In describing his time of religious crisis, the Vicar remarks: "I was in that frame of mind of uncertainty and doubt that Descartes demands for the quest for truth. This state is hardly made to last. It is disturbing and painful. It is only the self-interest of vice or laziness of soul which leaves us in it. My heart was not sufficiently corrupted to enjoy myself in it."[125]

It is plain to see how the traumatic genesis of philosophic wonder can explain the failure to ascend philosophically. The Vicar continues: "Doubt about the things it is important for us to know is too violent a state for the human mind; it does not hold out in this state for long, it decides in spite of itself one way or the other, and prefers to be deceived rather than to believe nothing."[126] The Vicar, whom Jean-Jacques calls a "man of peace,"[127] goes on to elaborate the need for *religion naturelle* in a post-Christian epoch. At stake in this teaching is the fundamental question of the right life and whether it consists in faith or reason. The Vicar admits in the first lines of the profession: "I am not a great philosopher, and I care little to be one. But I sometimes have good sense, and I always love the truth."[128] The answer to the question of the right life is therefore complicated by the nature or temperament of the given individual. For the Vicar who is not constituted for endurance in philosophic questioning, his love of truth is satisfied by the revelation of natural religion, even at the risk of self-deception.

The same does not appear to be the case for Émile, whose ordinary nature is presented as the reason for his failure to ascend philosophically. There is, accordingly, a difference between an education designed to lead the potential philosopher to philosophy and the independent ascent to philosophy itself. Likewise, there is certain irony in how Émile is provided an education which takes Sophie as the object of romantic love. For Émile is not one who "raises himself." Rather, he requires to be "raised." This is another way of saying that Émile does not ascend from the love of bodies to the love of Ideas. The last lines of the book cement this point, as they communicate Émile's plea that Jean-Jacques continue to serve as a guide for him to imitate.[129] The sense in which philosophy is a universal possibility for human beings is therefore mediated by the inequalities of nature that make one kind of life happier than another for a given human being. In the same sense that Plato's Socrates insists that the potential for philosophy resides "in each of us," we remain consistent with both Plato and Rousseau to assert that philosophy is a universal possibility for human beings, but all human beings do not possess the capacity to actualize the maximum of human possibility.[130]

VII. TIME AND PHILOSOPHY

If it can be said that philosophy begins in trauma, it is because an event within the order of quotidian experience reactivates, by the process of *après-coup*, the primal enigma of the good which originally shattered the presocial order of preservation that Rousseau identified with the pure state of nature; the same order of experience that belongs in principle to the *infans* "before" seduction. In the schema of Rousseau, the most cursory reading of his oeuvre reveals the question of human happiness as the guiding question of his work. Take, for example, the conclusion to the dedicatory letter of the *Second Discourse* where he indicates his intention to write in the voice of "a true Patriot [. . .] who envisions no greater happiness for himself than that of seeing all of you happy."[131] Beginning from the order of quotidian experience, the question of happiness—*bonheur*, the *summum bonum* of classical philosophy—splits the primal enigma of the good between the two foundations of the ordinary: *the ordinary course of things* belonging to quotidian experience and *the ordinary course of life* belonging to the condition of pure nature.

These two foundations are "ordinary" in the etymological sense that they give order to the human soul. In the abstract condition of pure nature, the soul is ordered by its purely physical needs. The order of quotidian experience is then achieved *après-coup*, after the implantation of those *causes étrangeres* that spur the derivation of *amour-propre* from *amour de soi*. At its origin, this order is one of profound disorder. It is the order of experience in which, to reference Rousseau, the "love of order" is constantly at issue.[132] In words closer to Laplanche, it is the order of experience in which the subject is constituted by a tension between the internal *étrangèreté* of the unconscious and its maintenance by the external *étrangèreté* of the other who is, in turn, maintained by its own internal *étrangèreté*. What Rousseau calls the "love of order" is thus, in the register of the general theory of seduction, the expression of an effort by the drive to master the twofold *étrangèreté* of the other: the external other and the other within.

In mapping the process of philosophical seduction, this fundamental split between the two foundations of the ordinary can also be described in terms of two temporal orders, which I call the *sanstemporal* (S) and the *historical* (H). Strictly speaking, the order of pure nature is a time without time, as Rousseau described the human being of pure nature as having no knowledge of death and therefore "no idea of the future, however near it may be."[133] With reference to the process of primal seduction and repression, we can also identify two respective orders of temporality, two orders of the extraordinary, which I call the *timeless* (ψ) and the *transhistorical* (Φ). I call these orders extraordinary because they participate in the ordinary as modes of disruption. On the diagonal axis of the ordinary, the sanstemporal (S) belongs to the pure state of nature or the *infans*, whereas the historical (H) belongs to quotidian experience, the temporality of the lived present, autobiographical time, or the time of historical record. On the intersecting axis of the extraordinary, the timeless (ψ) then belongs to the unconscious or what Freud called "the unalterability by time of the repressed,"[134] while the transhistorical (Φ) belongs to the enduring questions of philosophy, which transcend times and places (Figure 4.1).

In note 10 of the *Second Discourse*, Rousseau made a point of saying that worldly travel of the kind undertaken by Plato, Thales, and Pythagoras is necessary, not just "to shake the yoke of National prejudices," but "to get to know men by their conformities and their differences, and to acquire that universal knowledge that is not exclusively of one Century or one country but of all times and all places." Rousseau called this knowledge "the common science of the wise."[135] This is to suggest that the education toward philosophy

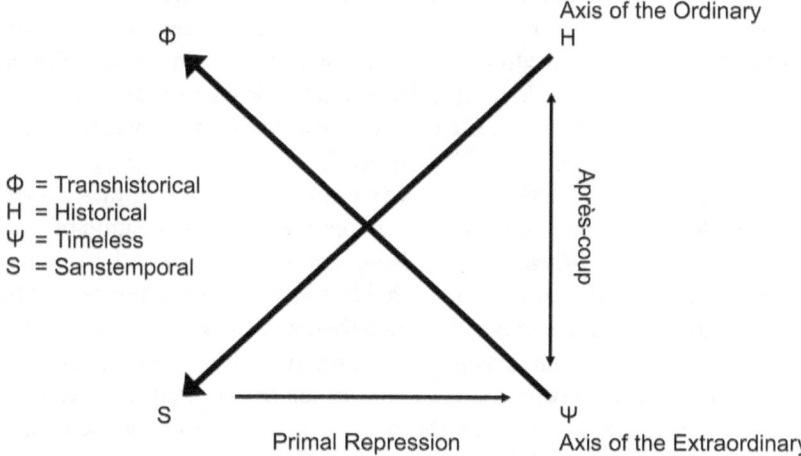

Figure 4.1 Philosophical Seduction

should include anthropology in its method; but its object should be knowledge of a transhistorical, universal kind. That this knowledge concerns human happiness is affirmed by Rousseau in Book II of *Émile* where he defines "human wisdom" as "the road of true happiness."[136] Insofar as the love of wisdom aims at transhistorical knowledge about the highest human good, the process by which the drive takes wisdom as its object is therefore explained by the seductive power of the question of happiness, which reactivates at the level of quotidian experience the primal enigma of the good. Philosophy as such then emerges as a way of viewing historical existence from a standpoint that is split between the transhistorical and the timeless; at once outside of history, abstracted from all times and places, but rooted in the *étrangereté* of the message of the other, which is transmitted across generations. Concisely stated, the transhistorical is a product of the timeless. One could even call it a symptom in the syncretic sense suggested by the "divine madness" of Socrates. From the transhistorical mode of questioning, philosophy thereby issues into history. Its various doctrines are so many attempts to master the timeless enigma of the good: the primal source-object of the drive for wisdom, the drive for knowledge of the life that is best for human beings.

VIII. THE NEW COPERNICANISM

Let us now return to the love of order that is implicitly at issue in quotidian experience. In this mode of temporality, we are situated within a continuum of events that inform or condition our thoughts and actions. The sense of having a continuum of experience is what makes this mode of temporality ordinary. I also call this mode historical because, in the spirit of Herodotus, it is the temporal stratum of human inquiry. The love of order is, accordingly, either the libidinal response to a disturbance within the continuum of quotidian experience, or it is the love of a determinate form of order that is called "good," perhaps not good in itself or good absolutely; but good for the one who, as the subject of history, calls it "good."

Now, according to Rousseau, the love of order is in itself neither good nor evil. It develops with the genesis of *amour-propre* as a modification of instrumental reason. In the *Moral Letters*, Rousseau calls *reason* "the faculty of ordering all the faculties of our soul suitably to the nature of things and their relations with us."[137] Since reason is understood as a faculty of order, that is, a faculty of calculation about arrangement, it requires the supplement of moral sentiment to calculate correctly about the order of the soul. For Rousseau, such sentiment can be known only through the inward turn to conscience, "in the silence of the passions." This is what he called in the *First Discourse* "*la véritable Philosophie.*"[138] However, it is not the contents of conscience that

I want to focus on, but the Vicar's criticism of attempts "to establish virtue by reason alone." As Rousseau has the Vicar put it: "Virtue, they say, is the love of order. But can and should this love win out in me over that of my own well-being? Let them give me a clear and sufficient reason for preferring it. At bottom, their alleged principle is a pure play on words; for I say that vice is the love of order, taken in a different sense."[139]

Let us note before continuing that the Vicar describes the difference between vice and virtue in ways that are comparable to the opposition in classical astronomy between Ptolemy and Copernicus, the respective figures of geocentrism and heliocentrism, who occupy some importance in Laplanche's effort "to show the movement through which, on the basis of an initial Copernicanism (a gravitation of the human child in the orbit of the sexual adult), man enclosed himself, in a Ptolemaic system."[140] The Vicar goes on to remark: "There is some moral order wherever there is sentiment and intelligence. *The difference is that the good [Copernican] man orders himself in relation to the whole, and the wicked [Ptolemaic] one orders the whole in relation to himself. The latter makes himself the center of all things; the former measures his radius and keeps to the circumference*."[141]

For the Vicar, God names the center. Virtue is the orientation of a life around the divinity. Vice is the attempt to make oneself the center of divine attention or to occupy the position of the divine itself. But what is the divine, if not the name of an enigma? If, by an operation of translation, the Ptolemaic position is treated in the Abrahamic sense, the attempt to make oneself the center of all things can be understood as the expression of a wish for the satisfactions of omnipotence. Is this a wish to be alleviated from the unconscious feeling of infantile helplessness, understood by Freud as a return of the repressed? This may well be the case. But more radically, the Ptolemaic position can be understood as the expression of a wish to be alleviated of the drive to translate. In this sense, it is a wish to master or abolish the message of the other; to close in on oneself by becoming the absolute master of the message.

Consider, in this connection, how the traumatism of the message could account for the great declarations, repeated as if by compulsion, of the "end of philosophy." In this same manner, the compulsive pull of "Ptolemaic" recentering can account for Rousseau's criticism of the degenerate *philosophe* who "only has to put his hands over his ears and to argue with himself a little in order to prevent Nature, which rebels within him, from letting him identify with the man being assassinated."[142]

The centering pull of Ptolemaic closure is therefore contrasted with the decentering force of Copernican opening. Much like the Socratic art of turning souls, the work of primal philosophy points to a new Copernican revolution in philosophy: a way of reopening the *étrangereté* of the message, a way of restoring our relation to the primal seductions of the other. Indeed, it is the through the reinstatement of the trauma of primal enigmas that the love of order may be turned toward transhistorical questioning about the timeless human problems.

IX. AIMS OF PRIMAL PHILOSOPHY

One could make a separate study of the ways that philosophy, through its history, through the work of what Hegel would call its world-historical figures, has gone astray from primal questioning or questioning about the primal. Such a study would have to trace the foundational question of philosophy through the historical vicissitudes of the classical connection between human happiness and the life of philosophic reason, going back at least to the crucial difference between Plato and Aristotle on the relation of the good to the genesis of philosophic wonder. I shall not venture further down that path here, except to say that when the possibility of philosophy is understood in view of the general theory of seduction, it no longer becomes a problem to explain how the idea of the good enters into human life or how the love of wisdom becomes attached to questioning about the good. This problem was fundamentally at issue in Rousseau's intention to end where Descartes began.

As a matter of method, Rousseau's reversal of Descartes was required to address the subordination of ethics to ontology—hence, the sundering of the good from the foundations of philosophy—that is characteristic of the Cartesian legacy through Heidegger and Badiou. It is a corollary of the Cartesian view that philosophy is founded by a heroism of the decision—to found philosophy on the model of mathematics and the experimental sciences, as in Descartes; to the announce "another beginning" founded on the thinking of being, as in Heidegger; or, as in Badiou, to found philosophy on four conditions of truth in science, politics, art, and love. In each of these examples, there is some confusion between the meaning of philosophy itself and the doctrines in which it issues. Descartes reduced philosophy to a system founded on the method of doubt; Heidegger translated the product of this method, the *cogito sum*, into the foundational question of being; and Badiou has defined philosophy as "that singular discipline of thought that has as its point of departure the conviction that there are truths."[143] That this definition of philosophy is itself the expression of a truth indicates its basis in the apparently circular conviction that there are truths—the operative word being that of *conviction*.

As Badiou has also stated: "The sole task of philosophy is to show that we must choose."[144] On the basis of this proposition, it could be said that the responsibility of the philosopher consists in clarifying the parameters of a choice; in showing what is at stake in the making of a decision. From the standpoint of primal philosophy, however, the exigency of the decision is what remains of the love of wisdom when love is displaced from the definition of philosophy by its transference to one of its conditions. According to this model, philosophy itself is predicated upon an act of the will, expressed by Badiou as the act of fidelity to the truth of an event. One could argue in these terms that the will of the philosopher is motivated by a crisis within the conditions of philosophy—of which love is one condition. But we still require an account of the genesis of love; foremost, the mode of love specific to the love of wisdom—and this invariably returns us to the fundamental anthropology of seduction: the fundamental anthropological situation and the ineluctable universality of primal seduction.

In the tradition of Plato and Rousseau together with Laplanche, it is evident that philosophy is not possible (or possible simply) as an act of the will. Its possibility resides, rather, in a form of compulsion rooted in the twofold demand of the drive. Whereas Descartes and his epigones attempt to found philosophy on the identification of a choice and the heroism of a decision, the love of wisdom cannot itself be reduced to a choice between decision and compulsion, as this formulates a false choice for the obvious reason that one does not choose a compulsion. Even if the task of the philosopher is in part to clarify the choices among which we must choose (a task which I do not dispute), the decision cannot be more than arbitrary without the capacity to rank our choices according to their goods. Insofar as the human good is at stake, we are thus again returned to the situation of primal seduction and the implantation of enigmatic messages in the infant by the adult.

Against the decisionistic method of Descartes, Rousseau proposed a return to the practice of Socratic ignorance. To repeat a line from Book I of *Émile:* "If we knew how to be ignorant of the truth, we would never be the dupe of lies."[145] This line takes on a particular resonance when read in association with Badiou's conviction that philosophy depends for its existence on the fidelity to a truth—namely, the truth that there are truths which are themselves the decisive products of events. Between Badiou and Rousseau one may therefore oppose the difference between conviction and ignorance. The practice of Socratic ignorance is not itself the consequence of a decision, an inaugural act of will, but of a compulsion—the kind of which Socrates owed to his daimonion, a voice not unlike the voice of conscience in Rousseau, the universality of which primal seduction traces originarily to the *étrangèreté* of the message of the other.[146]

In reading Rousseau together with Laplanche, my thought is that the practice of philosophy has as its possibility, and consequently, as its aim, a reinstatement of the Copernican situation of primal seduction—the originary situation which inspires, by the operation of *après-coup*, the love of wisdom understood as a love of order that takes its bearings at the level of quotidian experience from the question of human happiness, the highest human good. There are then two fundamental ways, adapted from the general theory of seduction, in which the primal situation may be reactivated: (1) through a provocation of the transference, in a sense liberated from the clinic, as in the instance of Rousseau's illumination or the Socratic art of turning souls; and (2) through a practice of analysis or "detranslation," as required by the allegorical Glaucus statue, which Rousseau used to indicate the problem of disentangling what is natural in the human being from everything that is not.[147]

With respect to the provocation of the transference, the generalization of seduction points to an equally general operation, according to which the process that occurs within the analytic situation is but a species of the genus, which is "already, 'in itself,' outside the clinic." Insofar as "the fundamental dimension of the transference is the relation to the enigma of the other," Laplanche distinguishes this "ordinary" mode of transference as "the multiple relation to the cultural," that is, "the cultural message," which is "before, beyond, or after analysis."[148] As we have seen, it is precisely this "ordinary" dimension of the transference that accounts for the *après-coup* of Rousseau's illumination.

Laplanche additionally identifies two contrasting dimensions of the transference. One is "filled-in" (*en plein*), the other is "hollowed-out" (*en creux*). Through the offer of analysis, the analyst first opens up the "hollow" of an "interior benevolent neutrality," a reflexively achieved neutrality concerning the analyst's own enigma.[149] Into this hollow, the analysand may then place something "filled-in" or "hollowed-out." If the transference is filled-in, the analysand places into the hollow of the analyst "the positive reproduction of forms of behavior, relationships, and childhood imagos," for example, the repetition of unconscious wishes, fantasies, or childhood scenes; either translated or repressed. If the transference is hollowed-out, the analysand deposits into the hollow of the analyst "*another hollow*, the enigma of his own primal situation"; hence, a relation to the *étrangèreté* of primal enigmas, leading to the enigma of the primal itself.[150]

It is, accordingly, the hollowed-out transference that establishes the paradigm of philosophical seduction, as it reinstates the primal relation to the enigmatic messages upon which the possibility of philosophy turns. In other words, whereas the analyst provokes a transference through the offer of a hollow within the confines of the clinic, the philosophical practitioner of the art of turning souls offers the hollow of a question, or a multitude of questions, all of which require for their illumination the primal enigma of the good. It is for this reason that a philosophical seduction must involve the provocation of a transference; one which aims at a reinstatement of the primal situation of infantile helplessness in relation to the enigmatic address of the other. Otherwise stated, if philosophy begins in wonder, the art of philosophical seduction must then consist in holding open the hollow of a question in order to provoke a transference of the primal, indeed, the enigma of the primal; a transference which the philosopher provokes through the use of ignorance or Socratic irony, so as not to fill up the transference with messages compromised by the philosopher's own unconscious.

As for the practice of analysis in relation to philosophy, Laplanche says of the analytic situation: "If the situation is the locus of a reactivation of the relation to enigmas emanating from the other, that effort can be accomplished only by way of a deconstruction, a detranslation of the myths and ideologies through which the ego constructed itself in order to master those enigmas."[151] To the extent that the dynamics of the clinic can be expanded to the cultural domain in which philosophy participates, I propose to think the imperative of analysis in terms of a double process through which the potential philosopher is freed for philosophy. On one side, this process corresponds to a detranslation of the "myths and ideologies" that constitute the ego of the potential philosopher, the subject of philosophy; on the other, it consists in a progressive detranslation of the history of philosophy itself, the artifact of human efforts to master the timeless enigmas at the source of philosophic questioning.

All of this in the name of making plans: a proposal for future work in the further development of a psychoanalytic approach to the practice of philosophy. Let me therefore conclude this chapter with a comment on the future. I previously cited Badiou's suggestion that "the future of philosophy always takes the form of a resurrection," along with his further claim that "the great declarations about the death of philosophy [. . .] are most likely the rhetorical means to introduce a new path, a new aim, within philosophy itself."[152] By questioning into the possibility of philosophy, I have also opened up the claim that philosophy has gone astray. In a sense, it has lost its responsibility to itself, through the historical vicissitudes that have resulted in the disavowal or repression of the primal link between the question of human happiness and the possibility of philosophy itself.

It is a corollary of this proposition that the future of philosophy depends upon a working-through of the melancholy attitude that became increasingly pervasive through the history of philosophy in the twentieth century, culminating in the respective claims of Wittgenstein and Heidegger that happiness is either "nonsense" or "the greatest nihilism," along with their attendant efforts to bring philosophy to an end by a process of destruction. As Wittgenstein said of his own attitude toward his work in philosophy: "I destroy, I destroy, I destroy—."[153] It was no less Heidegger's intention to subject the history of ontology to *Destruktion* in order to retrieve the question of being, "to reattain the originary experiences of being belonging to metaphysics."[154] In the sense communicated by Badiou, it was therefore necessary on the part of Heidegger to announce the end of metaphysics in order to initiate "another beginning" consisting in a resurrection of the thinking of being.

I leave to one side the question of whether the destructive efforts of Heidegger and Wittgenstein are symptomatic of attempts to arrest the trauma of primal enigmas at the source of philosophic questioning. Instead, I want to concentrate on what is fundamentally at stake in Rousseau's reversal of Descartes: his legacy-as-task to end where Descartes began. It follows from Rousseau's effort to rethink the meaning of first philosophy that the endeavor to renew the question of being as the mode of originary experience is founded, rather, on a misrecognition of the primacy of being with regard to philosophic questioning. The meaning of being is of concern to human beings only *après-coup*, on the condition that questioning into being is considered desirable or good. On this point, let us simply note together with Laplanche that even for the being who issues being as a question, "the 'I am situated,' *Dasein*," this is a question for the adult philosopher who is irremediably decentered by the primacy of childhood.[155] Anterior to the *Seinsfrage* is, accordingly, the primal enigma of the good and the question of how it enters into human life, which is answered by seduction.

What is finally at stake in Rousseau's reversal of Descartes is the possibility of reopening the primal source of philosophic questioning, a reinstatement of the enigmatic address emanating from the other; hence, a reappropriation of the enigma of the primal, a reactivation of the "drive to translate," a neo-genesis of philosophic wonder. As the study of the genesis of philosophy itself, primal philosophy aims at a renewal of philosophy subtracted from its doctrines; a restoration of philosophy itself. This is what Rousseau called genuine philosophy: the love of order that requires, paradoxically, the holding open of a rupture within the ordinary; the turning of the soul toward the enigma of the good; the pursuit of self-knowledge, which is in fact a pursuit of ignorance in the spirit of Socrates. Understood this way, philosophy is not itself a doctrine, but an activity of the soul, which participates in a transhistorical mode of investigation—one that has its origin in the *après-coup* of the timeless enigma of the good.

NOTES

1. Rousseau, OC 3:106/Bordes 110.
2. Freud, *Project for a Scientific Psychology*, GW N:444–48/SE 1:352–56. See Laplanche, VM 64ff/38ff; NFP 108ff/109ff.
3. See Freud, *Studies on Hysteria*, GW 1:292–94/SE 2:288–90.
4. Freud, *Project for a Scientific Psychology*, GW N:448/SE 1:356.

5. See Freud, "The Aetiology of Hysteria," GW 1:427/SE 3:192–93.
6. Laplanche, NFP 88/88 (Laplanche's emphasis).
7. Freud, Letter of September 21, 1897, BWF 283–284/264–65.
8. Laplanche, SEX 97–98/102. See also "la situation originaire" in Laplanche, NFP 90/89–90.
9. Laplanche, VM 75/46.
10. Rousseau, OC 4:245/E 37.
11. Rousseau, OC 4:350–51n/E 112n.
12. From M. J. Gaberel's *Rousseau et les Genevois* (1858, 143–44), and quoted in Barzun (2000, 386).
13. Laplanche, SEX 95/99.
14. Laplanche, NFP 89/89.
15. Laplanche, NFP 61/58–59.
16. Laplanche, NFP 89/89; 60/58.
17. Laplanche, NFP 89/89 (emphasis added).
18. Laplanche, "The Unfinished Copernican Revolution," RCI xxvi–xxvii/EO 75. See also Laplanche, NFP 97–98/97–99.
19. Laplanche, NFP 89/89.
20. Laplanche, NFP 90/89–90.
21. See, for example, Laplanche, NFP 125–29/126–30.
22. Laplanche, NFP 111–15/112–16; 128–29/129–30.
23. Laplanche, "The Unfinished Copernican Revolution," RCI xxxv/EO 83.
24. Laplanche, "Short Treatise on the Unconscious," ESIH 67–68/EO 84.
25. Laplanche, "Short Treatise on the Unconscious," ESIH 69/EO 85–86. Cf. Freud, Letter of December 6, 1896, BWF 219/208: "A failure of translation—this is what is known clinically as 'repression.'"
26. Freud, "Repression," GW 10:250/SE 14:147 (Strachey's emphasis).
27. Freud, "Repression," GW 10:250/SE 14:147.
28. Freud, "Repression," GW 10:250/SE 14:148.
29. Laplanche, VOC 396–98/333–34. See Freud, "The Unconscious," GW 10:279–80/SE 14:180–81.
30. Rousseau, OC 4:261/E 48 (my emphasis).
31. Laplanche, "Interpretation between Determinism and Hermeneutics: A Restatement of the Problem," RCI 407–8/EO 158.
32. Laplanche, "Short Treatise on the Unconscious," ESIH 74/EO 89 (Laplanche's emphasis).
33. Laplanche, "Short Treatise on the Unconscious," ESIH 79/EO 92; "Implantation, Intromission," RCI 358/EO 136.
34. Laplanche, NFP 124–25/124.
35. Freud, Letter of December 6, 1896, BWF 219/208.
36. Laplanche, "Short Treatise on the Unconscious," ESIH 80/EO 93.
37. Laplanche, NFP 132–34/134–36. See also "The Drive and its Source-Object: Its Fate in the Transference," RCI 239/EO 129. Cited hereafter as "The Drive and its Source-Object."
38. Laplanche, "The Drive and its Source-Object," RCI 239/EO 129.

39. Lacan (1966), 597.
40. Laplanche, P-III 69; "The Drive and its Source-Object," RCI 239/EO 129; NFP 141–43/144–45.
41. Freud, "Instincts and Their Vicissitudes," GW 10: 219/SE 126.
42. Freud, "Instincts and Their Vicissitudes," GW 10:219/SE 126–27 (translation corrected).
43. Detailed in Freud, "Instincts and Their Vicissitudes," GW 10:210–232/SE 14: 109–40. Cf. Laplanche, VM 22–41/10–24.
44. See Freud, *Three Essays on the Theory of Sexuality*, GW 5:67–69/SE 7:167–69. Cited in Laplanche, VM 22ff/10ff.
45. See, for example, Laplanche, "The Drive and Its Source-Object," RCI 238–39/EO 128–29. The theory of leaning-on is initially developed by Laplanche in VM.
46. See, for example, Laplanche NFP 134; EO 238/128.
47. See, esp., Laplanche, "The Drive and its Source-Object," RCI 238–39/EO 128–29.
48. See, for example, Laplanche, "The Unfinished Copernican Revolution," RCI xxii–xxv/EO 71–73; "Time and the Other," RCI 380–81/EO 256; "Short Treatise on the Unconscious," ESIH 103/EO 108.
49. Freud, *Beyond the Pleasure Principle*, GW 13:29/SE 18: 29–30. I do not wish to pursue the point here, but the general theory of seduction allows us to subvert the dichotomy between sexual and nonsexual psychoneuroses, insofar as this distinction marks the *proton pseudos* of Freud's initial motivation to theorize "beyond the pleasure principle."
50. This point is developed by Jonathan Lear (2000, esp., 77–78). However, Lear maintains a theory of mental functioning which concentrates on the mind's tendency to disrupt itself, understood as an endogenous capacity of mind. As Lear's overall theory owes much to Aristotle, this aspect should be reconsidered in view of the primacy of the other in Laplanche's explanation of human psychogenesis and the mechanisms of defense. It is, of course, a truism with Aristotle that the geocentric view of the cosmos appears correct from the standpoint of earthbound experience. For related comments in Laplanche, see "The Unfinished Copernican Revolution," RCI iii–xxxiv/EO 52–83.
51. Laplanche, "The Drive and its Source-Object," RCI 240/EO 130.
52. The isomorphism of *ratio cognoscendi* and *ratio essendi* may be translated, respectively, as "ground of knowing" and "ground of being."
53. Laplanche, SEX 95/99.
54. Rousseau, OC 3:162/SD 159.
55. Laplanche, SEX 95/99. See also "Transference: Its Provocation by the Analyst," RCI 417–437/EO 214–33.
56. Freud, *Project for a Scientific Psychology*, GW N:448/SE 1:356.
57. Freud, *Project for a Scientific Psychology*, GW N:445–47/SE 1:353–55.
58. See Freud, Letter of April 6, 1897, BWF 248/234.
59. Laplanche cites three additional statements by Freud to the same effect. See P-VI 64–66/57–59.
60. Laplanche, P-VI 68/61.

61. For Freud's rejection of Jung on the temporal priority of the present in the formation of fantasies, see Freud, "From the History of an Infantile Neurosis," GW 12:137/SE 17:102–3; cf. Carl Jung, "The Theory of Psychoanalysis" in *Freud and Psychoanalysis*, vol. 4 of *The Collected Works of C. G. Jung*, trans. R. F. C. Hull, ed. Herbert Read, Michael Fordham, and Gerhard Adler (New York: Pantheon Books, 1961), 168.

62. Laplanche, P-VI 169–71/154–55 (Laplanche's emphasis).
63. Freud, *New Introductory Lectures*, GW 15:81/SE 22:74.
64. Freud, "The Unconscious," GW 10:286/SE 14:187.
65. Freud, *Beyond the Pleasure Principle*, GW 13: 27–28/SE 18:28.
66. Freud, *New Introductory Lectures*, GW 15:80/SE 22:73.
67. For Laplanche on *auto-théorisation*, see, for example, NFP 58–59/162–63; "Short Treatise on the Unconscious," ESIH 92/EO 103; "Psychoanalysis, Time, and Translation," STD 176.
68. Freud, "Negation," GW 14:13/SE 19:236–37.
69. Freud, "Negation," GW 14:13, 11/SE 19: 236, 235.
70. Freud, "Negation," GW 14:13, 11/SE 19: 237.
71. Laplanche, P-VI 110/99.
72. Freud, "Negation," GW 14:13–14/SE 19:237.
73. Laplanche, P-VI 110/99–100.
74. Rousseau, OC 4:261/E 48 (my emphasis).
75. Rousseau, OC 3:134/SD 134.
76. It is consistent with Rousseau's principles that in the Fourth Walk of the *Reveries*, the Solitary Walker argues (1) "the truth owed is that which concerns justice" and (2) "the obligation to tell the truth is founded on its usefulness." Here, "general and abstract truth" is called "the most precious of all goods," whereas "particular and individual truth is not always a good." It would seem the utility of a truth therefore depends on its particular effect in relation to a given individual or kind of individual. It follows that a truth deemed harmful for a certain kind of individual cannot be owed as a matter of justice. In other words, justice requires withholding a truth deemed harmful, as "injustice consists only in the harm done to someone else" (OC 1:1026–27/SW 30–31; cf. Plato, *Republic*, 331eff). For additional commentary, see Meier (2016, 149–54) and (Gourevitch, 2012, 489–518).
77. Rousseau, OC 3:123/SD 125.
78. Rousseau, OC 3:132/SD 131.
79. Rousseau, OC 3:111/SD 114.
80. Plato, *Theaetetus*, 155c.
81. Plato, *Theaetetus*, 155d.
82. Plato, *Theaetetus*, 151a.
83. Aristotle, *Metaphysics*, A.1.980a21-27, A.2.982b12-20. The Greek for "desire" is *oregontai*, meaning "reach after," "grasp at," or "stretch out for."
84. Plato, *Phaedo*, 99d-e. Cf. Aristotle, NE 1105b12-16.
85. Aristotle, *Metaphysics*, A.1.993b7-9: "Since difficulty also can be accounted for in two ways, its cause may exist not in the objects of our study but in ourselves."
86. Plato, *Republic*, 485b. See also *Symposium*, 207a; *Phaedrus*, 247b-c.

87. Plato, *Republic*, 501d.
88. Plato, *Republic*, 475b, 485b; 486a.
89. Plato, *Republic*, 505a, 509b.
90. Aristotle, *Metaphysics*, Λ.7.1072a21ff; esp., Λ.7.1072a26-28, 1072a34-72b1, 1072b3, and 1072b20-23.
91. This appears as a version of the Euthyphro question. Is thinking beautiful because it is lovable, or is it lovable because it is beautiful?
92. Plato, *Symposium*, 202d-e; *Phaedrus*, 244a.
93. Immediately upon recalling his illumination, Rousseau admits to the fallibility of his memory, which is to say, the plausibility of embellishment. He notes: "Although I have a lively remembrance of the impression I received from it, its details have escaped me since I set them down in one of my four letters to M. de Malesherbes" (OC 1:351/C 294).
94. Rousseau, OC 1:351/C 294.
95. Rousseau, OC 1:225/C 189.
96. Rousseau, OC 1:237/C 198–99.
97. Rousseau, OC 1:394/C 331.
98. Rousseau, OC 1:1135/C 575.
99. Rousseau, OC 1:1135/C 575.
100. Starobinski ([1971] 1988, 141–42/115) said of Rousseau: "It took Kant to 'think Rousseau's thoughts,' as Eric Weil has written (and I would add: it took Freud to 'think' Rousseau's feelings)." It likewise could be said that it has taken Laplanche to rethink these same thoughts root and branch.
101. Rousseau, OC 4:1044/FICT 165.
102. This cuts a level deeper than Rousseau's claim that Pythagoras was the first to resort to the internal doctrine (OC 3:47/OBS 42). Whereas Pythagoras taught secret lessons in atheism while making public sacrifices to Jupiter, the "Fiction" addresses the beginning of religion in response to the opening of philosophic wonder.
103. Rousseau, OC 4:1044–45/FICT 165–66.
104. To say nothing of its function as the axis of Copernican motion. See section VIII of this chapter.
105. Rousseau, OC 3:6/FD 6.
106. Rousseau, OC 3:30/FD 27.
107. Rousseau, OC 4:348/E 110.
108. Rousseau, OC 4:767/E 408.
109. Plato, *Republic*, 518d3-7.
110. Plato, *Republic*, 517c.
111. Plato, *Republic*, 518b-c.
112. Plato, *Republic*, 518c.
113. Plato, *Republic*, 531e4-5.
114. Plato, *Republic*, 533a1-5.
115. Plato, *Republic*, 516e-517a.
116. Plato, *Republic*, 505e.
117. Plato, *Republic*, 505a-c.
118. Plato, *Republic*, 507b.

119. Plato, *Republic*, 508e.
120. See my interpretation of Plato's *Symposium* in Fain (2015).
121. Plato, *Theaetetus*, 150d8.
122. Laplanche, "Transference: Its Provocation by the Analyst," RCI 430/EO 226.
123. Laplanche, "Transference: Its Provocation by the Analyst," RCI 431-32/EO 228.
124. Laplanche, "Transference: Its Provocation by the Analyst," RCI 432/EO 228-29.
125. Rousseau, OC 4:567/E 267.
126. Rousseau, OC 4:568/E 268.
127. Rousseau, OC 4:565/E 266; viz. Luke 10:6.
128. Rousseau, OC 4:565/E 266.
129. These lines are spoken by Émile in announcement that he is soon to be a father: "But remain the master of the young masters. Advise us and govern us. We shall be docile. As long as I live, I shall need you. I need you more than ever now that my functions as a man begin. You have fulfilled yours. Guide me so that I can imitate you. And take your rest. It is time" (OC 4:868/E480).
130. Plato, *Republic*, 518c. For a suggestive account of how the education of Émile adumbrates the *Republic*'s "three waves" of reform in founding the *kallipolis*, see Cooper (2008, 177–201). Cooper also suggests that despite the philosophic character of Émile's education, the impetus toward philosophy may not be aimed primarily at Émile but at the reader of the text (2008, 200). I am in full agreement with this suggestion. I add only that Cooper does not connect Émile's failure to raise himself with his continuing need for imitation, nor does Cooper provide the fundamental anthropology of seduction which can explain the possibility of philosophy itself.
131. Rousseau, OC 3:121/SD 123. Examples are so numerous as to make additional citations superfluous.
132. See, for example, Rousseau, OC 3:145/SD 144; OC 4:598, 602, 636/E 282, 291–92, 314; OC 4:935–36/LtB 28.
133. Rousseau, OC 3:143–44/SD 142–43.
134. Freud, *New Introductory Lectures*, GW 15:81/SE 22:74.
135. Rousseau, OC 3:213/SD 210.
136. Rousseau, OC 4:304/E 80.
137. Rousseau, OC 4:1090/ML 182.
138. Rousseau, OC 3:30/FD 28.
139. Rousseau, OC 4:602/E 291.
140. Laplanche, "Short Treatise on the Unconscious," ESIH 103/EO 109.
141. Rousseau, OC 4:602/E 291–92 (emphasis added).
142. Rousseau, OC 3:156/SD 153.
143. Badiou, PE 128.
144. Badiou, PIP 5.
145. Rousseau, OC 4:269/E 54.
146. For the voice of Socrates' daimonion, see Plato, *Apology*, 31c-d.
147. I borrow this line of thought from Laplanche. Cf. Laplanche, "Goals of the Psychoanalytic Process," ESIH 236/BSIM 197.

148. Laplanche, "Transference: Its Provocation by the Analyst," RCI 426/EO 222.
149. Laplanche, "Transference: Its Provocation by the Analyst," RCI 433/EO 229.
150. Laplanche, NFP 157/161; "Transference: Its Provocation by the Analyst," RCI 433/EO 229.
151. Laplanche, "Goals of the Psychoanalytic Process," ESIH 237/BSIM 198.
152. Badiou, REPP 17–18/6.
153. Wittgenstein, CV 19.
154. Heidegger, SZ 26. See also "On the Question of Being," GA 9:417/PATH 315.
155. Laplanche, "Responsibility and Response," ESIH 163/BSIM 136.

Chapter 5

Philosophy and Responsibility

I. PRIMACY OF RESPONSE

I would like to conclude with some observations concerning the paradoxical relationship between the philosophical and political ends of the responsibility of the philosopher. These comments are not meant to be exhaustive. It will suffice that they follow in accord with the correct orientation to the question concerning the possibility of philosophy.

The first thing to say is that *philosophy is possible*. It has neither end nor beginning apart from the humanity that founds it in the universality of primal seduction. Whether so many claims about the end of philosophy are attempts to introduce something new into philosophy, as suggested by Badiou; or whether these attempts are altogether the symptom of an unconscious wish to be alleviated of the traumas at the source of philosophic questioning, as proposed in the reading of Rousseau together with Laplanche; it is nevertheless the case that the possibility of philosophy persists through the implantation of timeless enigmas, the residues accrued by the failure of the child to translate messages transmitted by the adult for whom they also bear enigmas. These enigmas constitute the unconscious, the internal other, which functions as the source-object of the drive, understood essentially as a drive to translate, to master the enigmas of the other, both the external other and the other within. On the basis of Rousseau's principles, it is accordingly the primal enigma of the good that serves as the unconscious source of the drive for wisdom, the love of order that is founded *après-coup* through the seduction of happiness, the question of the highest human good.

Provided this account of the possibility of philosophy, how should we understand the responsibility of the philosopher? In what sense is the responsibility of the philosopher informed by the possibility of philosophy itself?

In answering these questions, I shall not try to draw a theory of responsibility from whole cloth. I rather want to build upon a line of inquiry initiated by Laplanche in consideration of the primordial response to the enigmatic address of the other: the responsive "answer to" (*répondre à*), which, as a matter of course, prefigures the possibility of any responsible "answer for" (*répondre de*).[1]

Beginning from the primacy of childhood, more radically decentered by the message of the other than even the temporal decentering of Heideggerian Dasein (which presupposes active temporalizing, not endogenous to the *infans*), what is essential is the treatment of the message by the child and the "always inadequate *response*," the failure of translation that accounts for the formation of the sexual unconscious. As Laplanche never tired of insisting, the unconscious "should not in any way be reduced to a preexisting biological id."[2] It rather consists in the residues of untranslated messages, which instigate the enlarged sexuality of the drive: "The sexuality that, in infancy at least, can transform any region or function of the body, and even activity in general, into an 'erotogenic zone.'"[3]

In the context of philosophy, this plasticity of the drive explains how wisdom can become an erotogenic object, an object that is correspondingly the source of a certain "love of order," but one that takes its fundamental bearing from the question of human happiness, the drive for which is rooted in the primal enigma of the good. Indeed, however distant wisdom is from human grasp, its attainment is the highest sense in which I take Freud's original suggestion that happiness is modeled on the satisfaction of the drive.[4]

As for the primacy of *response*, it first emerges as the effort of translation by the child in answer to the enigma of the sexual implanted by the other. The enigma therefore issues a demand. It requires that the child answer to the other in the mode of a question, that is, a double question: "What does it want from me, this external other, this other within me?" This question is foundational for, if not identical to, what Rousseau called the voice of conscience. It consists essentially in a libidinal demand regarding knowledge of the good. As ineluctable as the fundamental anthropological situation, this is how the question of happiness enters into human life as an erotogenic object: through a process of seduction that begins with a primal decentering by the message of the other, "a fundamental Copernicanism," and the twofold demand of a response.[5]

I note that Laplanche advances the distinction between "responsibility" and "response" in connection with a brief and somewhat obligatory comment about the phenomenology of Emmanuel Lévinas, whose work Laplanche claims not to have followed after reading his early book of 1930, *Théorie de l'intuition dans la phenomenologie de Husserl*.[6] Despite their shared interest in notions of alterity, Laplanche and Lévinas did not correspond during their lifetimes. Laplanche explains that, from the first, Lévinas was not radically Copernican enough. As a consequence, he did not keep pace with Lévinas's publication history, nor did Lévinas influence his thinking.[7] It seems that Lévinas is worth mentioning, for Laplanche, only in view of a question initiated by Freud concerning our responsibility for whatever immoral wishes may lurk behind our dreams. Laplanche argues that the answer to this question is complicated by the general theory of seduction, which indicates the priority of the other in the formation of the unconscious, and therefore the priority of an alien sexuality as anterior to the formation of any human subject who could be called "responsible." To the extent that Laplanche engages Lévinas in this regard, it is mainly to include him among a list of thinkers whose doctrines have remained insufficiently Copernican; hence, insufficiently responsive to our primal decentering by the other. This provokes Laplanche to ask, as if in passing: "How is one to achieve a perception of Copernicanism [. . .] in philosophy, a universe of thought that, from Descartes to Kant, to Husserl, to Heidegger, and to Freud, is irremediably Ptolemaic?"[8]

In a sense, this is the question I have been asking all along. What is fundamentally at stake concerns the difference between the artifacts of philosophic reason in contrast to the opening of wonder in which philosophy begins. To state the point as sharply as possible: philosophy is not itself a doctrine, but an activity of the soul which participates in a transhistorical mode of investigation; one that has its origin in the *après-coup* of the timeless enigma of the good.

Now, with respect to Lévinas and the other "Ptolemaics," Laplanche is not engaged in a quarrel between the ancients and the moderns, which could be construed to break along the lines of Copernicus and Ptolemy. However, it is notable that, in the aforementioned list, the "Ptolemaic" thinkers all belong to the lineage of Descartes; including Freud, about whom Laplanche has argued: "Despite a good start, he remains centered, and centered on the self. Everything he says about the ego perched upon the id is situated in a perspective of recentering. Not, to be sure, a recentering in relation to consciousness, but a recentering in relation to our biological being, which allegedly would be the very foundation of the id."[9] Applied to the context of philosophy, there is a related question concerning why philosophy tends to go astray, toward Ptolemaic thinking, not only in the manner of Cartesianism, but beginning with Aristotle's fundamental split from Plato on the operation of the other in the genesis of wonder.

This question is another version of the question that appears at the start of chapter 1, that is, the question of whether the effort to ascend philosophically, toward *logos,* terminates inevitably in the production of a *mythos.* This question now requires some refinement. I want to distinguish the *function* of mythosymbolic thinking in response to messages emanating from the other, in contrast to the *use* of mythosymbolic thought in matters concerning the responsibility of the philosopher. Where the latter is concerned, I shall distinguish the political responsibility of the philosopher from the responsibility of the philosopher with respect to philosophy itself. As we know, in keeping with Laplanche, it is a consequence of the profound asymmetry within the primal situation that the question of "bearing responsibility" finds its root in the anteriority of a response; specifically, a response that has its exigency within the domain of the sexual in distinction from the vital order of biology. It is an important implication of this insight that responsibility as such is irreducible to responsibility for bare life, self-preservation, or its existential variant as "being-toward-death." Before proceeding to the responsibility of the philosopher, it is therefore necessary to address the rootedness of this responsibility in the primacy of response, which Laplanche connects to the function of mythosymbolic thinking in the effort by the *infans* to translate the enigmas of the other, that is to say, enigmas charged with traumatizing sexuality.

II. PRIMAL RESPONSIBILITY

In the world of Rousseau studies, there is a single figure in the twentieth century whose name seems unavoidable, that of Claude Lévi-Strauss (1908–2009), the French anthropologist who more than once announced his intellectual debt to Rousseau—the man he called his "master."[10] It is therefore remarkable that Laplanche calls upon Lévi-Strauss in order to elaborate some key elements in the connection between psychoanalysis and mythosymbolic thought, not only in reference to the sexual theories of children that have sometimes seemed to reduce the whole of psychoanalysis to the myths of Oedipus and castration, but more fundamentally (one could say, formatively) in the efforts of the little human to answer the enigmatic address of the other. The former is only of tangential interest here, so I shall concentrate on the later, the *function* of mythosymbolic thought in efforts by the *infans* to translate the enigmas of the other.

The key text in this regard is "Psychoanalysis: Myths and Theory" (1999).[11] There, Laplanche cites two complementary lines from Lévi-Strauss. The first comes from *La pensée sauvage* (1962): "The exigency of order [. . .] is at the base of all thought." (Lévi-Strauss actually writes: "*la base de la pensée que nous appelons primitive, mais seulement pour autant qu'elle est à la base de toute pensée,*" that is, "the base of the thought which we call primitive, but only in so far as it is the base of all thought."[12]) However indirect, "the exigency of order at the base of all thought" has clear resonance with Rousseau's notion of "the love of order," which emerges in response to the disruptive genesis of *amour-propre*—the so-called exit from "pure nature." The second line from Lévi-Strauss then comes from a later work, *La potière jalouse* (1985), and is presented by Laplanche as a refinement of the first. Here Lévi-Strauss suggests that mythosymbolic thought has as its function "relieving intellectual uneasiness and even existential anxiety," specifically, with respect to "an anomaly, contradiction, or scandal."[13] In combination, Laplanche suggests: "The myth proposes a scheme for a new translation with the purpose of confronting the 'existential' anxiety provoked by enigmatic elements that present themselves as 'anomaly, contradiction, or scandal.'"[14] In other words, "mytho-symbolic scenarios have as their principal function allowing the child arriving in the (human) world to deal with the enigmatic messages emanating from the adult other."[15] These messages are disruptive of human mental functioning for the very reason that they are infused with unconscious sexuality, which has escaped mastery by translation. Mythosymbolic formations are therefore "proposed in order to frame, bind, and ultimately repress the sexual."[16]

Binding the sexual. This is the fundamental function of mythosymbolic thought in the child's response to messages emanating from the other. Let us now take one step backward. It is imperative to recognize that the process of translation does not begin *ex nihilo*. It occurs within the context of the adult world, which is *in medias res* a world structured by the apparatus of culture. In effect, culture furnishes the *infans* with an abundance of "codes" (the term is Laplanche's), the meanings of which are not self-evident, but in need of translation. Take for example the function of totemic systems, which were of interest to both Freud and Lévi-Strauss. In Freud, totemic prohibitions are bound up with Oedipal tensions consummating in the murder of the primal father. In Lévi-Strauss, by contrast, totemism is regarded as a relational system of classification and exchange. Totemism is therefore a method of relieving various aspects of "intellectual uneasiness" or "existential anxiety," which spur the reciprocal need for order within human society. Totemic symbols are, of course, derived from any number of natural kinds, the most common of which come from the animal realm—an observation that prompts a question, for Laplanche, concerning the function of animality as a point of reference in the self-translating, self-theorizing activities of human beings.

Laplanche's most concise statement on this topic appears at the end of an October 23, 1997 lecture titled "Biologism and Biology." The theme of this lecture is precisely the "going-astray" (*fourvoiement*) of Freud's thought toward a "Ptolemaic" biologism, which has tended to cover over his fundamental insights about the genesis and vicissitudes of human sexuality. Laplanche observes how, for the ancient Greeks, animality is associated with the lowest part of human nature, designated in Plato as the epithumetic or appetitive part of the soul. According to the schema of the *Republic*, it is the bestial part that requires taming by what is most divine in us, namely, *nous* or "intellect," the seat of *logos* or reason. I note that Laplanche elides the chance to comment on the function of daimonic *erōs* in elevating the human being to its most divine potentiality. Moreover, in the context of the dialogue, the tripartite division of the soul is presented as a heuristic by Socrates, who never certifies it with the stamp of "truth," as it pertains to the analogy of city and soul. Nevertheless, the point for Laplanche is to see how the ancient Greeks tended to identify human sexuality with our animal or bestial nature. As he points out: "For the Greeks the beast is a sexual beast. Zeus takes the form of the bull or the swan to seduce his lovers."[17]

In several places throughout his works, Laplanche also cites the modern example of Hobbes, for whom the wolf serves as a symbol of human cruelty, as in his use of the Latin proverb *homo homini lupus*, "man is a wolf to man."[18] Within our working nexus of associations, it is significant that Laplanche acknowledges Freud's use of this same adage in *Civilization and Its Discontents* (1930), where it appears in conjunction with his account of the sadistic elements of the so-called death drive, understood as a metabiological or metacosmological force. Even more relevant, however, is Laplanche's analysis of Hobbes' dictum, as it points to the reasons underlying Rousseau's rejection of Hobbes, for whom it is claimed the human being is by nature wicked or intrepid, which is to say, naturally disposed to cruelty or violence. For Rousseau, this claim serves as the example *par excellence* of those thinkers who have failed to go back far enough in their efforts to reach the genuine state of nature. Needless to say, Rousseau finds fault with Hobbes for importing into nature characteristics or behaviors that emerge exclusively as a consequence of interactions within human society.

What interests Laplanche runs along similar lines. Much like Rousseau's doctrine that the human being is "good" by nature, Laplanche argues for "the absolute heterogeneity of sadistic aggression in humans in relation to any animality," meaning that, "neither the Thirty Years War nor Auschwitz nor Cambodia can be attributed to the 'biological animal' in us."[19] As the detranslation of Hobbes' adage goes to show, there is nothing to demonstrate that the attack of the wolf expresses cruelty or destructiveness of the kind pursued and enjoyed for its own sake—for some innate or adaptive reason. Stated in short, the wolf is not a "wolf." The cruelty attributed to the wolf is rather a kind of fiction or fantasy, which Laplanche describes as "a biological alibi disguising something that ultimately has nothing to do with biology."[20] The wolf is therefore an emblem of human cruelty; a product of the primary process of condensation and displacement, which serves to bind the disruptive, destructive, and even violent character of the sexual to a mythosymbolic form. This is also to say—in a manner consistent with Rousseau—that human cruelty is neither "natural" nor "animal" nor "instinctual" nor "biological." Instead, it is *sexual* and linked to fantasies inhabiting the unconscious. In Laplanche's words: "It is man alone who is a *Lupus* for man."[21]

This brings us back to the question of responsibility; specifically, its rootedness in the response of the *infans* to the *étrangèreté* of the other. First, with regard to the formation of mythic constructions, it is not so much a matter of "inevitability" as it is one of "going-astray." This is directly a consequence of the "exigency of order," a libidinal demand, which is produced by the disruptive effects of implanted enigmas, and which finds satisfaction in binding the sexual to mythosymbolic forms. I say this is less a matter of "inevitability" than of "going-astray" in order to emphasize the sense in which bound forms of the sexual are contingent formations (impermanent, however solidified or intractable); and may, for this reason, be subjected to a process of detranslation-retranslation, the aim of which is to open up the possibility of a renewed relation to the unconscious and its constitution by the enigmas of the other.

To say that responsibility is rooted in the anteriority of response is therefore to recognize a libidinal demand of the drive to "take care of" the timeless enigmas of the other—the unbound remainders of messages that return *après-coup*, in the afterwardness of an event, in order to be mastered for the very reason that they have escaped translation. Between the "answer for," which would be "responsibility," and the anteriority of the "answer to," which belongs to the category of "response," I therefore interpolate a third term. In the precise sense that the primal consists in the attempt to translate the other's message, this demand with regard to the *après-coup* of unbound enigmas is what I propose to call *primal responsibility: the taking care of the après-coup of timeless enigmas, the taking care of the return of the primal repressed.*[22]

The primal responsibility of the philosopher may thus be understood as the demand to take care of the *après-coup* of those timeless enigmas that constitute the enduring questions of philosophy. Fundamentally, this means reopening our relation to the primal enigmas of the other in order to make possible the detranslation of drives that have been subject to repression or translation, thereby rendering unconscious the unbound sexuality of those enigmatic messages that continue to attack us in their *étrangèreté*.

In this same spirit, Hobbes' answer for the Thirty Years War could be the subject of an intensive analysis in which the figure of the *Lupus* is understood as a pivotal step in the philosophic effort to master the *après-coup* of untranslated messages that were bound up with the religious antagonism between Christian churches that either do or do not give credence to the Pope. In this sense, the *Lupus* is the symbol of Hobbes' effort to bind the remainders of unbound sexuality that had erupted into a kind of proxy war through the ideological conflicts between Protestants and Catholics. Thus, the figure of the *Lupus* served to bind the untranslated residues of enigmatic messages—the disruptive *étrangèreté* that constitutes the compulsive force (or *Zwang*) of religious belief—to a mythic form that could be mastered, first in thought, then in practice, by the power of the sovereign. In effect, the unbound sexuality—that is, the animus—of religious violence could be tamed if it could first be rendered into something understandable in light of codes already made available by culture; in this case, the wild animality of the wolf, whose hallmark is traceable to the Roman dramatist Plautus (c. 254–184 BCE).[23] If human beings are, as it were, wolves to other humans, this "natural" propensity for violence could only be tamed by force. Leaving aside whether the wolf as such could ever be so controlled, Hobbes recommends the transfer of liberty to a sovereign who will control the animal within by fear.

As Rousseau knew all-too-well, however, Hobbes' political solution was founded upon the wrong metaphor. Through the work of detranslation-retranslation that guides the argument of the *Second Discourse*, Rousseau dismantled the Hobbesian artifice in order to assert a new myth—the conjectural history of the human species—for the purpose of unbinding the violent affects of *amour-propre* from the figure of nature in the wolf. Rousseau thus exemplifies the primal responsibility of the philosopher to open up the possibility for us to truly know ourselves according to the Delphic maxim, *gnōthi seauton*, but with the added determination of rebinding our sexuality (our *amour-propre*) to the figures of freedom, equality, natural goodness, and perfectibility discovered in the pure state of nature. In this way, Rousseau established the principles of happiness for human beings: the notion that human beings are free, perfectible, and therefore educable by nature. What follows is the dissolution of the myth that we are so innately dangerous that peace can only be achieved, not by reason or the general will, but by sovereign force. With Rousseau, at least, there is reason to hope.

III. RESPONSIBILITY OF THE PHILOSOPHER

I come now to the *use* of mythosymbolic thought in connection to the responsibility of the philosopher. If mythic constructions function to encode the residues of enigmatic messages that persist in attacking us in their *étrangèreté*, myth can also function to propose a scheme for a new translation, the aim of which is to satisfy our "love of order" by relieving the "intellectual uneasiness" or "existential anxiety" that is provoked by the unbound residues of the other's message. Along these lines, one could speak of both the *use* and *abuse* of myth, where the Hobbesian *Lupus* serves as an example of how the *abuse of mythic thought* in the discourse of philosophy results in leading the philosopher astray, away from the primal responsibility to take care of the *après-coup* of the timeless enigmas of philosophy itself. In the case of Rousseau, by contrast, the *use of mythic thought* is in the service of philosophy, as in his use of the conjectural history of the human species to confront the likes of Hobbes, Descartes, and Aristotle. In Hobbes, Rousseau confronts the *Lupus*, the natural basis of politics; in Descartes, the *cogito sum*, the foundation of philosophy; and in Aristotle, the genesis of wonder, the possibility of philosophy itself. In each of these examples, Rousseau's use of myth serves a dual purpose: to reopen our relation to the primal and, in doing so, to correct the errors that have led philosophers astray. It is thus an outcome of my thesis that, in the context of Rousseau, the philosophical and political ends of the responsibility of the philosopher converge in the use of myth to answer for the *après-coup* of the timeless enigmas of philosophy.

To expand this point, it is first necessary to comment on the derivation of the responsibility of the philosopher from the primal responsibility to take care of the *après-coup* of timeless enigmas. I start from the premise that the responsibility of the philosopher is rooted in the possibility of philosophy itself, which is to say, in the *après-coup* of enigmas implanted by the other—foremost, the enigma of the good. With its roots in the scene of primal seduction, the responsibility of the philosopher is therefore activated, at the level of ordinary quotidian experience, by the invocation of moral or ethical questioning, the height of which concerns the question of human happiness (one could say, the offer of a "hollow"), as it reinstates the drive to answer the enigma of the good.

It is precisely this traumatic character of the beginning of philosophy, rooted in the *après-coup* of the enigma of the good, that inaugurates the responsibility of the philosopher, the demand to answer for the question of human happiness. Stated with maximal concision, whereas the *responsibility* of the philosopher consists in "answering for" the transhistorical question of happiness, this responsibility derives from the *primal responsibility* to "take care of" the timeless enigma of the good. The alternative is to say that philosophy is without responsibility; that philosophy escapes responsibility; that philosophy is inherently *reckless* or *irresponsible*—or that it ought to be, which would amount to a kind of "cryptoresponsibility" of the philosopher.

Recall for a moment the position of Badiou, who has argued: "By definition, philosophy, when it truly appears, is either *reckless* or it is nothing."[24] This line is consistent with Badiou's regard for Nietzsche, whose teaching Deleuze called: "Irresponsibility—Nietzsche's most noble and beautiful secret."[25] At bottom, these notions celebrate the heroism of decision as a pure resolution of the will.

As for whether philosophy is somehow beyond responsibility, the positions of Nietzsche and Badiou differ only by differences of degree from Aristotle, who made possible the separation of philosophy from politics by scrubbing the enigma of the good from the genesis of philosophic wonder. Without accounting for the function of the good in turning the soul toward philosophy,

philosophy becomes a caricature of itself, beginning with the thesis that philosophy grows of its own accord out of a natural desire to know. This position anticipates the kind of irresponsibility that Hannah Arendt attributed to Heidegger when she wrote, on the occasion of his eightieth birthday, that Heidegger's engagement with National Socialism was not unlike the misstep of Thales, who was so engrossed in looking at the stars that he fell into a well.[26] To adopt terms familiar to Aristotle, what requires to be explained is not the definition of philosophy as *theōria* purged of *phronēsis*, that is, Aristotle's conception of the highest life; but rather the process by which *phronēsis* is purged from the definition of philosophy—and deeper still, the process by which the artifacts of philosophy become detached from philosophy itself.

There is much one could say about this, but here I want to focus on the responsibility of the philosopher—in terms borrowed from Laplanche—as the "guardian of the enigma" and "guarantor of the transference." As I have tried to show in the reading of Rousseau together with Laplanche, it is the offer of the hollow of a question concerning the meaning of happiness that serves to reinstate the relation of primal seduction in which the enigma of the good takes hold *après-coup* as an object of philosophic wonder. Insofar as "the art of turning souls" aims to reactivate the scene of primal seduction, it serves as the analogue to the offer of analysis, as it involves the deliberate attempt to invoke a rupture within the order of the psyche belonging to the potential philosopher. There is, accordingly, some measure of violence in the work of philosophical seduction. For the same reason Meletus claimed that Socrates was guilty of corrupting the youth and creating new gods, the seduction of the potential philosopher carries with it the risk of tremendous disruption to both the individual psyche and the structures it may share with the established order of society.

Insofar as the responsibility of the philosopher consists in questioning into happiness, the practitioner of the art of turning souls must therefore stake a wager that the primal responsibility for the possibility of philosophy, hence, the seduction of the potential philosopher into the practice of philosophy, will outweigh whatever risks are posed to the whole of human happiness—for the individual and society, to say nothing of the philosopher who may live under political conditions hostile to philosophy.[27] It is, after all, the enigmatic character of the good itself that explains Rousseau's decision to employ, in the *Second Discourse*, the *doctrine intérieur* in order to elide direct discussion of "the root" which anchors the genesis of philosophic wonder. For this same reason, Rousseau warned in the *First Discourse* with respect to the excesses of Enlightenment: "Scorned ignorance will be replaced by a dangerous Pyrrhonism."[28] There is nothing more dangerous to human happiness than Pyrrhonism about the good.

IV. THE PARADOX OF RESPONSIBILITY

These observations now put us in position to see how the enigma of the good engenders a paradox between the philosophical and political ends of the responsibility of the philosopher. On one hand, the political and philosophical responsibilities of the philosopher converge in the question of human happiness and in taking responsibility for this question. As we have seen, the question of happiness serves as the foundational question of philosophy, which in turn inspires a libidinal demand to answer for the best way to live. On the other hand, questioning into happiness leads to questioning about the good, which is inherently disruptive, if not destructive, of the mythosymbolic or ideological structures—broadly speaking, the plural *doxai*—that constitute the common basis of society and, hence, the "Ptolemization" or subjective ordering of the individual psyche. This puts the philosopher in the paradoxical position of having to take responsibility for the destructive effects of philosophic questioning, while at the same time preventing the excesses of philosophic doubt from taking hold in the manner of a "dangerous Pyrrhonism" concerning knowledge of the good.

Bear in mind that Rousseau perceived himself to be living under historical conditions dangerous to human happiness. The advancement of the scientific Enlightenment threatened to replace the love of virtue with sheer ambition in commerce and trade, just as the traditional sources of moral order were giving way to the Hobbesian doctrine of human life as a "restless desire for power after power, that ceaseth only in death."[29] As Leo Strauss once remarked about the related doctrine of John Locke, the life of laboring for pleasure after pleasure is a "joyless quest for joy."[30] Moreover, the overwhelming demand for scientific certainty, joined with the inherent instability of scientific progress, increasingly threatened to replace the moderate disposition of Socratic ignorance with the wayward fluctuations of uncertain knowledge.

There is thus a paradox of "Enlightenment" when the effort to replace opinion with scientific knowledge reverts to the untethered sway of opinion. Under such tenuous conditions for human happiness, Rousseau perceived the need for caution in taking responsibility for those who raise themselves toward philosophy, while at the same time offering an answer to the multitude about what is in the interest of their happiness. To formulate this as a principle: philosophy addresses itself equally to all, as a universal possibility of human experience; but because it recognizes that not all human beings will raise themselves to engagement in philosophy—indeed, because it recognizes that philosophy is dangerous—it is therefore the responsibility of the philosopher to persuade the multitude to love the image of their happiness. Rousseau's use of myth or fable is therefore in the service of the twofold responsibility of the philosopher: to seduce the potential philosopher into the practice of philosophy, while at the same time offering the multitude a desirable image of their happiness.

V. REVOLUTION AS SEDUCTION

If the responsibility of the philosopher consists in answering for happiness, this likewise means that philosophy is responsible for the creation of a desire—one should say the *drive*—for the genuine happiness of human beings. In a moment, I will characterize Rousseau's express depiction of the philosopher as the hero of happiness. But first, to take a singular example, Rousseau remarked about the Lawgiver of the *Social Contract:* "Anyone who dares to institute a people must feel capable of, so to speak, changing human nature."[31] To "change human nature" means, in effect, the creation of a desire for a certain kind of life; here, a uniquely collective life governed by the general will.

To anticipate a point that I shall comment on below, I note that there is no single definition of happiness in Rousseau. Instead, the promise of happiness tends to function as a kind of enigmatic signifier designed to lead the reader to inquire into happiness by taking as a guide Rousseau's investigation into various kinds of lives.[32] Among the most obvious examples, one could cite the Citizen in the *Social Contract*, the lives of rural virtue depicted in *Émile*, and the life in exile from society found in the *Reveries of the Solitary Walker*. Where the happiness of the Citizen is concerned, the demand of the Lawgiver to "change human nature" prompts the following incisive question. Rousseau asks:

> How will a blind multitude, which often does not know what it wills because it rarely knows what is good for it, carry out an undertaking as great, as difficult as a system of legislation? By itself the people always wills the good, but by itself it does not always see it. The general will is always right, but the judgment which guides it is not always enlightened. It must be made to see objects as they are, sometimes as they should appear to it.[33]

Once again it is possible to hear the teaching of Socrates. For just as sight cannot be put into blind eyes, the blind multitude requires enlightenment by a process of seduction. Likewise, insofar as sound judgment requires true knowledge and attunement to the good, democratic politics and so the public happiness depends upon the art of turning souls to educate the general will—that which is "always right," but "not always enlightened."

In making this distinction between what is "good" and what is "right," Rousseau treats these terms in a manner consistent with the enigmatic character of the good itself. As Rousseau argues in the *Second Discourse*, the force of "right" requires to be established on "other foundations," namely, the general will, which serves to supplement the two sources of natural right, *amour de soi* and *pitié*, two sentiments increasingly stifled upon our exit from pure nature.[34] If the task of the Lawgiver is to engender in the people a desire to live in accordance with the general will, the need to (so to speak) "change human nature" is undoubtedly the work of a Lawgiver-Sage, a master of the art of turning souls, much like the figure of Rousseau depicted by Chassonneris' *carte de la Révolution*. However mythical this figure may be—and Rousseau's *bona fides* are borne by history—it is along these lines that I now turn to the figure of the philosopher as *the hero of happiness*.

VI. THE HERO OF HAPPINESS

I have in mind a passage from the *Discourse on Heroic Virtue*, which Rousseau frankly called, in the *avertissement* to the reader, a "very bad" piece of writing.[35] I quote:

> The Philosophers do, I admit, claim to teach men the art of being happy and, as if they could expect to form nations of Wise Men (*nations de Sages*), they preach to Peoples a chimerical felicity which they themselves do not possess, and the idea and taste for which Peoples never acquire. Socrates saw and deplored the misfortunes of his fatherland; but it remained for Thrasybulus to end them; and Plato, after wasting his eloquence, his honor and his time at a Tyrant's court, was compelled to relinquish to another the glory of delivering Syracuse from the yoke of tyranny. The Philosopher may give the Universe some salutary instructions; but his lessons will not ever correct either the Great who despise them, or the People which does not understand them. This is not the way men are governed, by abstract views; they are only made happy by being constrained to be so, and they have to be made to experience happiness in order to be made to love it: this is the Hero's care and talents; often it is with force in hand that he puts himself in the position of receiving the Blessings of men whom he begins by compelling to bear the yoke of the laws so that he might eventually subject them to the authority of reason.[36]

Originally composed in the winter of 1750/1751, the manuscript of this *Discourse* remained unpublished until 1768, when it saw light in a defective edition that was corrected only posthumously in 1782. I suspect that Rousseau's discontent with this piece stems from a certain lack of control or attempted obfuscation in his terminological apparatus; in particular, his depiction of the Philosopher in contrast to the figures of the Wise Man (i.e., the Sage) and the Hero. I add as a preface to these remarks that the Sage, the Philosopher, and the Hero all belong together with the aforementioned list of figures through which Rousseau investigates the varieties of happiness that are suited to different kinds of lives. However incomplete, this list should also include the Lawgiver of the *Social Contract* and the Savoyard Vicar of *Émile*, in addition to the Human Being of Pure Nature who is distinguished from the primitive sociality of the so-called Savage of the Golden Age. As a detailed comment on the differences between these figures would cause a long digression, I restrict myself to saying that the various kinds of lives may be arranged along a spectrum. At one end is the solitary happiness and self-sufficiency that belongs to the Human Being of Pure Nature; at the opposite extreme is the analogue of the Solitary Walker. In the center is the fully corrupted *homme vulgaire*.

It is, however, not immediately clear that the Solitary Walker exemplifies the happiness of the philosophic life. In Rousseau's depiction, this figure finds his greatest satisfaction, not in taking responsibility for happiness, as does the Hero, but rather in a kind of postphilosophical enjoyment of the sentiment of existence—a sort of precursor to Heideggerian *Gelassenheit*, which seems mainly like a consolation for the personal suffering Rousseau endured as a consequence of his philosophic efforts to answer for the happiness of others.[37] In this respect, the Solitary Walker exemplifies the exit from philosophy, rather than its culmination or fulfillment. As Rousseau has the Solitary Walker admit: "I have sometimes thought rather deeply, but rarely with pleasure, almost always against my liking, and as though by force. Reverie relaxes and amuses me; reflection tires and saddens me; thinking always was a painful and charmless occupation for me."[38] I treat this here, not as a closure, but rather as an opening to the question of whether the philosophic life is itself a happy life. To anticipate the terms of a response: philosophy is by definition the love of wisdom, which is to say, the pursuit of wisdom; and as long as wisdom is lacking for the philosopher, the philosophic life can be only the pursuit of happiness; at best, the approximation of happiness, insofar as wisdom is required for happiness.[39]

As for the difficulties in Rousseau's distinction between the Hero, the Philosopher, and the Sage, it should be observed that the "care and talents" of the Hero are devoted to the happiness of the People. The Hero works to make the People experience happiness in order to make them love it, even if by force. Heroism is, accordingly, "free of all personal interest." It "has the felicity of others as its sole object, and their admiration as its sole reward."[40] However, Rousseau contradicts this statement almost immediately when he admits in a few more paragraphs that the desire for "personal glory" motivates the Hero's care for public happiness.[41] Opposite the Hero is then the Sage for whom "attending to his own felicity" is regarded as "the Sage's sole care."⁴² Yet just a few pages later, Rousseau contradicts himself again when he asks his audience of "illustrious Citizens" to judge "who deserves the palm of Heroism more, the Warriors who rushed to your defense, or the Sages who do everything for your happiness."⁴³ This confusion is then compounded by Rousseau's reference to the figure of the Sage as a fantasy produced by the Philosopher's desire to create "nations of Wise Men." Perhaps today it is still astonishing that, however benevolent, such wise solipsists could form any community at all. For Rousseau, at any rate, the joke is on the Philosopher who appears as the figure of a farce; as one who may care for the happiness of others, but inexpertly and clumsily. Rousseau adds: "The Philosopher may give the Universe some salutary instructions; but his lessons will not ever correct either the Great who despise them, or the People which does not understand them."⁴⁴ Finally, as if to multiply our difficulty, although I think the distinction is quite clear, Rousseau writes: "Nothing is as categorical as ignorance, and doubt is as rare among the People as assertion is among true Philosophers (*les vrais Philosophes*)."⁴⁵ Thus, we have Rousseau's distinction between the ambivalent motivations of the Hero, the farcical Philosopher, the alternatively solipsistic or benevolent ambitions of the Sage (an ambivalent image of the Philosopher's ego ideal), and the "true Philosopher" who knows when not to speak.

Now, knowing when not to speak is a function of Socratic ignorance, the prudential doubt that comes with knowing what one does not or cannot know. This is crucially important with respect to knowledge of the good, as the understanding of ignorance should inform how the true Philosopher answers for happiness at a given time and place. In this precise sense, ignorance is the font of prudence—what the ancient Greeks called *phronēsis*. However, it should be emphasized that because the good itself is enigmatic, it cannot tell us what to do. In Rousseau's terms, it functions rather as the call of conscience; in psychoanalytic terms, a libidinal demand organized around the desire of the other, which directs the philosopher by a power of compulsion toward the timeless problems of philosophic questioning, the primal source-objects of the philosophic drive.

As for knowing when not to speak, let us recall in this regard not only Rousseau's use of the *doctrine intérieur*, but also the aim of the *Second Discourse* "to disentangle what is original from what is artificial in man's present Nature, and to know accurately a state which no longer exists, which perhaps never did exist, which probably never will exist, and about which it is nevertheless necessary to have exact Notions *in order accurately to judge of our present state*."⁴⁶ In order to accurately judge our present state, it is necessary to confront our ignorance—and this requires the art of turning souls in order to restore our relation to the primal enigmas of philosophy. Knowing when not to speak is thus essential to the responsibility of the philosopher, insofar as this responsibility consists in a process of seduction; the aim of which consists in reinstating our relation to the enigma of the good for the purpose of rethinking the timeless human problems. It is, accordingly, the responsibility of the philosopher to offer the hollow of a question in order to restore the primal situation in which the problems of philosophy take hold.

Rousseau's "return to nature" is the prime example of his use of myth or fable to uphold the responsibility of the philosopher, the hero of happiness, who "can realize his own happiness only by working for that of others."[47] In this connection, Rousseau explicitly includes Socrates and Epictetus as examples of the true Philosopher who demonstrates heroic virtue, defined as the "strength of soul or fortitude [. . .] in being able always to act forcefully [. . .] with the firmness that *dispels illusions and overcomes the greatest obstacles*."[48] From this it follows that the true Philosopher expresses heroic virtue though the use of ignorance in the art of turning souls, that is, the work of philosophical seduction, which aims with fortitude at the dissolution of those "illusions" that present the "greatest obstacles" to human happiness. In fact, it seems Rousseau prepared this line of thought in the Preface to the *First Discourse*, where the glory of philosophy is found in answering for "those truths that affect the happiness of humankind." As Rousseau wrote in the spirit of the Hero: "I do not care whether I please Wits or the Fashionable. [. . .] One ought not to write for such Readers when one wants to live beyond one's century."[49]

This brings me to one last remark on the relation between philosophy and history. Insofar as philosophy itself participates in transhistorical questioning into the timeless human problems, the primal responsibility of the philosopher to reopen our relation to the primal can be appreciated according to the model, developed by Laplanche, of a spiral, configured as a helix, in which every progress forward is achieved through a motion of return, "by passing through, on the horizontal axis, the same enigmatic signifiers."[50] Within the history of philosophy, these "enigmatic signifiers" are themselves the timeless enigmas of philosophic questioning (Figure 5.1). The

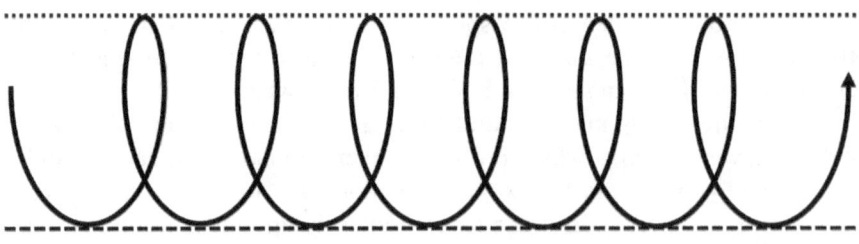

······ = Axis of the Transhistorical   --- = Axis of the Timeless   ▬▬ = Arrow of History

Figure 5.1   History of Philosophy.

recursive motion of the spiral thus exemplifies the *après-coup* of enigmatic messages, which are required to undergo the process of detranslation–retranslation, that is, the process of rethinking the timeless enigmas according to our contemporary time and place. For his part, Rousseau initiates this effort by constructing a return to the pure state of nature—the condition "before" seduction, which lays bare the interhuman process according to which the primal enigma of the good, hence, the idea of moral or political inequality, enters into human life as a message from the other. Having thus implanted the enigma of his message, it is then for us to raise ourselves to the practice of philosophy.

NOTES

1. Laplanche, "Responsibility and Response," ESIH 165/BSIM 138.
2. Laplanche, "Responsibility and Response," ESIH 163, 164–65/BSIM 136, 137.
3. Laplanche, SEX 6/2.
4. See Freud, *Civilization and Its Discontents*, GW 14:433–34, 437/SE 21:76, 78.
5. Laplanche, "Goals of the Psychoanalytic Process," ESIH 231/BSIM 193.
6. Laplanche, "Responsibility and Response," ESIH 163, 162–63/BSIM 135–36. This book is significant for its role in introducing Husserl to Francophone audiences.
7. Laplanche, "Responsibility and Response," ESIH 163/BISM 135. The reference to Lévinas appears obligatory given wide recognition of his doctrine of "responsibility for the other." For an insightful foray into the implications of Laplanche for Lévinasian ethical theory, see Butler (2005). For a development of coordinate themes in ethical theory and psychoanalytic practice, see Chetrit-Vatine (2012). The arguments I have presented here are likewise likely to provoke associations to Lévinas's "ethics as first philosophy." However, an explanation of my differences would require a separate monograph.
8. Laplanche, "Responsibility and Response," ESIH 162/BISM 135.
9. Laplanche, "Responsibility and Response," ESIH 161–62/BSIM 135.
10. Lévi-Strauss (1955), 476/389. Cf. Lévi-Strauss (1973), 45/33: "the founder of the human sciences."
11. First presented at the January 23, 1996 meeting of the Association psychanalytique de France.
12. Lévi-Strauss (1962), 17. Quoted in Laplanche, "Psychoanalysis: Myths and Theory," ESIH 287/BSIM 239.
13. Laplanche, "Psychoanalysis: Myths and Theory," ESIH 287/BSIM 239. See also "Psychoanalysis as Anti-Hermeneutics," ESIH 260/BSIM 217; "Biologism and Biology," P-VII 138/124.
14. Laplanche, ESIH 287/BSIM 239.
15. Laplanche, ESIH 288/BSIM 240.
16. Laplanche, ESIH 290/BSIM 241.
17. Laplanche, "Biologism and Biology," P-VII 138/124.

18. See Laplanche, "Biologism and Biology," P-VII 138–39/124–25; "The So-called Death Drive: A Sexual Drive," ESIH 212–15/BSIM 177–80; "Responsibility and Response," ESIH 166–69/BSIM 139–41.

19. Laplanche, "The So-called Death Drive: A Sexual Drive," ESIH 215/BSIM 179.

20. Laplanche, "Responsibility and Response," ESIH 167/BSIM 139.

21. Laplanche, "The So-called Death Drive: A Sexual Drive," ESIH 214/BSIM 178.

22. I derive this point from Laplanche's observation that images of political violence operate, at the level of the unconscious, on a spectrum with images in literature devoted to sadomasochism. In this connection, he indicates a "demand to treat, or *take care of*, the same unconscious drives in ourselves—even to silence them" (Mehlman's emphasis). By extending this insight to the notion of *primal responsibility*, I am going beyond Laplanche who, in the very next sentence, writes: "I have not presented a theory of responsibility [. . .]" (ESIH 171/BSIM 143).

23. Plautus, *Asinaria*, 495.

24. Badiou, SM 69/71.

25. Deleuze (1962), 25/21.

26. Arendt (1971) 1978, 301–3.

27. As this line of thought ventures further into philosophical esotericism and the art of exoteric writing, I shall simply cite a remark by Leo Strauss, which points to how the need of philosophy gains legitimacy under conditions of tyranny. As Strauss wrote in a footnote to his study of Xenophon's *Hiero:* "If the social fabric is in order, if the regime is legitimate according to the generally accepted standards of legitimacy, the need for, and perhaps even the legitimacy of, philosophy is less evident than in the opposite case" ([1948] 2000, 121 n. 50). In this connection, Strauss also writes: "The correction of tyranny consists in nothing else than the transformation of the unjust or vicious tyrant who is more or less unhappy into a virtuous tyrant who is happy" ([1948] 2000, 69). These lines point more or less directly to Strauss's own treatment of the responsibility of the philosopher as responsibility for happiness.

28. Rousseau, OC 3:9/FD 8.

29. Hobbes, "Of the difference of Manners," L 70.

30. Strauss, NRH 251.

31. Rousseau, OC 3:381/SC 69.

32. Jonathan Lear has convincingly argued that Aristotle employs the question of happiness, the highest good, to seduce his audience into contemplating the organization of one's life "taken as a whole" (2000, 22).

33. Rousseau, OC 3:381/SC 69.

34. Rousseau, OC 3:125–126/SD 127.

35. Rousseau, OC 2:1262/DHV 305.

36. Rousseau, OC 2:1263–1264/DHV 306.

37. Recall Rousseau's motto, *vitam impendere vero*, as well as his comment to Bordes on the dire rhetoric of the *First Discourse:* "I spared not myself, but the truth, in order to have it get through more readily and to make it more useful" (OC 3:106/Bordes 110).

38. Rousseau, OC 1:1061–1062/R 7:58.

39. For Rousseau, much turns on whether or in what respect *rêverie* is identified with philosophical activity, in contrast to reflection (*réflexion*), thinking (*penser*), and meditation (*méditation*). The cited passage continues: "Sometimes my reveries end in meditation, but more often my meditations end in reverie; and during these wanderings, my soul rambles and glides through the universe on the wings of imagination, in ecstasies which surpass every other enjoyment" (OC 1:1062/R 58). In the Second Walk, the narrator also speaks of "my solitary walks and of the reveries that fill them when I leave my head entirely free and let my ideas follow their bent without resistance and without constraint" (OC 1:1002/R 9). It is remarkable how clearly these lines resonate with the fundamental rule of free association in psychoanalysis.

In this spirit, it is also tempting to connect the notion of reverie-sans-constraint to Badiou's Nietzschean inflection that "philosophy, when it truly appears, is either *reckless* or it is nothing." Let us therefore note that, for the Solitary Walker, the "enjoyment" (*jouissance*) he finds in the sentiment of existence bears all the hallmarks of the "oceanic feeling," described by Freud in *Civilization and Its Discontents*, as "a sensation of 'eternity,' a feeling of something limitless, unbounded," which serves as "the source of religious energy," but which traces the "feeling of an indissoluble bond, of being one with the external world as a whole," back to the undifferentiated state of the infantile psyche (GW 14:421–45/SE 21:64–68). For the Solitary Walker, the sentiment of existence is likewise described as a state of the soul "in which time is nothing for it; in which the present lasts forever without, however, making its duration noticed and without any trace of time's passage" (OC 1:1046/R 46). Is this not the expression of a wish to return to the condition of pure nature; the condition "anterior" to that of primal seduction? Or does it rather describe a stage in the philosophical ascent to transhistorical questioning, rooted in the timelessness of primal enigmas?

Permit me one further quotation. The Solitary Walker asks: "What do we enjoy in such a situation? Nothing external to ourselves, nothing if not ourselves and our own existence. As long as this state lasts, we are sufficient unto ourselves, like God" (OC 1:1047/R 46). This is exactly the form of happiness the Solitary Walker describes as the enjoyment of *far niente*, of "doing nothing" (OC 1:1042/R 42); and it may well be that this is the end toward which Rousseau points in his reversal of Descartes. However, it behooves the reader to consider in this connection the Savoyard Vicar's rejection of the "Ptolemaic" ordering of the human soul, that is, the moral order in which the individual "makes himself the center of all things," that is, "like God." In the enjoyment of *far niente*, we are, I think, very far from the Socratic notion of a philosophical ascent that aims at "friendship with the gods" (Plato, *Symposium*, 212a). For a highly nuanced, but rather opposite reading, see Meier (2016), esp. Chapter 4: *Beisichselbstsein*, 104–5, 116–18, 120.

40. Rousseau, OC 2:1264/DHV 306–7.
41. Rousseau, OC 2:1264/DHV 307.
42. Rousseau, OC 2:1263/DHV 306.
43. Rousseau, OC 2:1269/DHV 311.
44. Rousseau, OC 2:1263/DHV 306.
45. Rousseau, OC 2:1265/DHV 308.

46. Rousseau, OC 3:123/SD 125 (my emphasis).
47. Rousseau, OC 2:1273/DHV 316.
48. Rousseau, OC 2:1273/DHV 315. "Of what use is justice with tyrants, prudence with the insane, temperance in misery? But all events honor a man of strength or fortitude, happiness and adversity contribute equally to his glory, and he rules no less in chains than on the Throne. Regulus's martyrdom in Carthage, Cato's feast upon being denied the Consulship, Epictetus's equanimity upon being crippled by his master, are no less illustrious than the triumphs of Alexander and of Caesar; and if Socrates had died in his bed, one might now wonder whether he was anything more than a skillful Sophist" (OC 2:1274/DHV 316).
49. Rousseau, OC 3:3/SD 4.
50. Laplanche, "Transference: Its Provocation by the Analyst," RCI 435/EO 231.

Abbreviations and Works Cited

References to works in translation are first to the original language edition, followed by the English translation when available. These translations are occasionally modified.

ADORNO

AP "Die Aktualität der Philosophie" (1931). In GS 1. / "The Actuality of Philosophy." *Telos* 31 (1977): 120–33.
AT *Ästhetische Theorie* (1970). In GS 7. / *Aesthetic Theory*. Translated by Robert Hullot-Kentor. Edited by Gretel Adorno and Rolf Tiedemann. New York: Continuum, 2002.
DA *Dialektik der Aufklärung: Philosophische Fragmente* (with Max Horkheimer). Frankfurt am Main: Fischer Taschenbuch Verlag, (1944/47) 1988. / *Dialectic of Enlightenment: Philosophical Fragments*. Translated by John Cumming. New York: Continuum, 1999.
DTP "Diskussion über Theorie und Praxis" (with Max Horkheimer, 1956). In Horkheimer, Max. *Gesammelte Schriften, vol. 13: Nachgelassene Schriften 1949–1972*, edited by Alfred Schmidt and Gunzelin Schmid Noerr, 32–72. Frankfurt am Main: S. Fischer, 1985–96. / *Towards a New Manifesto*. Translated by Rodney Livingstone. New York: Verso, 2011.
GS *Gesammelte Schriften*. 20 vols. Frankfurt am Main: Suhrkamp, 1970–86.
MM *Minima Moralia: Reflexionen aus dem beschädigten Leben* (1951). In GS 4. / *Minima Moralia: Reflections on a Damaged Life*. Translated by E. F. N. Jephcott. New York: Verso, 2005.
ND *Negative Dialektik* (1966). In GS 6. / *Negative Dialectics*. Translated by E. B. Ashton. New York: Continuum, 1973.

BACON

AL *The Advancement of Learning* (1605). In BW 3.
BW *The Works of Francis Bacon.* 14 vols. Edited by James Spedding, Robert Leslie Ellis, and Douglas Denon Heath. London: Longman, 1858–74.
NO *The New Organon* (1620). Edited by Lisa Jardine and Michael Silverthorne. New York: Cambridge University Press, 2000.

BADIOU

AFP *The Adventure of French Philosophy.* Translated and edited by Bruno Bosteels. Brooklyn, NY: Verso, 2012.
AM *Abrégé de métapolitique.* Paris: Seuil, 1998. / *Metapolitics.* Translated by Jason Barker. New York: Verso, 2005.
BI "A Short Chat with Alain Badiou." Interview by Genoa Mungin with Jesse Allen Sawyer. *InDigest.* Accessed online, March 10, 2014.
CD *Casser en deux l'histoire du monde?* Paris: Les Conférences du Perroquet, 1992.
CON *Conditions*, Paris: Editions du Seuil, 1992. / *Conditions.* Translated by Steven Corcoran. New York: Continuum, 2008.
CSC "Comments on Simon Critchley's *Infinitely Demanding*" (with Simon Critchley). *Symposium: Canadian Journal of Continental Philosophy/ Revue canadienne de philosophie continentale* 12, 2 (2008): 9–17.
CT *Court traité d'ontologie transitoire.* Paris: Seuil, 1998. / *Briefings on Existence: A Short Treatise on Transitory Ontology.* Translated and edited by Norman Madarasz. Albany, NY: SUNY Press, 2006. Citations to CT refer to this volume, unless otherwise noted.
EE *L'être et l'événement.* Paris: Seuil, 1988. / *Being and Event.* Translated by Oliver Feltham. New York: Continuum, 2005.
ETH *L'éthique: essai sur la conscience du mal* (1993). Caen: Nous, 2003. / *Ethics: An Essay on the Understanding of Evil.* Translated by Peter Hallward. New York: Verso, 2001.
IT *Infinite Thought: Truth and the Return to Philosophy.* Translated and edited by Oliver Feltham and Justin Clemens. New York: Continuum, 2005.
LM *Logiques des mondes: l'être et l'événement, 2.* Paris: Editions du Seuil, 2006. / *Logics of Worlds: Being and Event, 2.* Translated by Alberto Toscano. New York: Continuum, 2009.
MP *Manifeste pour la philosophie.* Paris: Seuil, 1989. / *Manifesto for Philosophy: Followed by Two Essays: "The (Re)turn of Philosophy Itself" and*

"Definition of Philosophy." Translated and edited by Norman Madarasz. Albany, NY: SUNY Press, 1999.
PE *Philosophy and the Event* (with Fabien Tarby). Translated by Louise Burchill. Cambridge: Polity Press, 2013.
PIP *Philosophy in the Present* (with Slavoj Žižek). Translated by Peter Thomas and Alberto Toscano. Edited by Peter Engelmann. Malden, MA: Polity, 2009.
REPP *La relation énigmatique entre philosophie et politique*. Meaux: Germina, 2011. / *Philosophy for Militants*. Translated by Bruno Bosteels. New York: Verso, 2012.
RP *La république de Platon: dialogue en un prologue, seize chapitres et un épilogue*. Paris: Fayard, 2012. / *Plato's Republic: A Dialogue in Sixteen Chapters, with a Prologue and an Epilogue*. Translated by Susan Spitzer. Malden, MA: Polity, 2012.
SM *Second manifeste pour la philosophie* (2009). Paris: Flammarion, 2010. / *Second Manifesto for Philosophy*. Translated by Louise Burchill. Malden, MA: Polity, 2011.
TW *Theoretical Writings*. Translated and edited by Ray Brassier and Alberto Toscano. New York: Continuum, 2004.
WN "Who is Nietzsche?" *Pli* 11 (2001): 1–11.

DESCARTES

A-T *Oeuvres de Descartes*. 9 vols. Edited by Charles Adam and Paul Tannery. Paris: J. Vrin, 1964–74. All citations to Descartes are from AT. English translations reference *The Philosophical Writings of Descartes*. 3 vols. Translated by John Cottingham, Robert Stoothoff, Dugald Murdoch. New York: Cambridge University Press, 1984–91.

DIDEROT AND D'ALEMBERT

DP *Discours préliminaire des éditeurs* (by Jean le Rond d'Alembert, 1751). In ENC 1. / *Preliminary Discourse to the Encyclopedia of Diderot*. Translated by Richard N. Schwab with Walter E. Rex. Chicago: University of Chicago Press, 1995.
ENC *Encyclopédie, ou dictionnaire raisonné des sciences, des arts et des métiers, etc.* (1751–72), 17 vols. Edited by Denis Diderot and Jean le Rond d'Alembert. University of Chicago: ARTFL Encyclopédie Project, 2017. Edited by Robert Morrissey and Glenn Roe. Retrieved from encyclopedie.uchicago.edu.

FREUD

BWF *Briefe an Wilhelm Fliess, 1887–1904*. Edited by Jeffrey Moussaieff Masson. Frankfurt am Main: S. Fischer, 1986. / *The Complete Letters of Sigmund Freud to Wilhelm Fliess, 1887–1904*. Translated and edited by Jeffrey Moussaieff Masson. Cambridge, MA: Belknap Press of Harvard University Press, 1985.

GW *Gesammelte Werke*. Edited by Anna Freud with Marie Bonaparte, et al. 17 vols. London: Imago, 1940–52; vol. 18 and *Nachtragsband*, Frankfurt am Main: S. Fischer Verlag, 1987. Citations to the *Nachtragsband* are identified as GW N:[page].

SE *The Standard Edition of the Complete Psychological Works of Sigmund Freud*. Translated and edited by James Strachey. London: The Hogarth Press, 1953–74.

HEGEL

E-I *Enzyklopadie der philosophischen Wissenschaften im Grundrisse* (1817). In W 8. / *Encyclopedia of the Philosophical Sciences in Basic Outline, Part I: Science of Logic*. Translated by Klaus Brinkmann and Daniel O. Dahlstrom. New York: Cambridge University Press, 2010. Citations are to section numbers common in both editions.

PhG *Phänomenologie des Geistes* (1807). In W 3. / *Phenomenology of Spirit*. Translated by A. V. Miller. New York: Oxford University Press, 1977.

PR *Grundlinien der Philosophie des Rechts* (1820). In W 7. / *Elements of the Philosophy of Right*. Translated by H.B. Nisbet. Edited by Allen W. Wood. New York: Cambridge University Press, 1991.

VPW *Vorlesungen über die Philosophie der Weltgeschichte: Berlin 1822/1823*. Edited by Karl-Heinz Ilting, Hoo Nam Seelmann, and Karl Brehmer. Hamburg: F. Meiner Verlag, 1996. / *Lectures on the Philosophy of World History, Volume 1: Manuscripts of the Introduction and the Lectures of 1822–1823*. Translated and edited by Robert F. Brown and Peter C. Hodgson. New York: Oxford University Press, 2011.

W *Werke*. 20 vols. Edited by Eva Moldenhauer and Karl Markus Michel. Frankfurt: Suhrkamp Verlag, 1969–.

HEIDEGGER

B *Besinnung* (1938–39). In GA 66. / *Mindfulness*. Translated by Parvis Emad and Thomas Kalary. New York: Continuum, 2006. Citations follow the pagination in GA.

BdZ *Der Begriff der Zeit* (1924). In GA 64. / *The Concept of Time*. Translated by Ingo Farin with Alex Skinner. New York: Continuum, 2011. Citations follow the pagination in GA.
BzP *Beiträge zur Philosophie (Vom Ereignis)* (1936–38). In GA 65. / *Contributions to Philosophy (Of the Event)*. Translated by Richard Rojcewicz and Daniela Vallega-Neu. Bloomington: Indiana University Press, 2012.
EM *Einführung in die Metaphysik* (1935). In GA 40. / *Introduction to Metaphysics*. Translated by Gregory Fried and Richard Polt. New Haven: Yale University Press, 2000. Citations follow the marginal pagination in GA.
EoP *The End of Philosophy*. Translated by Joan Stambaugh. New York: Harper & Row, 1973.
FT "Die Frage nach der Technik" (1954). In GA 7. / *The Question Concerning Technology and Other Essays*. Translated by William Lovitt. New York: Harper & Row, 1977.
GA *Gesamtausgabe*. Frankfurt am Main: V. Klostermann, 1975–.
GaP *Grundbegriffe der aristotelischen Philosophie* (1924). In GA 18. / *Basic Concepts of Aristotelian Philosophy*. Translated by Robert D. Metcalf and Mark B. Tanzer. Bloomington: Indiana University Press, 2009.
GdP *Die Grundprobleme der Phänomenologie* (1927). In GA 24. / *The Basic Problems of Phenomenology*. Translated by Albert Hofstadter. Bloomington: Indiana University Press, 1982.
N *Nietzsche*. 2 vols. (1936–46). In GA 6.1–2.
ON *Ontologie (Hermeneutik der Faktizität)* (1923). In GA 63. / *Ontology—The Hermeneutics of Facticity*. Translated by John van Buren. Bloomington: Indianan University Press, 1999.
PATH *Pathmarks*. Edited by William McNeill. Cambridge: Cambridge University Press, 1998.
S-G "Nur noch ein Gott kann uns retten: *Spiegel*-Gespräch mit Martin Heidegger am 23 September 1966." *Der Spiegel* 30 (Mai, 1976): 193–219. / "Only a God Can Save Us Now: An Interview with Martin Heidegger." *Graduate Faculty Philosophy Journal* 6, 1 (Winter 1977): 5–27.
SZ *Sein und Zeit*. Elfte, unveränderte Auflage. Tübingen: Niemeyer, (1927) 1967. / *Being and Time*. Translated by John Macquarrie and Edward Robinson. New York: Harper and Row, 1962.
U-XII-XV *Überlegungen XII–XV (Schwarze Hefte 1939–1941)*. In GA 96. / *Ponderings XII–XV: Black Notebooks 1939–1941*. Translated by Richard Rojcewicz. Bloomington: Indiana University Press, 2017.

HOBBES

DC *On the Citizen [De Cive]* (1642). Translated and edited by Richard Tuck and Michael Silverthorne. New York: Cambridge University Press, 1998.

EL *De Corpore Politico, or The Elements of Law* (1650). In HW 4.
HW *The English Works of Thomas Hobbes of Malmesbury.* Edited by Sir William Molesworth. 11 vols. London: John Bohn, 1839–45.
L *Leviathan* (1651). Edited by Richard Tuck. New York: Cambridge University Press, 1996.
T Thucydides. *History of the Grecian War, vol. 1* (1629). In HW 8.

KANT

AA *Gesammelte Schriften.* Berlin: Preussische Akademie der Wissenschaften, 1910–.
GMS *Grundlegung zur Metaphysik der Sitten* (1785). In AA 4. / *Grounding for the Metaphysics of Morals*, 3rd ed. Translated by James W. Ellington. Indianapolis: Hackett, 1993.
KrV *Kritik der reinen Vernunft* (1781). Edited by Jens Timmermann. Hamburg: Felix Meiner Verlag, 1998. / *Critique of Pure Reason* [*First Critique*]. Translated and edited by Paul Guyer and Allen W. Wood. New York: Cambridge University Press, 1998.

LAPLANCHE

BSIM *Between Seduction and Inspiration: Man.* Translated by Jeffrey Mehlman. New York: The Unconscious in Translation, 2015.
EO *Essays on Otherness.* Edited by John Fletcher. New York: Routledge, 1999. This volume contains essays which are either published or forthcoming in English translations of Laplanche's complete works from The Unconscious in Translation.
ESIH *Entre séduction et inspiration: l'homme.* Paris: PUF, 1999.
NFP *Nouveaux fondements pour la psychanalyse: la séduction originaire.* Paris: PUF, 1987. / *New Foundations for Psychoanalysis.* Translated by David Macey. Cambridge, MA: Basil Blackwell, 1989. This volume is also available in English translation by Jonathan House (New York: The Unconscious in Translation, 2016).
P-III *Problématiques III: La sublimation.* Paris: PUF, 1980.
P-VI *Problématiques VI: L'après-coup.* Paris: PUF, 2006. / *Après-coup.* Translated by Jonathan House and Luke Thurston. New York: The Unconscious in Translation, 2017.
P-VII *Problématiques VII: Le fourvoiement biologisant de la sexualité chez Freud, suivi de Biologisme et biologie.* Paris: PUF, 2006. / *The Temptation of Biology: Freud's Theories of Sexuality.* Translated by Donald Nicholson-Smith. New York: The Unconscious in Translation, 2015.

RCI *La révolution copernicienne inachevée: travaux 1967–1992* (1992). Paris: PUF, 2008.
SEX *Sexual: la sexualité élargie au sens freudien: 2000–2006*. Paris: PUF, 2007. / *Freud and the Sexual: Essays 2000–2006*. Translated by John Fletcher, Jonathan House, and Nicholas Ray. Edited by John Fletcher. [U.S.]: International Psychoanalytic Books, 2011.
STD *Jean Laplanche: Seduction, Translation, Drives*. Translated by Martin Stanton. Edited by John Fletcher and Martin Stanton. London: Institute of Contemporary Arts, 1992.
VM *Vie et mort en psychanalyse*. Paris: Flammarion, 1970. / *Life and Death in Psychoanalysis*. Translated by Jeffrey Mehlman. Baltimore: The Johns Hopkins University Press, 1976.

MACHIAVELLI

DL *Discourses on Livy* (1531). Translated by Harvey C. Mansfield and Nathan Tarcov. Chicago: University of Chicago Press, 1996.
P *The Prince* (1532), 2nd ed. Translated by Harvey C. Mansfield. Chicago: University of Chicago Press, 1998.

NIETZSCHE

BGE *Jenseits von Gut und Böse* (1886). In KSA 4. / *Beyond Good and Evil: Prelude to a Philosophy of the Future*. Translated by Walter Kaufmann. New York: Vintage Books, 1966. Citations refer to section numbers in KSA.
eKGWB *Digitale Kritische Gesamtausgabe Werke und Briefe*. Based on KSA. Edited by Paolo D'Iorio. Retrieved from www.nietzschesource.org. Citations to Nietzsche's letters are formatted as eKGWB/BVN-[year], [letter number].
FW *Die fröhliche Wissenschaft* (1882). In KSA 3. / *The Gay Science: With a Prelude in Rhymes and an Appendix of Songs*. Translated by Walter Kaufmann. New York: Vintage Books, 1974.
KSA *Kritische Studienausgabe*. 15 vols. Edited by Giorgio Colli and Mazzino Montinari. Berlin: Walter de Gruyter, 1967–.
NF *Nachgelassene Fragmente: 1885–1887*. In KSA 12. Citations refer to page numbers.
WP *The Will to Power*. Translated by Walter Kaufmann and R.J. Hollingdale. New York: Vintage Books, 1967. Citations refer to section numbers.

Z   *Thus Spoke Zarathustra: A Book for None and All*. Translated by Walter Kaufmann. New York: Penguin Books, 1966.

ROUSSEAU

Bordes   "Preface of a Second Letter to Bordes" (1753). In VGa.
C   *The Confessions* (1782–89). In CW 5.
CW   *The Collected Writings of Rousseau*. 12 vols. Translated and edited by Christopher Kelly and Roger Masters, et al. Hanover, NH: University Press of New England, 1990–2010.
D   *Rousseau, Judge of Jean-Jacques: Dialogues* (1782). In CW 1.
DHV   *Discourse on this Question: "What is the Virtue a Hero Most Needs and Who are the Heroes who have Lacked this Virtue?"* [*Discourse on Heroic Virtue*] (1750–51). In VGa.
E   *Émile, or On Education* (1762). Translated by Allan Bloom. New York: Basic Books, 1979.
EOL   *Essay on the Origin of Languages* (1781). In VGa.
FD   *Discourse on the Arts and Sciences* [*First Discourse*] (1750). In VGa.
FICT   "Fiction or Allegorical Fragment on Revelation" (n.d.). In CW 12.
LNR   *Letter by Jean-Jacques Rousseau of Geneva about a New Refutation of his Discourse by a Member of the Academy of Dijon* [*Letter about a New Refutation*] (1752). In VGa.
LR   *Last Reply by J.-J. Rousseau of Geneva* (1751). In VGa.
LtB   *Letter to Christophe de Beaumont* (1762). In CW 9.
LtdA   *Letter to M. d'Alembert on the Theatre* (1758). In *Politics and the Arts*. Translated by Allan Bloom. Ithaca, NY: Cornell University Press, 1960.
LtP   *Letter to Philopolis* (c. 1755). In VGa.
LtV   *Letter to M. de Voltaire* (1756). In VGa.
ML   *Moral Letters* (1757–58). In CW 12.
OBS   *Observations by Jean-Jacques Rousseau of Geneva On the Reply Made to his Discourse* (1751). In VGa.
OC   *Oeuvres complètes*. 5 vols. Edited by Bernard Gagnebin and Marcel Raymond. Paris: Gallimard, Bibliothèque de la Pléiade, 1953–1995.
OMdW   "The Orchard of Madame de Warens" (1739). In CW 12.
PN   *Preface to "Narcissus"* (1752–53). In VGa.
R   *The Reveries of the Solitary Walker* (1782). In CW 8.
SC   *Of the Social Contract* (1762). In VGb.
SD   *Discourse on the Origin and Foundations of Inequality among Men* [*Second Discourse*] (1755). In VGa.

VGa *The Discourses and Other Early Political Writings.* Translated and edited by Victor Gourevitch. Cambridge: Cambridge University Press, 1997.

VGb *The Social Contract and Other Later Political Writings.* Translated and edited by Victor Gourevitch. Cambridge: Cambridge University Press, 1997.

WITTGENSTEIN

BT *The Big Typescript, TS 213* (1933–37). German with English translation by C. Grant Luckhardt and Maximilian A. E. Aue. Malden, MA: Blackwell, 2005.

CV *Culture and Value: A Selection from the Posthumous Remains* (1977). Edited by Georg Henrik von Wright with Heikki Nyman. Revised edition by Alois Pichler. German with English translation by Peter Winch. Cambridge, MA: Blackwell, 1998.

LoE "A Lecture on Ethics." *The Philosophical Review,* 74, 1 (1965): 3–12.

NB *Notebooks, 1914–1916.* Edited by G. H. von Wright and G. E. M. Anscombe. German with English translation by G. E. M. Anscombe. New York: Harper and Rowe, 1961.

PI *Philosophical Investigations* (1953), 4th ed. German with English translation by G. E. M. Anscombe, et al. Malden, MA: Wiley-Blackwell, 2009.

TLP *Tractatus Logico-Philosophicus* (1921). German with English translation by D. F. Pears and B. F. McGuinness. New York: Routledge & Kegan Paul, 1963.

OTHER WORKS CITED

Arendt, Hannah. (1971) 1978. "Martin Heidegger at Eighty." In *Heidegger and Modern Philosophy: Critical Essays*, edited by Michael Murray, 293–303. New Haven: Yale University Press.

Aristotle. 1926–. *Works.* Cambridge, MA: Harvard University Press.

Aubenque, Pierre. 2008. "The Science without a Name." Translated by Anna Strelis. *Graduate Faculty Philosophy Journal* 29 (2): 5–50.

Barzun, Jacques. 2000. *From Dawn to Decadence: 500 Years of Western Cultural Life, 1500 to the Present.* New York: HarperCollins.

Brandwood, Leonard. 1976. *A Word Index to Plato.* Leeds: W. S. Maney & Son.

Burke, Edmund. (1759) 1963. "A Letter from M. Rousseau of Geneva, to M. d'Alembert, of Paris, Concerning the Effects of Theatrical Entertainments on the

Manners of Mankind." In *Edmund Burke: Selected Writings and Speeches*, edited by Peter J. Stanlis, 89. Garden City, NY: Anchor Books.

Butler, Judith. 2005. *Giving an Account of Oneself*. New York: Fordham University Press.

Cassirer, Ernst. 1951. *The Philosophy of the Enlightenment*. Translated by Fritz C. A. Koelln and James P. Pettegrove. Princeton, NJ: Princeton University Press.

Castoriadis, Cornelius. (1988) 1991. "The 'End of Philosophy'?" In *Philosophy, Politics, Autonomy: Essays in Political Philosophy*. Edited by David Ames Curtis. New York: Oxford University Press.

Chetrit-Vatine, Viviane. 2012. *La séduction éthique de la situation analytique*. Paris: PUF. / 2014. *The Ethical Seduction of the Analytic Situation: The Feminine-Maternal Origins of Responsibility for the Other*. Translated by Andrew Weller. London: Karnac.

Condillac, Etienne Bonnot de. (1746) 1973. *Essai sur l'origine des connaissances humaines, précédé de L'archéologie du frivole, par Jacques Derrida*. Paris: Galilée. / 2001. *Essay on the Origin of Human Knowledge*. Translated and edited by Hans Aarsleff. New York: Cambridge University Press.

Cooper, Laurence D. 2008. *Eros in Plato, Rousseau, and Nietzsche: The Politics of Infinity*. University Park, PA: Pennsylvania State University Press.

Critchley, Simon. 2000. "Demanding Approval: On the Ethics of Alain Badiou." *Radical Philosophy* 100: 16–27.

———. 2007. *Infinitely Demanding: Ethics of Commitment, Politics of Resistance*. New York: Verso.

Crowell, Steven. 2008. "Meaning-taking: Meaning and Normativity in Heidegger's Philosophy." *Continental Philosophy Review* 41 (3): 261–76.

Dahlstrom, Daniel O. 2011. "Thinking of Nothing: Heidegger's Criticism of Hegel's Conception of Negativity." In *A Companion to Hegel*, edited by Stephen Houlgate and Michael Baur, 519–36. Malden, MA: Blackwell Publishing.

Deleuze, Gilles. 1962. *Nietzsche et la philosophie*. Paris: PUF. / 1983. *Nietzsche and Philosophy*. Translated by Hugh Tomlinson. New York: Columbia University Press.

Dent, N. J. H. 1988. *Rousseau: An Introduction to His Psychological, Social, and Political Theory*. New York: Basil Blackwell.

Driscoll, J. T. 1911. "Miracle." In *The Catholic Encyclopedia*. New York: Robert Appleton Company. Retrieved from www.newadvent.org/cathen/10338a.htm.

Epictetus. 1928. *The Encheiridion*. In *The Discourses as Reported by Arrian, The Manual, and Fragments, vol. 2*. Translated by W.A. Oldfather. Cambridge, MA: Harvard University Press.

Fain, Lucas. 2011. "Heidegger's Cartesian Nihilism." *The Review of Metaphysics*, 64 (3): 555–79.

———. 2015. "The Solonian Legacy in Socrates." *Helios*, 42 (1): 209–43.

———. 2018. "Philosophy and the Problem of Beauty in Heidegger's Translation of 'Justice.'" *Graduate Faculty Philosophy Journal* 39 (1): 39–75.

Force, Pierre. 2003. *Self-Interest before Adam Smith: A Genealogy of Economic Science*. New York: Cambridge University Press.

Fuchs, Hans-Jürgen. 1977. *Entfremdung und Narzißmus. Semantische Untersuchungen zur Geschichte der Selbstbezogenheit als Vorgeschichte von französisch "amour-propre."* Stuttgart: Metzler.
Foucault, Michel. 1984. "What Is Enlightenment?" In *The Foucault Reader*, edited by Paul Rabinow, 32–50. New York: Pantheon Books.
Gaberel, M. J. 1858. *Rousseau et les Genevois*. Geneva, Paris: J. Cherbuliez.
Gonzalez, Francisco J. 2006. "Beyond or Beneath Good and Evil? Heidegger's Purification of Aristotle's Ethics." In *Heidegger and the Greeks: Interpretive Essays*, edited by Drew Hyland and John Panteleimon Manoussakis, 127–56. Bloomington: Indiana University Press.
Gouhier, Henri. 1970. *Les méditations métaphysiques de Jean-Jacques Rousseau*. Paris: Vrin.
Gourevitch, Victor. 1988. "Rousseau's Pure State of Nature." *Interpretation: A Journal of Political Philosophy*, 16 (1): 23–59.
———. 2012. "A Provisional Reading of Rousseau's *Reveries of the Solitary Walker*." *The Review of Politics* 74 (3): 489–518.
———. 2013. "On Strauss on Rousseau." In *The Challenge of Rousseau*, edited by Eve Grace and Christopher Kelly, 147–67. New York: Cambridge University Press.
Habermas, Jürgen. (1983) 1990. *Moral Consciousness and Communicative Action*. Translated by Christian Lenhardt and Shierry Weber Nicholsen. Malden, MA: Polity Press.
Hadot, Pierre. (1995) 2002. *What Is Ancient Philosophy?* Translated by Michael Chase. Cambridge, MA: Harvard University Press.
Hawking, Stephen and Leonard Mlodinow. 2010. *The Grand Design*. New York: Bantam.
Husserl, Edmund. (1906–7) 2008. *Collected Works, vol. 13, Introduction to Logic and Theory of Knowledge*. Translated by Claire Ortiz Hill. Dordrecht: Springer.
Johnston, Adrian. 2013. *Prolegomena to any Future Materialism, Volume One: The Outcome of Contemporary French Philosophy*. Evanston, IL: Northwestern University Press.
Kelly, Christopher. 2003. *Rousseau as Author: Consecrating One's Life to the Truth*. Chicago: University of Chicago Press.
Kelly, Christopher and Roger Masters. 1989–1990. "Rousseau on Reading 'Jean-Jacques': *The Dialogues*." *Interpretation: A Journal of Political Philosophy*, 17 (2): 239–53.
Kennington, Richard. 2004. *On Modern Origins: Essays in Early Modern Philosophy*. Edited by Pamela Kraus and Frank Hunt. Lanham, MD: Lexington Books.
Kierkegaard, Søren. (1846) 1987. *Two Ages: The Age of Revolution and the Present Age, A Literary Review*. Translated and edited by Howard V. Hong and Edna H. Hong. Princeton: Princeton University Press.
Kuehn, Manfred. 2001. *Kant: A Biography*. New York: Cambridge University Press.
Lacan, Jacques. 1966. *Écrits*. Paris: Éditions du Seuil. / 2006. *Écrits*, the first complete edition in English. Translated by Bruce Fink with Héloïse Fink and Russell Grigg. New York: W.W. Norton & Co. Citations follow the French edition.

———. 1986. *Le séminaire de Jacques Lacan. Livre VII, L'éthique de la psychanalyse (1959–1960)*. Paris: Éditions du Seuil. / 1992. *The Seminar of Jacques Lacan. Book VII, The Ethics of Psychoanalysis (1959–1960)*. Translated by Dennis Porter. W.W. Norton & Co.

Lear, Jonathan. 2000. *Happiness, Death, and the Remainder of Life*. Cambridge, MA: Harvard University Press.

Lévi-Strauss, Claude. 1955. *Tristes Tropiques*. Paris: Plon. / 1961. *Tristes Tropiques*. Translated by John Russell. New York: Criterion Books.

———. 1962. *La pensée sauvage*. Paris: Plon.

———. 1973. *Anthropologie structurale deux*. Paris: Plon. / 1976. *Structural Anthropology, vol. 2*. Translated by Monique Layton. Chicago: University of Chicago Press.

Lloyd, G. E. R. 1989. *The Revolutions of Wisdom: Studies in the Claims and Practice of Ancient Greek Science*. Berkeley: University of California Press.

Lyotard, Jean-François. 1989. "Liminaire sur l'ouvrage d'Alain Badiou *L'etre et l'evenement*" (with Philippe Lacoue-Labarthe, Jacques Rancière, and Alain Badiou). *Le Cahier* (*Collège international de philosophie*) 8: 201–68.

Marks, Jonathan. 2005. *Perfection and Disharmony in the Thought of Jean-Jacques Rousseau*. Cambridge: Cambridge University Press.

Masters, Roger. 1968. *The Political Philosophy of Rousseau*. Princeton, NJ: Princeton University Press.

Meier, Heinrich. 1984. "Rousseaus Diskurs über den Ursprung und die Grundlagen der Ungleichheit unter den Menschen: Ein einführender Essay über die Rhetorik und die Intention des Werkes." In Jean-Jacques Rousseau. *Diskurs über die Ungleichheit/Discours sur l'inégalité: Kritische Ausgabe des integralen Textes, mit sämtlichen Fragmenten und ergänzenden Materialien nach den Originalausgaben und den Handschriften*, translated and edited with commentary by Heinrich Meier, xxi–lxxvii. Paderborn: F. Schöningh.

———. (2011) 2016. *On the Happiness of the Philosophic Life: Reflections on Rousseau's "Rêveries" in Two Books*. Translated by Robert Berman. Chicago: The University of Chicago Press.

Neuhouser, Frederick. 2008. *Rousseau's Theodicy of Self-love: Evil, Rationality, and the Drive for Recognition*. New York: Oxford University Press.

Orwin, Clifford. 1998. "Rousseau's Socratism." *The Journal of Politics*, 60 (1): 174–87.

Page, Carl. 1995. *Philosophical Historicism and the Betrayal of First Philosophy*. University Park, PA: The Pennsylvania State University Press.

Pascal, Blaise. (1670) 1947. *Pensées sur la religion, et sur quelques autres sujets*. Edited by Louis Lafuma. Paris: Delmas. / 1995. *Pensées*. Translated by A.J. Krailsheimer. New York: Penguin Books.

Plato. 1914–. *Works*. Edited by Jeffrey Henderson. Cambridge, MA: Harvard University Press.

Plautus, Titus Maccius. 1966–80. *Asinaria*. In *Works, vol. 1*. Translated by Paul Nixon. Cambridge, MA: Harvard University Press.

Rorty, Richard. 1989. *Contingency, Irony, and Solidarity*. New York: Cambridge University Press.

———. 2004. "Philosophy as a Transitional Genre." *Pragmatism, Critique, Judgment: Essays for Richard J. Bernstein*. Edited by Seyla Benhabib and Nancy Fraser. Cambridge, MA: MIT Press.

Rosen, Stanley. 1969. *Nihilism: A Philosophical Essay*. New Haven: Yale University Press. Reprint. 2000. South Bend, IN: St. Augustine's Press.

———. 1980. *The Limits of Analysis*. New York: Basic Books.

Salkever, Stephen G. 1977–78. "Interpreting Rousseau's Paradoxes." *Eighteenth-Century Studies*, 11 (2): 204–26.

Starobinski, Jean. 1971. *Jean-Jacques Rousseau: La transparence et l'obstacle suivi de Sept essais sur Rousseau*. Paris: Gallimard. / 1988. *Jean-Jacques Rousseau: Transparency and Obstruction*. Translated by Arthur Goldhammer. Chicago: University of Chicago Press.

Strauss, Leo. (1935) 1996. *The Political Philosophy of Hobbes: Its Basis and Its Genesis*. Translated by Elsa M. Sinclair. Chicago: University of Chicago Press.

———. (1948) 2000. *On Tyranny: Including the Strauss–Kojève Correspondence*. Edited by Victor Gourevitch and Michael S. Roth. Chicago: University of Chicago Press.

———. 1953. *Natural Right and History*. Chicago: The University of Chicago Press.

———. 1959. *What Is Political Philosophy?* Chicago: The University of Chicago Press.

Thomas-Fogiel, Isabelle. (2005) 2011. *The Death of Philosophy: Reference and Self-Reference in Contemporary Thought*. Translated by Richard A. Lynch. New York: Columbia University Press.

Tuck, Richard. 1999. *The Rights of War and Peace: Political Thought and the International Order from Grotius to Kant*. New York: Oxford University Press.

Vattimo, Gianni. (2003) 2004. *Nihilism & Emancipation: Ethics, Politics, & Law*. Translated by William McCuaig. Edited by Santiago Zabala. New York: Columbia University Press.

———. (2009) 2011. *A Farewell to Truth*. Translated by William McCuaig. New York: Columbia University Press.

Velkley, Richard L. 2002. *Being after Rousseau: Philosophy and Culture in Question*. Chicago: The University of Chicago Press.

Weber, Max. (1919) 1996. "The Profession and Vocation of Politics." In *Weber: Political Writings*, edited by Peter Lassman and Ronald Speirs, 309–69. New York: Cambridge University Press.

Westmoreland, Peter. 2013. "Rousseau's Descartes: The Rejection of Theoretical Philosophy as First Philosophy." *British Journal for the History of Philosophy* 21 (3): 529–48.

Williams, David Lay. 2007. *Rousseau's Platonic Enlightenment*. University Park, PA: The Pennsylvania State University Press.

Wilson, Nelly. 1983. "Discourses on Method and Professions of Faith: Rousseau's Debt to Descartes." *French Studies: A Quarterly Review*, 37 (2): 157–67.

Yovel, Yirmiyahu. 1998. "Kant's Practical Reason as Will: Interest, Recognition, Judgment, and Choice." *The Review of Metaphysics* 52 (2): 267–94.

Index

Adorno, Theodor, 11, 17–29, 46; and Auschwitz, 19, 23, 28, 29; and Badiou, 27–29, 38, 44–45; and decisionism, 26; and demand, 20, 22; and Foucault, 19; and happiness, 23–24; and Hegel, 18–20; and Heidegger, 17–23, 26–28, 31; and historicism, 26; and Kant, 18, 20–23; and melancholy science, 24–27, 44, 46; and messianism, 19–22, 23, 29, 31, 45; and negative dialectics, 18–19, 23, 26–27, 29; and Nietzsche, 19; and ordinary experience, 23; and philosophy, 17–20, 27; and possibility of philosophy, 18; and responsibility, 17–22, 26; and Rousseau, 80. See also *Dialectic of Enlightenment*; impossibility
Alembert, Jean le Rond d', 73
amour-propre: and *amour de soi*, 95–98, 121–23; and drive, 121–23, 125–26; and narcissistic libido, 123; and philosophy, 57, 100–101, 103, 113–16, 132–33, 142–43, 146, 148
analytic philosophy, 34
anxiety, 16–17, 43, 63, 165, 168
après-coup (*Nachträglichkeit*), 114, 121, 124–25, 143, 145, 146, 151, 154, 161, 163, 167, 169–70, 177;
double movement of, 126–29; of the good, 131–32, 134; and Rousseau's illumination, 137, 152; versus *Zurückphantasieren*, 129
Arendt, Hannah, 170
Aristotle, 8, 16, 150, 169–70; *Categories*, 58; and first philosophy, 57–58, 113; and mathematics, 58, 92; *Metaphysics*, 57–58, 91–92, 136; and natural desire to know (or understand), 41, 91–92, 135–36, 170; and philosophic wonder, 92, 100–101, 135–36; versus Plato, 135–36, 163; and Rousseau, 80–82, 86–87, 88, 90–94, 96, 100–101, 115, 133, 169
art, 24
art of turning souls (*periagogē tēs psychēs*), 140–44, 145, 149, 152, 170–76
Aubenque, Pierre, 104n10

Bacon, Francis, 13n23, 17, 35, 63, 66, 71
Badiou, Alain, 11, 27–47, 150–51, 153, 161, 169; and Adorno, 27–29, 38, 44–45; and Auschwitz, 28; and Cantor, 33, 43; and decisionism, 34–38, 151; and Descartes, 31–32,

36; and ethic of truths, 32–33, 38, 44, 46, 150–51; and event, 33, 35–37, 45, 151; and future of philosophy, 27–28; and the Good, 39–40; and happiness, 43, 45; and Hegel, 29; and Heidegger, 28–31, 33; and Kant, 38; and Machiavelli, 35–37; and mathematics, 32–38, 40; and metaphysical domination of the one, 30; and Nietzsche, 37–38, 43, 47; nonbeing of the one, 31–33; and ontology, 33–36, 44, 46, 153–54; and Plato, 39; and possibility of philosophy, 28–29, 39; and recklessness, 27, 32, 36–38, 169. *See also* impossibility
beauty, 101, 131, 136, 143
being: primacy of, 154; qua being, 16, 29–30, 33, 36, 40, 57–58, 86, 134, 143. *See also* first philosophy
Beyond the Pleasure Principle (Freud), 125, 129
biologism, 165–67
Bowlby, John, 121
Brandwood, Leonard, 110n169
Burke, Edmund, 106n70
Butler, Judith, 177n7

Cantor, Georg, 33, 43
capitalism, 6, 41, 43
Cartesian nihilism, 39–42
Cassirer, Ernst, 106n75
Castoriadis, Cornelius, 47n1
Categories (Aristotle), 58
causes étrangeres (alien or foreign causes), 95–96, 98, 101, 114–16, 122, 126, 127, 131–33, 142, 146
Chassonneris, Hugues, 1–4, 173
Chetrit-Vatine, Viviane, 177n7
childhood (primacy of), 154, 162. *See also* fundamental anthropological situation; primal seduction; primal situation; *Project for a Scientific Psychology*
compulsion, 129, 151, 175; to repeat, 27, 125, 149

Condillac, Etienne Bonnot de, 73
conscience: and Heidegger, 17, 21, 23; and Rousseau, 139–40, 142, 148, 151, 162, 175
conviction, 47, 123, 150–51
Cooper, Laurence D., 159n130
Copernican (decentering), 148–50, 162–63
crisis, 6–7, 11; and Cartesian method, 41–42; moral, 41; philosophy in, 15–47 (*passim*), 151; responsibility in, 17–22
Critchley, Simon, 21, 52n131
Crowell, Steven, 49n47
culture, 19, 55, 165, 168
culture industry, 2, 24

Dahlstrom, Daniel O., 48n8
death, 23; being-for, 31, 33, 43; being-toward, 31, 63, 164; fear of, 24, 26, 31, 62–63, 65, 94; and philosophy, 62–63, 65–67; of philosophy, 15, 17, 27
death drive, 166
decisionism, 9, 11, 22, 26, 33–38, 43, 77–78, 151. *See also* heroism of decision
Deleuze, Gilles, 10, 169
Delphic imperative, 82, 140, 168. *See also* philosophy and self-knowledge
demand, 97; Adorno, 20, 22; libidinal, 162, 167, 171, 175; of the other, 22–23, 127; of philosophy, 15, 167; for translation, 114–15, 127; twofold, 127–29, 139, 151, 162. *See also* drive
Dent, N. J. H., 109n166
Descartes, René, 9, 145, 150, 163; and Badiou, 31–32, 36; and *cogito sum*, 41, 56, 78, 150, 169; and *esprit de système*, 60, 73; and first philosophy (or metaphysics), 11, 58–59, 69; and *générosité*, 59, 77; and mathematics, 9, 32, 42, 56, 59, 63, 67–68; and Nietzsche, 59; reversal of Aristotle, 58; and Rousseau, 40, 56–103

(*passim*), 115, 134, 145, 150–51, 154, 169; and tree of philosophy, 58–59, 62, 68, 75–77. *See also* Cartesian nihilism; ethics and ontology
detranslation, 152–53, 166–68, 177. *See also* translation
Dialectic of Enlightenment (Horkheimer and Adorno), 2–3, 7
Diderot, Denis, 5
Discourse on Heroic Virtue (Rousseau), 102, 173
drive (*pulsion*, *Trieb*), 116, 119–20, 127, 139, 151, 161–62, 167, 169, 172; and *amour-propre*, 121–23, 125–26; genesis of, 123–26; libidinal economy of, 132–33; for meaning, 125, 127; temporal structure of, 129; to translate, 125, 130, 133, 149, 154, 161; for wisdom, 148, 161. *See also* sexuality
Durkheim, Émile, 6

Emma (Freud's case of). *See Project for a Scientific Psychology*
enigma: of the good, 115, 127, 130, 131–34, 141–44, 146, 148, 152, 154, 161–63, 169–70, 171, 176–77; guardian of, 144–46, 170; of the other, 144, 152; of the primal, 133, 152–54. *See also* primal enigma
enigmatic message (or signifier), 114, 118–33 (*passim*), 151–52, 165, 167, 168, 172, 176–77
enlightenment, 89, 172. *See also Dialectic of Enlightenment*
Enlightenment, 6–12, 17, 19, 26, 27, 43, 97, 113, 132, 140, 170; paradox of, 20, 171
Epictetus, 102, 176
erōs, 166; and drive, 45; for philosophy, 136, 137, 140–43. *See also* philosophical eros
esotericism. *See* interior doctrine
esprit de système, 60, 73, 113, 140
ethical experience, 23, 80

ethics and ontology, 31–33, 39–40, 42, 46, 56, 65, 76, 150
étrangèreté, 116, 121, 126, 127, 146, 148–49, 151–52, 167, 168
eudaimonia. *See* happiness
event, 117, 131, 133, 137–38, 146, 167; Badiou's concept of, 33, 35–37, 45, 151; Heidegger's concept of (*Ereignis*), 33, 40
extraordinary, 78, 135; axis of, 147

Fain, Lucas, 12n16, 49n47, 53n154, 105n45, 159n120
"Fiction, or Allegorical Fragment on Revelation" (Rousseau), 138
first philosophy (*prōtē philosophia*), 11, 38, 55–71, 76–77, 79–80, 86, 88, 95, 101–2, 113, 127, 134–35, 154. *See also* primal philosophy
Fliess, Wilhelm, 115, 121, 128
Force, Pierre, 109n167
Foucault, Michel, 19
foundations (plural, split), 126, 129, 132, 146–47. *See also* "origin and foundations"
freedom: from moral-juridical good, 88; and philosophy; 45; from philosophy (or love of wisdom), 7, 12, 45, 48n8, 59–60; and Rousseau, 93
Freud, Sigmund, 165; *Beyond the Pleasure Principle*, 125, 129; drive theory, 45–46; and Fliess, 115, 121, 128; and happiness, 162; "Instincts and their Vicissitudes," 123; "Negation," 130; *New Introductory Lectures on Psychoanalysis*, 129–30; *Project for a Scientific Psychology*, 114, 128; theory of seduction, 11, 114–15; "The Unconscious," 129
Fuchs, Hans-Jürgen, 109n167
fundamental anthropological situation, 116–18, 126, 135, 151, 162. *See also* primal situation
fundamental anthropology of seduction, 151

future: messianic, 23; and philosophy, 44–45; of philosophy, 10–12, 15, 27–28, 31–32, 153

general will, 1, 8, 172–73
Genet, Jean, 45
Glaucus allegory, 81–83, 103, 116, 120, 152
"going-astray," 165, 167
Gonzalez, Francisco J., 49n42
good, 88–89; beyond being, 39, 136, 141–43; enigma of, 115, 127, 130, 131–34, 141–44, 146, 148, 152, 154, 161–63, 169–70, 171, 176–77; and happiness, 89, 101, 115, 127, 133; introduction of, 130–34; and mathematics, 59, 63–64; as object of desire, 101; and paradox, 88; and possibility of philosophy, 43, 134–44, 150–52, 154; as a question, 101; versus right, 24–25, 172–73; and Rousseau, 99, 140–43; as source-object of drive, 127; timelessness of, 129–31. *See also* Badiou and the Good; Ideas (Platonic)
Gouhier, Henri, 103n2
Gourevitch, Victor, 107–8n122, 109n138, 157n76
guardian of the enigma, 144–46, 170

Habermas, Jürgen, 8–9
happiness, 172; and Badiou, 43, 45; versus *Befriedigung*, 16; as *eudaimonia*, 4, 7, 16, 43; and Freud, 162; as *Glücklichkeit*, 7; as *Glückseligkeit*, 16, 47–48n4, 53n162; and the good, 89, 101, 115, 127, 133; and Hegel, 16, 27; Heidegger and Wittgenstein on, 7, 16–17; as *jouissance*, 43–44; and Kant, 9, 16; and philosophy, 7, 11–12, 16, 42–47, 47–48n4, 66–67, 79–80, 86, 89, 95, 99–101, 115, 148, 151–53, 174; promise of, 3, 23–24, 172; as a question, 12, 80, 86, 99, 115,

133, 146, 148, 162, 169, 171; and Rousseau, 65, 95, 146, 161–62, 168, 170–77; seduction of, 11, 161; and Socratic philosophy, 3, 43
Hawking, Stephen, 17
Hegel, G. W. F., 15–20, 27, 46, 48n8, 150; and Badiou, 29
Heidegger, Martin, 6–8, 10–11, 15–47, 56–57, 63, 113, 150, 153–54, 162–63, 170, 174; and Adorno, 17–23, 26–28, 31; and anticipatory resoluteness, 21–22, 28; and authenticity, 16–17, 21–22, 28, 31; and Badiou, 28–31, 33; and *cogito sum*, 150; and conscience, 17, 21, 23; *Destruktion*, 6, 48n8, 153; *Gelassenheit*, 6, 48n8, 174; and happiness, 7, 16–17; and Hegel, 15–17, 27; and Hobbes, 31; and Kant, 21–23; and Nietzsche, 7, 30–31; and nihilism; 7, 10, 153; and poetry, 29; possibility higher than actuality, 20–21; and responsibility, 21–22; and Wittgenstein, 6–7, 10. *See also* Cartesian nihilism; impossibility
helplessness (*Hilflosigkeit*), 118, 144, 149, 152
Herodotus, 4, 12n16, 148
heroism of decision, 52n131, 150–51, 169. *See also* decisionism
"hero of happiness," 173–76
historicism, 10, 26, 83
Hobbes, Thomas, 24–26; and Heidegger, 31; and Laplanche, 166–68; and Rousseau, 8, 85–86, 166, 168–69, 171
hollow (of a question), 152–53, 169–70, 176
Horkheimer, Max, 2–3, 7
Husserl, Edmund, 40, 57, 163

Ideas (Platonic), 17, 66, 97, 135–43 (*passim*), 145; and Bacon, 63; and Badiou, 39
imagination, 84, 94

implantation, 116, 120–22, 127, 133, 142–43, 146, 151, 161, 177
impossibility (higher than possibility), 20–23, 44–45
inequality, 71–72, 75–76, 88–89, 93, 101, 134, 177
instinct (*Instinkt*), 116, 123–25; and *amour de soi*, 121–23
"Instincts and their Vicissitudes" (Freud), 123
interior doctrine (*doctrine intérieur*), 67–72, 88, 102, 132, 143, 170, 175
internal foreign body (*corps étranger interne*), 122, 124, 127
irresponsibility, 10, 19, 169–70

Jefferson, Thomas, 25
Johnston, Adrian, 53n147
Jung, Carl, 129
justice. *See* Rousseau and justice

Kant, Immanuel, 16, 24, 26, 55, 158n100, 163; and Adorno, 18, 20–23; and Badiou, 38; and Habermas, 8–9; and Heidegger, 21–23; and Rousseau, 8–9
Kelly, Christopher, 105n53, 105n58, 105n61. *See also* Kelly and Masters
Kelly and Masters, 106n82
Kennington, Richard, 53n160
Kierkegaard, Søren, 16–17
Klein, Melanie, 121
Kuehn, Manfred, 103n1

Lacan, Jacques: and drive theory, 121–22; and *jouissance*, 44; and suture, 29
Laplanche, Jean, 11, 114; and biologism, 165–67; and Copernican (decentering), 148–50, 162–63; and event, 117; "going-astray," 165, 167; versus Heidegger, 162; and Hobbes, 166–68; versus Lacan, 121; versus Lévinas, 162–63; and Ptolemaic (centering), 149, 163, 165, 171; and Rousseau, 113–54 (*passim*), 161–77

leaning-on (*Anlehnung, étayage*), 116, 122, 124
Lear, Jonathan, 156n50, 178n32
leisure, 92, 100
Lévinas, Emmanuel, 162–63
Lévi-Strauss, Claude, 164–65
Lloyd, G. E. R., 12n15
Locke, John, 25, 61, 137, 171
love (moral), 101, 114, 127, 131, 133–34. *See also amour-propre*; sexuality
"love of order," 146, 148–50, 151, 154, 161–62, 164, 168
Lyotard, Jean-François, 34–35

Machiavelli, Niccolò, 35–37
Marks, Jonathan, 107–8n122
Marxism, 6, 25, 43, 45, 46
Masters, Roger, 106n86. *See also* Kelly and Masters
mathematics: and Aristotle, 58, 92; and Badiou, 32–38, 40; and Descartes, 9, 32, 42, 56, 59, 63, 67–68; and first philosophy, 38; and the good, 59, 63–64; and nature, 42, 64; and philosophy, 56, 66–68, 85
mathesis universalis, 41, 66
McCarthy, Paul, 24
Meier, Heinrich, 107–8n122, 157n76, 179n39
Menexenus (Plato), 87
messianism. *See* Adorno
metaphysics: destiny of, 16; destruction of, 30; end of, 154; and history, 19–20, 29; overcoming of, 6; revolution against, 10. *See also* philosophy
Metaphysics (Aristotle), 57–58, 91–92, 136
method and philosophy, 24–26, 28, 41–42, 45–46, 56–69, 74–76, 77–78, 82–86, 116–18, 126, 148, 150–51
miracles, 78
Moog, Robert, 35
"morality originates in sexuality," 127
myth, 92, 163–76 (*passim*); Laplanche on, 164–68; and philosophy, 2, 108,

168–71; Rousseau versus Hobbes, 167–68
mythosymbolic thought, 163–69, 171

narcissism: and *amour-propre*, 123; theory of, 122
nature: and artifice, 79–84; pure state of, 66, 78–101 (*passim*), 126, 129–33, 146–47, 168, 177
"Negation" (Freud), 130
Neuhouser, Frederick, 109n66
New Introductory Lectures on Psychoanalysis (Freud), 129–30
Nietzsche, Friedrich, 4, 24, 46, 169; and Badiou, 37–38, 43, 47; and Descartes, 59; and happiness, 43; and Heidegger, 7, 30–31; and nihilism, 6–7, 10, 67
nihilism, 6–7, 10, 27, 30, 39–47, 62, 67, 142, 153
normativity: and the infant's "first ideas"; 120; moral, 131; and the one; 30, 31. *See also* Habermas, Kant

ontology: Badiou and Heidegger, 30, 46, 153–54; Badiou's theory of, 33–36, 44; and ethics, 31–33, 39–40, 42, 46, 56, 65, 76, 150
"The Orchard of Les Charmettes" (Rousseau), 60, 73
ordinary, 135; axis of, 147; "course of life," 78, 91, 98, 126, 129, 132, 146; "course of things," 57, 77–78, 126, 129, 132, 146; foundations of, 126, 129, 132, 146–47; mode of transference, 152; temporality, 148. *See also* ordinary experience
ordinary experience, 33, 91; and Adorno, 23; and Rousseau, 57, 77, 91, 126
"origin and foundations," 57, 66, 75–77, 77–79, 85–87, 113, 132–33
Orwin, Clifford, 12n8
the other, 124, 146, 161; desire of, 102, 114, 117, 125, 127, 131, 143, 175; message of, 129, 148, 149, 151, 162, 177; primacy (priority) of, 115, 125, 131, 135–36, 144–45, 163; seduction of, 143, 149
Ovid, 132

Page, Carl, 107n117
Pascal, Blaise, 96–97
Phaedo (Plato), 65
Phaedrus (Plato), 135, 136
philosophes, 69; and Rousseau, 1, 5, 65, 149, 175
philosophical eros, 41, 46
philosophical experience, 41, 46, 57, 79
philosophical seduction, 144–48, 152–54, 170, 176
philosophy, 4, 148; as activity of soul, 154, 163; and Adorno, 17–20, 27; and *amour-propre*, 57, 100–101, 103, 113–16, 132–33, 142–43, 146, 148; and Badiou, 27–38; destruction of, 6–7, 15; end of, 6, 11, 15–17, 18, 26–27, 29, 46, 149, 161; foundational question of, 11, 55–57, 66, 80, 95, 130, 134, 150, 171; future of, 10–12, 15, 27–28, 31–32, 153; and happiness, 7, 11–12, 16, 42–47, 47–48n4, 66–67, 79–80, 86, 89, 95, 99–101, 115, 148, 151–53, 174; history of, 153, 176–77; and mathematics, 56, 66–68, 85; new Copernican revolution in, 149; "origin and foundations" of, 57, 66, 75–77, 77–79, 85–87, 113, 132–33; philosophic roots, 75–77, 127, 130, 132, 135; and poetry, 83–84; and politics, 56, 161, 164, 169–72; possibility of, 79–80, 86, 91–92, 99–103, 113, 115, 126–34, 134–44, 150–54; and postphilosophical culture, 10–11; and psychoanalysis, 123, 153–54; replaced by modern science, 17, 59–60, 67; and Rousseau, 70, 74, 89, 95, 138–40, 144–46, 154; and self-knowledge, 75, 81, 84, 154; and

time, 146–48; and trauma, 145–46; as universal human possibility, 129, 145–46, 171; and wisdom, 2–5, 7, 10, 42, 174. *See also* death; first philosophy; metaphysics; primal philosophy; Socratic philosophy
Plato, 17, 24, 150; versus Aristotle, 135–36, 163; and Badiou, 39; doctrine of Ideas, 17, 66, 97, 135–43 (*passim*), 145; *Menexenus*, 87; *Phaedo*, 65; *Phaedrus*, 135; and philosophic wonder, 92, 135–36; *Republic*, 34, 39, 81, 137–38, 140, 143, 165–66; and Rousseau, 86–87, 92, 94, 101, 115, 133, 136–44; *Symposium*, 96–97; *Theaetetus*, 135, 143
Platonism, 12n8, 30, 136–46
Plautus, Titus Maccius, 168
Plutarch, 66
poetry, 6, 97; and Heidegger, 29; and philosophy, 83–84
politics and philosophy, 56, 161, 164, 169–72. *See also* interior doctrine
Pontalis, J.-B., 119, 122
positivist legacy, 17
"Preface of a Second Letter to Bordes" (Rousseau), 68, 72, 113
Preface to "Narcissus" (Rousseau), 72, 102
the primal, 117, 167; reactivation of, 126, 127, 134–44, 146, 148, 152–54, 170
primal enigma, 133, 146, 148, 150, 152, 154, 161–62, 167, 175, 177
primal fantasy, 125
primal philosophy, 57, 134–36, 149, 150–54 (113–54 *passim*); and primal seduction, 135
primal repressed, 120–21, 129, 143, 167
primal responsibility, 164–70, 176
primal seduction, 116–18, 123, 131–33, 135, 142–45, 147, 149, 151, 161, 169–70, 179n39; and repression, 119, 122, 124, 147

primal situation, 117–20, 122, 129, 144, 152, 164, 176; and Rousseau, 119–20. *See also* fundamental anthropological situation
Project for a Scientific Psychology (Freud), 114, 128
psychoanalysis and philosophy, 123, 153–54
Ptolemaic (centering), 149, 163, 165, 171
Pyrrhonism, 3, 170–71

quarrel of ancients and moderns, 6, 8, 62, 65–66, 163

recklessness, 22, 26, 27, 32, 36–38, 169, 179n39
repression: Laplanche's translational theory of, 120–21, 128, 130, 132; primal, 118–21, 124, 127, 142
Republic (Plato), 34, 39, 81, 137–38, 140, 143, 165–66
response, 120; primacy of, 161–64; versus responsibility, 162, 167
responsibility, 153; and Adorno, 17–22; in crisis, 17–22; and Heidegger, 21–22; and melancholy science, 25; paradox of, 171–72; of the philosopher, 3–5, 10–11, 46, 56, 161–77; primal, 164–70, 176
revelation, 138, 145
reverie, 179n39
revolution as seduction, 172–73
rhetoric. *See* Rousseau and rhetoric
right versus good, 24–25, 172–73
Rorty, Richard, 11, 26, 38
Rosen, Stanley, 34, 107n117
Rousseau, Jean-Jacques: and *amour-propre* versus *amour de soi*, 95–98, 121–23; and animals compared to humans, 90–91, 93, 166–68; and *après-coup*, 137; and Aristotle, 80–82, 86–87, 88, 90–94, 96, 100–101, 115, 133, 169; "chain of wonders," 79, 84, 88, 92, 94,

95–101, 133; and conscience, 139–40, 142, 148, 151, 162, 175; critique of modern medicine, 62–63; and Descartes, 40, 56–103 (*passim*), 115, 134, 145, 150–51, 154, 169; *Dialogues*, 5, 69, 71, 73–75; *Discourse on Heroic Virtue*, 102, 173; Émile and philosophy, 145–46; "Fiction, or Allegorical Fragment on Revelation," 138; and first philosophy (or metaphysics), 11, 55–71, 76–77, 79, 86, 88, 101; and freedom, 93; and general will, 1, 8, 172–73; "genuine philosophy" (*la véritable philosophie*), 138–40, 154; and the good, 99, 140–43; and happiness, 65, 95, 146, 148, 151–53, 161–62, 168, 170–77; and Hobbes, 8, 85–86, 166, 168–69, 171; and Horkheimer and Adorno, 2–3; and human nature, 75–76, 79–94; and illumination, 136–40, 144–45, 152; and imagination, 84; and justice, 157n76, 180n48; and Kant, 8–9; and kinds of lives, 172–74; and Laplanche, 113–54 (*passim*), 161–77; and legacy-as-task, 56, 102, 113, 127, 134, 154; "love of order," 146, 148–50, 151, 154, 161–62, 164, 168; "mechanical prudence," 98–99; and method, 63, 77, 82–84, 86, 150; *Moral Letters*, 40, 56, 62, 65, 68, 148; and myth (or fable), 2, 92, 168–69, 171–72, 176; "natural goodness of man," 74, 82, 88, 142, 168; "The Orchard of Les Charmettes," 60, 73; "ordinary course of life," 78, 91, 98, 126, 129, 132, 146; "ordinary course of things," 57, 77–78, 126, 129, 132, 146; and ordinary experience, 57, 77, 91, 126; "origin and foundations," 57, 66, 75–77, 77–79, 85–87, 113, 132–33; and Ovid, 132; and paradox, 5, 9, 72–73, 82, 88–89, 117, 154; and perfectibility, 93, 95;

and *philosophes*, 1, 5, 65, 149, 175; the pivot, 3, 8–9, 55; and Plato, 86–87, 92, 94, 101, 115, 133, 136–44; and possibility of philosophy, 134–44, 150–54; "Preface of a Second Letter to Bordes," 68, 72, 113; *Preface to "Narcissus,"* 72, 102; and primal responsibility, 168; and primal situation, 119–20; and public good, 88, 132; and pure state of nature, 66, 78–101 (*passim*), 126, 129–33, 146–47, 168, 177; and reason, 90, 148; and *réflexion*, 99, 179n39; and reverie, 179n39; and rhetoric, 4, 55–56, 66, 68, 75–77, 86–87, 94, 139, 141; and root as metaphysics, 68–69, 72, 75–77, 84–86, 93, 102, 113, 132, 143, 170; Savoyard Vicar and philosophy, 145, 149; and seduction, 102–3, 113–14, 125, 138, 141–48, 151–54, 161, 170–72; and sentiment of existence, 98, 174; and Socrates, 3–5, 65–67, 81, 113, 142–43, 151, 154, 172, 173, 176; and Solitary Walker, 2, 10, 172, 174, 179n39; "sublime science of simple souls," 139–40; and synthetic method, 74; and system, 72–75; "true Philosopher," 175–76; use of myth (or fable), 92, 171, 176

Sade, Marquis de, 2
Salkever, Stephen G., 106n70
seduction, 136; Freud's theory of, 113–16, 118; of happiness, 11, 161; Laplanche's generalization of, 11, 118–19, 125, 127, 130, 138, 145, 146, 150, 152, 163; and moral love, 131; and Rousseau, 102–3, 113–14, 125, 138, 141–48, 151–54, 161, 170–72; and Socrates, 141; temporality of, 118, 127–31. *See also* philosophical seduction; primal seduction
the sexual, 162, 164–68. *See also* drive

sexuality: adult, 116, 132; as drive for meaning, 127; Freudian theory of, 45–46; infantile, 115–18, 122–23; and morality, 127; oral, 122–24, 130–31; and vital order, 121–22, 133
Socrates, 34, 63; and Rousseau, 3–5, 65–67, 81, 113, 142–43, 151, 154, 172, 173, 176; and seduction, 141
Socratic ignorance, 3, 47, 67, 70, 74, 151, 154, 171, 175
Socratic philosophy, 3–5, 6, 8–9, 10, 43, 65, 70, 75, 113, 148, 154, 172
source-object (of drive), 120, 124–25, 127, 131, 132, 139, 142, 148, 161
Spinoza, Baruch, 61
spiral (structure of retracement), 140
Starobinski, Jean, 107n98, 107n114, 138
Stendhal, 23
Strachey, James, 123
Strauss, Leo, 103n2, 107n117, 109n138, 109n141, 171, 178n27
Swift, Jonathan, 6. See also quarrel of ancients and moderns
Symposium (Plato), 96–97, 136

temporality, 33, 58, 114; and decentering, 162; of the drive, 129; of *Nachträglichkeit*, 114, 121, 124; ordinary, 148; of seduction, 118, 127–31. See also *après-coup*; time and philosophy; the timeless; transhistorical questioning
Theaetetus (Plato), 135, 143
Theremin, Léon, 35
Thomas-Fogiel, Isabelle, 47n1
Thucydides, 25
time and philosophy, 146–48, 176. See also temporality
the timeless: and the good, 129–31, 143, 147–48, 154, 163, 169; problems (of philosophy), 175–77
totemism, 165
transference, 114, 126, 144, 151–53, 170

transhistorical questioning, 150, 176
translation: versus hermeneutic interpretation, 121; Laplanche's theory of, 114, 119–21, 124–25, 162, 164–65. See also detranslation; drive; repression
trauma: of the good, 142, 169; and philosophy, 145–46; of primal enigmas, 150, 154; psychoanalytic theory of: 114, 125, 128; and Rousseau, 138
Tuck, Richard, 85

unconscious: of the philosopher, 153; psychoanalytic concept of, 118–21; timelessness of, 129–30, 147–48; as unmoved mover, 130
"The Unconscious" (Freud), 129

Vattimo, Gianni, 14n38
Velkley, Richard L., 103n2, 107n114
Voltaire, 69–70, 77–78

Weber, Max, 6, 47
Westmoreland, Peter, 103n2
Williams, David Lay, 12n8
Wilson, Nelly, 103n2
Winnicott, D. W., 121
wisdom: drive for, 133–34, 148, 161–62; and *erōs*, 136; as an object, 101, 116, 127, 133–34, 140, 143, 144, 148, 162; and philosophy, 2–5, 7, 10, 42, 174
Wittgenstein, Ludwig, 15–17, 46; destruction of philosophy, 6, 153–54; and Habermas, 9; and happiness, 7; and Heidegger, 6–7, 10
wonder (philosophic), 11, 90–92, 94, 95, 99–101, 113–16, 129–54 (*passim*), 163, 169–70. See also Rousseau and "chain of wonders"; Rousseau and illumination

Yovel, Yirmiyahu, 49n46

About the Author

Lucas Fain is a visiting scholar in the Elie Wiesel Center for Jewish Studies at Boston University. He has taught philosophy and social thought at Harvard University and the University of California, Santa Cruz. He was previously an affiliate scholar at the Boston Psychoanalytic Society & Institute.

www.ingramcontent.com/pod-product-compliance
Lightning Source LLC
Chambersburg PA
CBHW022012300426
44117CB00005B/148